Mainstream Multimedia

Mainstream Multimedia

APPLYING MULTIMEDIA IN BUSINESS

Roger L. Fetterman

Satish K. Gupta

Copyright © 1993 by Van Nostrand Reinhold

Library of Congress Catalog Card Number 93-21839
ISBN 0-442-01181-4

I(T)P Van Nostrand Reinhold is an International Thomson Publishing company.
ITP logo is a trademark under license.

Printed in the United States of America

Van Nostrand Reinhold   ITP Germany
115 Fifth Avenue   Königswinterer Str. 418
New York, NY 10003   53227 Bonn
                                         Germany

International Thomson Publishing   International Thomson Publishing Asia
Berkshire House,168-173   38 Kim Tian Rd., #0105
High Holborn, London WC1V 7AA   Kim Tian Plaza
England   Singapore 0316

Thomas Nelson Australia   International Thomson Publishing Japan
102 Dodds Street   Kyowa Building, 3F
South Melbourne 3205   2-2-1 Hirakawacho
Victoria, Australia   Chiyada-Ku, Tokyo 102
                                          Japan

Nelson Canada
1120 Birchmount Road
Scarborough, Ontario
M1K 5G4, Canada

16 15 14 13 12 11 10 9 8 7 6 5 4 3 2

Library of Congress Cataloging in Publication Data
Fetterman, Roger L.
    Mainstream multimedia : applying multimedia in business / Roger L. Fetterman,
Satish K. Gupta.
        p.   cm.
    Includes index.
    ISBN 0-442-01181-4
    1. Management information systems. 2. Information storage and retrieval
systems—Business. 3. Multimedia systems. I. Gupta, Satish K. II. Title.
HD30.213.F48   1993
658.4'038'011—dc20
                                              93-21839
                                           CIP

Contents

9. TECHNOLOGY INFRASTRUCTURE *163*

10. CONCLUSIONS *251*

MULTIMEDIA AND NETWORKING GLOSSARY *259*

INDEX *267*

List of Figures

10. CONCLUSIONS

Foreword

THE MESSAGE IS THE MEDIUM

Most people who read this book will be far more pragmatic than I. I see this as fitting because the movement of dreams to reality does not stop at the audiovisual richness of the desktop. As the authors know, it extends to the full panoply of communications needs. Ultimately, multimedia will be as obvious as air; namely, you will be aware of it only when it is missing.

At Massachusetts Institute of Technology (MIT) in 1978, I recall demonstrating something we called a "movie manual." This was a full-color, photo-illustrated, hypertext manual for the maintenance and repair of a bicycle. While it contained a certain luster for its time, it was not breathtaking. However, as soon as a viewer touched the illustration and saw and heard it turn into a video sequence, there would be gasps. That audio, video, and data should coexist and be synchronized was outside the realm of most people's imaginations.

Now, 15 years later, the pendulum has swung in the opposite direction, overcompensating for years of sensory deprivation in the computer milieu. Multimedia means anything and everything from video compression to fiber to the home to Madonna's latest contract. Computer vendors who squeeze a tiny bit of video onto their personal computer or workstation claim to be in the multimedia business, but in my mind are less so than Nintendo or Sega.

We failed to understand in 1978 that the three-way mix of media richness, information depth, and interactivity was not itself the message. The message is about "being digital."

This is perhaps most easily illustrated in common broadcast media: newspapers, magazines, radio, and television—point-to-multipoint communications. Today, all the intelligence in the system lies in the transmitter and the signal is delivered by truck, ether, copper, or fiber to a human being with no mechanical intermediary or receiver of the dumbest sort (e.g., television or fax).

Increasingly, all these media will be fully digitized, and in the not-too-distant future the "bits" will be delivered directly to their final destination. Media companies who enjoy being in the full spectrum of mass communications today will find that the "bits" of magazines, radio, and television will start to mingle together. Eventually, the information provider with broadcast model-based information and the medium of preference will be determined at the receiving end. If you did not have time to finish reading the newspaper printed in your home, for example, an audio signal will be delivered to your car automatically .

In point-to-point communications, the subject of this book, the same will hold true. Thus, the "bits" are more like models, coded differently by different machines at the request of different users. I know I am dreaming again but it is very important for the reader not to stop at the idea of audio, video, and data meeting at the screen and that being the end of the story. It is only the beginning. Multimedia is what you want, not what you get. It is the surface embodiment of something much deeper, which has to do with how we represent knowledge, telecommunicate it, and transcode it.

If you are a businessperson trying to make a purchase decision, don't look for the cheapest and prettiest face but rather for the most extensible and scalable system you can buy, perhaps paying a bit more today, to be in business tomorrow.

If you are a computer scientist, try to discover the fundamental ways to represent knowledge and understand learning.

If you are a student, do not limit your dreams.

Nicholas Negroponte
Cambridge, Massachusetts

Preface

This book is for the decision maker in business who is concerned about increasing the competence of his or her organization. In the global business environment of the 1990s, a higher level of performance has been mandated by domestic and foreign competitors that deliver high-quality products and services at commodity prices.

This book was written for business managers who need to develop the implementation strategies for applying multimedia capabilities in all aspects of their business operation. Planning for a 3- to 5-year horizon will help ensure that multimedia is applied effectively to increase the health and wealth of businesses in the 1990s. The book was designed to help answer the following questions:

- What is multimedia and why should we concern ourselves about it?

- When, where, and how should it be applied in business environments?

- How can cost and value be determined for justification purposes?

- How can I prepare my organization to capitalize on the potential of multimedia?

- How will multimedia computing and networking evolve over the next 5 years?

The phenomenon known as multimedia provides an opportunity to evolve to a business environment where information, learning modules, expert systems, and support systems can be provided in the context of the business processes of individuals and groups. The book provides the information needed by decision makers who are interested in implementing multimedia applications. It defines multimedia, reviews applications and technologies, and provides valuable insights into the cost and value of multimedia applications.

Technological change is constantly providing opportunities to make fundamental changes to the ways that we communicate and learn. In the early stages the capabilities of a phenomenon such as multimedia are understood by a few who are capable of applying it to situations at hand. As the community of interest grows, others develop visions of how the capabilities can be exploited by organizations to reduce costs, improve productivity, and increase sales. Such visionaries are beholden to the pioneers who struggled to show the value of their applications to an often skeptical business audience.

This book gave the authors an opportunity to share their visions of the potential improvements that multimedia can bring to the most fundamental activity in all business entities—the communication of information and the transfer of knowledge. When we began to collaborate, we were uncertain about our ability to work together. We didn't know where our deliberations would lead but both of us had a common desire to share our views of how multimedia would evolve in business environments in this decade. Each of us brought different skills, backgrounds, and experiences to the project.

Soon after his return to International Business Machines (IBM) headquarters in 1988, Satish Gupta found himself in a small group charged with determining technology areas of strategic importance to IBM. He and his boss, Dr. Terry Rogers, who is currently at Lotus Corporation, were determined to do the "right thing." Satish was asked to review two projects to see if they were of long term importance to IBM.

The first, a project called INFOWINDOWS, was based on the use of laser disc interactive motion video technology for corporate training applications. The approach had been proven to be very cost-effective by a number of customers and by IBM. Although the business plans had not been received with enthusiasm by management, Satish felt that continued involvement in the corporate training business would be important to IBM.

The second project, known as the Audio Video Computer (later renamed the Audio Visual Connection or AVC) used photorealistic images and high quality sound to enhance business presentations. The group had introduced a product called Story Board which lead to the use of personal computers in the business presentation. This group did not believe that analog video devices had any merit in the personal computer domain. The business case wasn't solid but AVC had more mainstream appeal since it extended the personal computer into a new application area.

After his review, Satish struggled to find common ground for the two projects. He didn't feel that the IBM bureaucracy would be able to manage such products in small, emerging markets with modest revenue potential. He concluded that AVC was more important strategically but neither project would lead to significant revenue opportunity.

The turning point came within a week as he was asked to evaluate a proposal from Intel Corporation asking IBM to participate in the deployment of a new technology called Digital Video Interactive or DVI®. The DVI group wanted to use Compact Disc Read Only Memory (CD-ROM) drives for motion video rather than video discs. They proposed to distribute movies on CD-ROM for playback on personal computers or television sets. This approach surpassed the Compact Disc Interactive or CD-I™ approach proposed by Sony and Philips for interactive entertainment and education. CD-I could not support motion video.

The DVI group showed Edit level video (which later evolved to Real Time Video or RTV) to Satish. Although they apologized for the quality of the video presentation on one quarter of the screen at 15 frames per second, he was most impressed. The video information was played directly from hard disk. The net result of examining the three projects was the realization of the opportunity to integrate digitized, motion video into computing independent of the storage or transport media.

Satish became convinced that a personal computer capable of handling audio and video data would become a "personal communicator." His debates with Terry Rogers strengthened his conviction. All three projects were to be pursued aggressively to establish a market position for IBM until the personal computer line and the entire product line absorbed multimedia computing.

Although there was support in the "new IBM," many people could see the pieces but few grasped the vision. Many times he thought of writing a book or paper to make it explicit. In 1991, Satish left IBM to join Media Vision.

Media Vision was founded by experienced entrepreneurs and totally focused on the business premise of multimedia. His new job provided the opportunity to test the strength of his convictions and to be rewarded handsomely if they were correct. The challenge of communicating the vision continued in his new position.

In 1989, I left Northern Telecom to establish a new career as an independent consultant to leading companies in information technology and telecommunications. In the course of preparing for a new way of life, I became more and more intrigued by the possibilities offered by multimedia. My explorations determined that a of community of bright, energetic people were counting on multimedia to provide a bright future. Few discussed the business implications and no one talked about networking multimedia. I decided to establish a consulting practise focused on business and strategic planning for computer or networking companies interested in exploiting multimedia.

Early in 1989, I met Scott Harmon and learned that he shared my dream of establishing a career based on the pursuit of multimedia. Scott introduced me to Randy Seger and the three of us shared information and understanding in our independent quests. Our interactions provided a rich ground for learning about the potential that multimedia offered in business environments. I also learned that many people in the multimedia community understood some of the pieces but few had a vision of what it could and would mean to organizations in the 1990s.

It was not the first time that I felt that the potential of a new capability was not understood by the practitioners or the business community. In 1980, I was involved with a program to define and develop a integrated computer/communications system at BNR Inc., the research and development arm of Northern Telecom and Bell Canada. The integration was at a functional level so a variety of applications could be developed that simultaneously used the capabilities of both the computer and the communications switch.

As I explored the concept with a number of companies, I realized that there was a suite of applications where the user made intensive use of the telephone and needed simultaneous access to computer files. Credit collection, market research, customer support, service, legal agencies, and other applications appeared to be excellent candidates.

Although the project failed for reasons that I won't go into, I was afforded a second opportunity in 1982 to exploit the lessons in my new role as Director of Strategic

Alliances at Northern Telecom. I was responsible for creating, implementing and managing alliances with all of the leading computer vendors. Through our programs with Sperry Univac, Digital Equipment Corp., Data General, Wang, and Hewlett-Packard, we evangelized the virtues of the signaling channel between host computers and private branch exchanges (PBXs).

No one paid much attention to our enthusiasm until Greg Borton, an engineering manager at Digital Equipment Corp. caught our fever and established a program. In 1986, Digital's development/marketing team coined the term "Computer Integrated Telephony" (CIT). Digital's efforts prompted all of the major suppliers of computers and communications switching equipment to establish PBX/computer integration programs.

Although it is satisfying to have been a proponent of the concept, I was often frustrated by my inability to convince my colleagues that it represented a significant business opportunity.

My consulting assignments provided many opportunities to learn more about multimedia applications and their impact on public and private networks. To my networking clients, I became the multimedia "expert," and to my computer clients the networking "expert." When I talked to colleagues in business—the potential users and buyers of multimedia computing—they didn't seem to know what it was, why it was valuable, and how they would use it.

With the support of Scott Harmon, Randy Seger, and others, I published a report entitled *Multimedia Applications, Market Opportunities and Networking Strategies* in 1991. I called Satish to ask him to review the report. When we met, we discussed the challenge of communicating the context and vision of applying multimedia in business environments. We agreed that multimedia wouldn't enjoy widespread success until large numbers of people understood this vision. I noted that Van Nostrand Reinhold was interested in publishing a multimedia handbook.

Although Satish was interested in writing a book, he was concerned that his duties at Media Vision would not allow him to contribute. I convinced him that we could make it work and that our combined experience and knowledge would be important to the undertaking. This book is presented in the hope that it will allow you to appreciate our vision and successfully apply multimedia computing in your organization.

Acknowledgments

By selecting certain individuals to thank, I run the risk of omitting some important contributors. There are many friends whose suggestions have been critical to my ability to complete this book. I thank them all for their support and patience and take full responsibility for any flaws in this book.

Naturally, the first person I must thank is Roger Fetterman who convinced me to start the book. I also thank Robert L. Brannon for reviewing the book and providing feedback. My wife Neera has been very patient and provided much encouragement. I could not have completed my task without her support. To Neera, I dedicate this book.

Satish K. Gupta

Over the past three years two people have shared their insight and wisdom, provided new inputs and challenged my thinking in many of the areas covered by this book. Scott Harmon and Randy Seger have been steadfast in their support of my endeavors to understand multimedia, applications and networking in business environments. I thank both for reviewing the manuscript at several stages in its development.

I would also like to thank my clients for assignments that always seemed to contribute to the base of information needed to undertake this effort. Their support and encouragement sustained me through some difficult times.

I thank Satish Gupta for introducing me to new ways to look at application requirements and solutions and for all of his contributions to the book.

Finally I thank my wife Lynn for being patient and steadfast in her support. This book is dedicated to her.

Roger L. Fetterman

Mainstream Multimedia

1

Introduction

The computer industry is in the midst of an evolutionary "leap forward" which is every bit as significant as the introduction of the personal computer in the business environment. Personal computers are being transformed from compute-intensive to communications-intensive devices that use the power of audio and video, which were the exclusive domain of the radio, television, and motion picture industries in the past.

While it is not the subject of this book, the television industry is undergoing a parallel transformation through the development of high-resolution, interactive, digital television devices. The discussion excludes Compact Disc Interactive (CD-I) and video games such as those provided by Nintendo because they are not based on personal computers.

WHAT IS DIGITAL MULTIMEDIA?

Multimedia is an old concept that has been given new meaning by the computer industry through their efforts to create multimedia-capable computing platforms.

Digital multimedia or multimedia is defined as the integration of up to six media data types—in an interactive, color computing environment as shown in Figure 1-1. Text, graphics, and animation are the traditional "synthesized" or "artificial-world" media data types from the digital domain of yesterday's personal computer platforms. Audio, images, and video are "real-world" media data types that only existed previously in the analog domain of radio and television technology. The real world-media must be digitized in order to operate in personal computers and digital networks as digital data types.

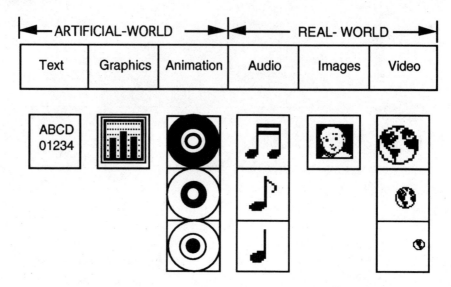

Figure 1-1. Multimedia combines "real-world" media with the media of the computer domain in an interactive computer environment. Source: Authenticity Incorporated.

The term "multimedia" is often used as an adjective to qualify computer products and technologies that use multiple media. Occasionally the term is used as a noun to refer to the evolving phenomenon that includes interactive use of multiple digitized media in all aspects of computing. Simply put, multimedia is a multisensory, participative experience with the emotional impact of audio, image, and video information that takes place in an interactive computing environment. When the term "multimedia" is applied to the personal computer, it will be referred to as *multimedia computing*.

Multimedia enables the addition of real-world media to any application on a personal computer or workstation to improve the effectiveness of the communication of information or the transfer of knowledge. In multimedia applications, the user/viewer can actively participate and control the flow of information. The user is also able to control the outcome of an action within the bounds established by the creator of the application.

Historically, audio, images, and video remained in the analog domain because of the vast amount of information contained in their media representations. Recent technological advancements have made it economically feasible to digitize and compress these real-world media so they can operate effectively in digital computer and networking environments. As a result, audio, images, and video media can be stored, retrieved, manipulated, and transported in the digital world, just as text, graphics, and animation. A new "digital world" is being fashioned through the convergence of the information technology, consumer electronics, and telecommunications industries.

WHY IS MULTIMEDIA IMPORTANT?

In the 1990s, the health and wealth of organizations will be measured by how well they create, manage, distribute, and use information. The application of multimedia and broadband networking capabilities can dramatically improve business communications by providing the desired information *when it is needed, where it is needed, and how it is needed*. The shift from a compute-intensive to a communications-intensive role for the personal computer will have as dramatic an impact on business operations as the invention of the computer itself.

Multimedia can revolutionize the way that information is communicated. The resultant changes in the way that work is carried out by organizations can generate a competitive edge by

• Increasing the overall competency of the workforce

• Improving productivity of individuals and workgroups

• Improving decision-making skills and processes

• Reducing the cost of operating the business

• Increasing sales revenues

The implementation of multimedia offers tremendous opportunities and technological challenges to the developers of personal computers, applications software, network servers, database systems, and networks. However, these areas are undergoing significant advances (as described in Chapter 9).

The interactive use of photorealistic images combined with dynamic media such as audio and video can get us closer to experiencing the information presented than can normally be achieved by the simple act of reading or seeing static media such as text or graphics.

An ancient Chinese proverb is particularly appropriate comment on the power of multimedia:

```
I Hear, I Forget

I See, I Remember

I Experience, I Understand
```

Audio and video have the power to evoke emotion. The personal computer has the power to support interactivity between the user and an application. There is a significant increase in retention, comprehension, and learning when multiple senses participate in the receipt of information.

Multimedia applications include Computer-Based Training (CBT) applications, product documentation, and maintenance manuals and systems that deliver task-specific information to individuals when, where, and how it is needed. Historically, multimedia capabilities enabled CBT and other applications to be implemented in a manner that was simply cheaper, faster, and/or better than traditional methods. CBT studies have shown that ideas and concepts that are experienced interactively are better understood and retained that those experienced passively in a lecture or book. As personal computers and workstations continue to deliver improved price/performance and it becomes easier to implement applications because of enhancements to operating systems and application tools, multimedia applications will become the norm rather that the exception.

It is far more cost-effective to deliver large quantities of information in manuals, references, and documentation in hypermedia format using Compact Disc Read Only Memory (CD-ROM) or other electronic storage mechanisms than it is to use paper. Hypermedia is a method of delivering information that provides multiple connected pathways through a body of information, allowing the user to jump easily from one topic to related or supplementary material. Information is much easier to find and the content can include audio, images, and motion video to make it easier for the user to understand complex ideas and concepts.

The addition of an audio or video clip to a text document or a spreadsheet can improve the information exchange between individuals.

Finally, when information, learning modules and support tools are delivered to the desktop in the context of the tasks and activities of an individual, the individual becomes more competent at his or her job sooner, has easier and quicker access to information, and is more effective at communicating with peers and management.

Communication is an essential element in all business organizations. The act of consuming, manipulating, and producing information is a group activity that must be done in the standard work environment of the group. Teams are seen by experts in the field of groupware and organizational change as the basic organizational building block for modern, innovative companies.

The document imaging industry has proven that productivity improvements of the order of 50 percent can be realized by making it easier to store and retrieve documents. Multimedia can provide similar benefits with the added bonus of making it easier to find specific information in a document. In addition, hypermedia capabilities allow the reader to follow paths of greatest interest and utility through a body of information.

Decision making must keep pace with the changing business environment. The restructuring of business in North America and around the world recognizes the need for decision-making activities to be handled by teams that are close to markets and customers, rather than in headquarters organizations (Johansen, Sibbet, Benson, Martin, Mittman, and Saffo 1991). Communication consumes significant amounts of time in modern businesses and can be facilitated and enhanced by using static and dynamic media.

Leading-edge companies such as Aetna Life and Casualty Company, Motorola Corporation, and Johnson & Johnson recognize that people are their most important asset. They are making investments in equipment and facilities in support of this belief. Motorola is investing in training to compete head-on with the Japanese—and win—in the consumer electronics market. Johnson and Johnson realizes an attractive return on investment (ROI) through investments in an employee wellness program. Aetna improved worker morale and performance by investing in a better workplace (Weddle 1990).

Why are these three companies important to multimedia? All three are living proof that the human capital concept is a valid option for generating a return on investment. Multimedia can be an investment in human capital which will pay dividends in multiple ways, as discussed in Chapter 7.

STATIC AND DYNAMIC MEDIA

Effective communication is an essential element of all successful organizations. In the past, businesses primarily communicated information with static media, which only use *space* (i.e., text, graphics, and images) to communicate information in the form of documents, drawings, and presentations. Dynamic media are time-based media (i.e., animation, audio, and video) which can add a powerful new emotional element to the communication process. Multimedia applications can use both *time* and *space* to communicate information content as shown in Figure 1-2.

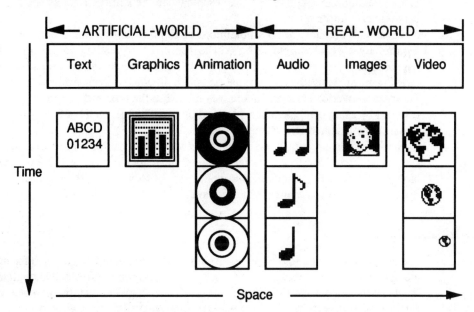

Figure 1-2. The addition of time-based media adds a new dimension to the effectiveness of business communication. Source: Authenticity Incorporated.

The characteristics of static media and dynamic media are discussed below.

Static Media

Static media, text, graphics, and images can only be perceived with our eyes, and are frozen in time. Paper has been the dominant vehicle for storing static media since the invention of movable type by Gutenburg in 1605. The printing process facilitated the "broadcast" of information by providing a time effective mechanism for transferring information from a few knowledgeable individuals to many receivers. In the nineteenth century, text and graphics were augmented by black-and-white images which added to the "communications power" of paper documents.

Initially computers began as a numerical character-based environment. They were designed to reduce the cost and increase the speed of labor-intensive computational functions. It wasn't until the 1980s that computers were used intensively for word and text processing (alphabetical character-based) applications. The addition of graphics and the introduction of the graphical user interface, first by Xerox PARC with the Star workstation and then by Apple with the Lisa and Macintosh personal computers, marked a major shift in how we interface with and use computers.

The shift from computing to desktop publishing created a demand for image handling capability which is being satisfied by a number of technological innovations. It is clear that the addition of graphics and images enhanced the ability of books and computers to communicate information.

Paper will continue to be a ubiquitous communications vehicle because it does not require any special equipment or skill to use it. Basic reading and writing skills in a relevant language are the only prerequisites. Paper has become so ubiquitous that many individuals are deluged with information, much of which may be irrelevant. However, the information overload problem and issues related to the timeliness of information may be resolved by using computers in a "demand printing" mode, which allows you to print up-to-date information as and when you need it.

Static media are used and will continue to be used in all aspects of business communications. However, the availability of inexpensive and easy to use scanners, audio tape recorders, video cameras, and compression technology is prompting the use of dynamic media to communicate information.

Dynamic Media

Audio, animation, and motion video use time as a critical dimension of information and are *dynamic* media. Audio includes voice, music, and sound effects. Although animation has been used for some time in personal computer applications, the personal computer enhancements needed for audio and video provide an even richer environment for the use of animation. The multimedia computer is capable of handling dynamic media in an interactive, programmable environment. As shown in Figure 1-3, the video cassette recorder (VCR) is dynamic but it is not interactive.

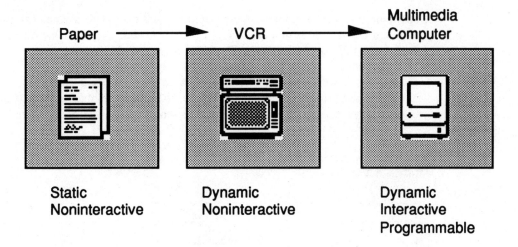

Paper → VCR → Multimedia Computer

Static Noninteractive

Dynamic Noninteractive

Dynamic Interactive Programmable

Figure 1-3. The multimedia computer enables interaction with dynamic media.

The characteristics of voice—tone, pitch, loudness, and intonation—add significant amounts of information to the message. For example, repeat the sentence—"I didn't say he was a thief"—several times with the emphasis on a different word each time. Note that the sentence takes on an entirely different meaning each time. The vocal nuances (affective response) often carry more information than the words themselves.

Many devices are available to facilitate the use of dynamic media in business communication. The most pervasive device is the telephone. Voice mail systems enable users of the telephone system to defer usage of information, as can be done with paper-based or electronic mail (e-mail) communications.

The addition of dynamic media enhances the "communications power" of the personal computer. Dynamic media can be more effective than static media in many applications. Voice-annotated comments from your boss about a document have a more significant impact than handwritten comments in the margin. The integration of digitized audio and video information, in our day-to-day business activities, will significantly enhance our ability to receive, process, and act on information.

The power of dynamic media is often attributed to the quantity of information that is transmitted between the sender and the receiver. The eye is able to digest the information in a full-color image that represents more than a megabyte of information in a fraction of a second. When we watch movies or television, our eyes assimilate information at more than 25 Mbyte/s.

In some instances, a single image can present all of the information that is needed. However, dynamic media helps to preserve the context by presenting information in the right sequence and at the appropriate tempo. Context provides additional information which is simply not provided in the individual pieces that make up information. Individual photographs of an incident may convey a partial meaning or even a completely different meaning than a full-motion video clip. For example, a photograph can show the gears that drive the rollers in a laser printer but a video clip can show the direction that each gear takes during a print cycle. The additional contextual information accounts for the increased effectiveness of communication that uses dynamic media.

Table 1-1 compares the characteristics of static and dynamic media. The impact of dynamic media on storage capacity and network bandwidth is much greater than static media so it may be necessary to make tradeoffs based on cost and value considerations.

Table 1-1. Dynamic Media Require Larger Storage Mechanisms and Higher-Bandwidth Networks than Static Media

	Static Media	Dynamic Media
Time	Discontinuous	Continuous
Senses	Seeing	Seeing and hearing
Storage mechanisms	Paper	Magnetic tape
	Magnetic/optical disk	Magnetic/optical disk
Data rate/quantity	1 kbyte per page	50 kbyte/s for audio
	1 Mbyte per image	25 Mbyte/s for video

Currently, the mechanisms used to create and access dynamic media are expensive compared to paper and pen. As a result, applications that exploit dynamic media are not accessible to broad audiences in business or consumer markets. The lack of ubiquitous access to dynamic media is a major inhibitor to broad acceptance of multimedia in business environments. This book was written to shed light on the factors that should be considered as individuals attempt to use multimedia capabilities to improve communications in their daily business environment.

TECHNOLOGY SHIFTS

Technological shifts and industry convergence make it a propitious time to move ahead with multimedia in business environments. There is a pervasive shift to an all-digital environment and previously unrelated industries and products—cameras, computers, stereo systems, photocopiers, telephones, television sets, VCRs, and typewriters—are converging to form a huge, unified information technology sector. The digitization of these technologies and their convergence into a single information sector is based on a common set of digital component technologies is depicted in Figure 1-4. The shift to an all-digital environment is providing the foundation for the development of multimedia computing.

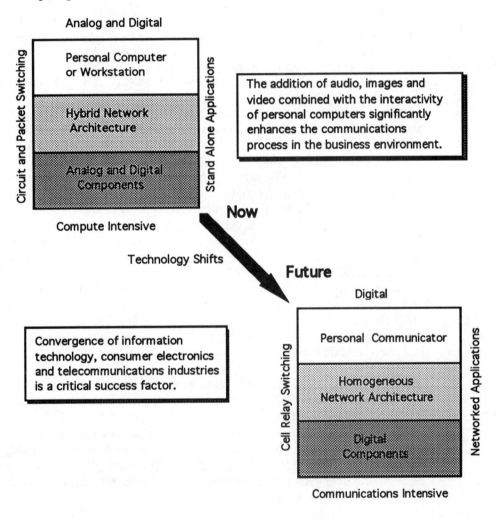

Figure 1-4. The shift to an all-digital environment and industry convergence is accompanied by a move to a homogeneous network architecture.

The shift to an all-digital environment in the fields of telephony, television, music, and photography is particularly important for multimedia. All of these technologies contribute to the growth of multimedia computing by reducing cost and enabling integration.

Telephony

Most of the backbone of the public telephone network has been digital for some time. The network is comprised of a hierarchy of bandwidths that extends to the gigabit/s range. The bandwidth of an individual channel for voice or data is 64 kbit/s. In North America, T1 is a digital transmission system that operates at 1.544 Mbit/s, allowing 24 voice channels to be multiplexed on a single line. T3 operates at 44.736 Mbit/s, which is equivalent to 28 T1 links.

Both T1 and T3 services are available to business on a widespread basis. The bandwidths of T1 and T3 are adequate for most emerging multimedia networking applications.

The introduction of Synchronous Optical Network (SONET) fiber optics introduces a new hierarchy in the backbone network which will extend from 155.52 Mbit/s eventually to 13.271 gigabit/s. SONET-based networks will provide the bandwidth needed to transport any and all media types including audio and video. There will no longer be any distinction between voice and data networks as the Broadband Integrated Services Digital Network (BISDN) will accommodate all types of traffic. The networks of the Interexchange Carriers (IECs) are largely fiber at this time. Fiber networks can and will be upgraded to SONET as the need arises.

The power of digital signal processing is being used to increase the bandwidth of existing copper facilities to residential and small-business users. Initially 1.544 Mbit/s and basic rate Integrated Services Digital Network (ISDN) (144 kbit/s) will be delivered over the existing copper facilities. American Telephone and Telegraph (AT&T) has announced that they can run 3 Mbit/s on two twisted pairs, which means that phone companies will be able to offer multimedia services on existing copper facilities. By the end of the decade, transmission rates of more than 10 Mbit/s will be possible. It will be possible to deliver multimedia information to small business and home office users even if fiber-optic links are not available.

It will be reasonable and feasible to provide high bandwidth digital service (i.e., bandwidths greater than 1.544 Mbit/s) to all public network subscribers using a hybrid fiber/copper network and powerful signal processing technologies. The long-term success of multimedia computing in the business environment hinges on the availability of ubiquitous, broadband, digital network services.

Television

High-definition television or HDTV is the next generation television system which offers enhanced picture and sound quality. It may be fully digital when the standard is finalized by the Federal Communications Commission (FCC) in 1993. The proposed American HDTV system makes use of a unique spectral notch or small band of frequencies that will avoid interference with present television signals or vice versa. An important feature of the newly designed digital system is the ability to carry a combination of data, video, and audio signals which can be varied instantaneously.

HDTV is important to multimedia because it makes use of so much advanced computer and microprocessor technology that it could have a massive positive impact on the cost and quality of memory devices, digital signal processors, and flat screen displays.

When HDTV sets are produced in quantity by the consumer electronics industry, the cost of high-resolution display technology will become very attractive. This will stimulate a shift to higher-resolution displays in multimedia computing.

Music

The music industry has been totally transformed by the introduction of the compact disc products. This fully digitized audio technology is responsible for the unprecedented quality that is achieved using inexpensive stereo equipment.

Digital Audio Tape (DAT) technology provides fully digitized audio in a medium that allows easy recording and reproduction. Very high quality sound reproduction is possible because of the use of digital technology.[1]

Compact disc (CD) technology has been a significant factor in success of multimedia computing because it resulted in the development of the CD-ROM. CD-ROM provides an inexpensive medium for publishing large amounts of digital audio and video information in addition to text, graphics, images, and animation.

Photography

Recent developments in photography validate the trend toward digitization. Canon introduced a camera that captures pictures directly on a floppy disk so that the pictures can be viewed on a computer display or a television screen. The images are recorded on the floppy disks in digital form. Similar products are available from Sony and Logitec.

Kodak introduced a concept called Photo CD which is being adopted by the suppliers of multimedia products. Developed jointly by Kodak and Philips Electronics NV, the Photo CD system combines the convenience and outstanding image quality of 35 mm photography with the benefits of digital technology on compact discs. Consumers will take pictures with a 35 mm camera. When they bring their film to the photofinisher for processing, they will have the option of ordering a Photo CD disc in addition to the prints, negatives, and slides they ordinarily receive.

Photographs that are "printed" on a compact disc (CD) can be viewed on a computer with a CD-ROM drive or a Photo CD player. Photo CD makes it easy for application developers to capture the images they need for business applications in digital form.

---

[1] The music industry feels threatened because it is easy to make copies with same quality as the original. As a result, the industry is pursuing legal and technical alternatives to protect the rights to their software by controlling all reproductions

Impact of Digitization

For the foreseeable future, the integration of *uncompressed* digital audio, images, and video will not be feasible. Digitized audio, images, and video must be compressed to be of practical use in personal computers and networks. The term "images" is used to mean photographs or bit-mapped images of text and/or graphics on the printed page. Refer to Chapter 9 for more information.

For example, 5 minutes of CD-quality audio requires more than 50 megabytes of storage. This would consume the entire disk drive on most personal computers. In addition, the transmission of the audio information requires a sustained rate of 1.2 Mbit/s. Four or five concurrent users would overload a traditional Ethernet local area network (LAN).

The challenge presented by video is even more imposing. Full-motion video with broadcast television quality requires 720 kbytes per frame at 30 frames per second (fps). One second of video consumes 21.6 Mbytes of storage. At 30 fps, television-quality full-motion video requires a bandwidth of more than 172.8 Mbit/s. At this rate, 5 minutes of video consumes 64.8 gigabytes of storage. Digitized video must be compressed more than 100 times to be of practical use in the computing environment.

Benefits of the Shift to Digital

The benefits of converting to an all-digital environment are compelling. Once all of the media are in digital form and compressed, they are of practical use in contemporary computer systems and networks. Audio, image, and video files can be processed by computers using existing input or output devices. The ability to manipulate, store, retrieve, and transmit real-world information enables the personal computer or workstation to play a major role in the business communication process.

Technological innovation in computing and digital signal processing has reduced the cost and increased the performance of the personal computers and multimedia support systems. As a result, it is feasible and reasonable to achieve an all-digital environment for multimedia computing.

An all-digital environment offers functionality that makes it much easier to develop multimedia applications in businesses with diverse computer equipment and networking systems. The functions described below could not be achieved in a hybrid analog/digital world

• Resolution independence or scalability

• Digital network compatibility

• Network bandwidth independence

• Magnetic/optical storage compatibility

• Selective access

• Content analysis

Resolution Independence or Scalability

Resolution independence or scalability means that audio or video quality is determined by the characteristics of the receiving device rather than that of the information source. The same digital video source can be used to present a low-quality picture on a low-resolution display and a higher-quality picture on a display with higher resolution.

The principle of scalability can be applied to the frame rate of full-motion video. Even though the source is 30 fps, the network and the personal computer may only be capable of handling 10 fps.

Digital audio is also scalable. For example, an audio source with a sample rate of 44 kHz and 16 bits per sample, can be played back at 22 kHz and 8 bits per sample. Once again, the quality of playback is determined by the receiver.

Thus a single copy of high-quality audio and video information on a multimedia file server can satisfy the quality requirements of an variety of personal computers and workstations. Scalability also means that the same source can deliver information over different networking schemes and that quality will be dictated by the capability of the network.

Digital Network Compatibility

Digitized "real-world" information can be transported to any location using existing data networks. Time-dependent media such as audio and video need a network that does not impose undue transmission delays. Transmission time and audio and video quality will vary with the bandwidth of the network.

Network Bandwidth Independence

The quality of the audio and video information for a given compression level varies directly with the lowest speed link of the end-to-end network serving the desktop. Once again, scalability can be used to adjust the delivery of information to correspond to the resources that are available.

Magnetic or Optical Storage Compatibility

Digitized multimedia information can be stored on a variety of mechanisms including diskettes, hard disk drives, flash memory cards, and digital tapes and optical disks so that it can be retrieved from any location at any time.

Selective Access

The searching and sorting techniques used for text and graphics can be extended to digitized audio, images, and video. Current database management products allow users to organize content based on the properties of data. Since multimedia databases are huge, effective search and retrieval techniques are important to the implementation of business applications.

In addition, hypermedia techniques can be used to browse through multimedia databases in a manner that is consistent with the interests of the individual. Hypermedia—an extension of a more commonly used term hypertext—is a method for delivering information that provides multiple connected pathways through a body of information, allowing the user to jump easily from one topic to related or supplementary material, which may be text, graphics, audio, images, or video.

Content Analysis

Digitized audio and video information can also be searched based on content. A considerable amount of research is being conducted to exploit the full potential of content analysis for digitized audio and video. In an exploratory effort, the MIT Media Laboratory has separated the fixed stage related content from the character content in an *I Love Lucy* television program. New scenes could be created by superimposing character content with stage content from other scenes in the program. In principle, brand new episodes could be created by reusing pieces from the old ones.

FROM COMPUTER TO COMMUNICATOR

Multimedia shifts the role of the personal computer from compute-to communications-intensive activities. In the short term, the input/output (I/O) capability of personal computers will be challenged by the introduction of real-world media. In the long term, computer manufacturers will add more communications processing power to their products to accommodate multimedia I/O requirements. The shift from personal computer to personal communicator is examined in the following sections.

Compute-Intensive Use of Computers

Todate, computers have been used primarily for compute-intensive applications, i.e., calculating consumes a large portion of the resources and time of a computer. The results have been presented in a brief and simple alphanumeric manner which fails to effectively represent the conceptual models from which they were derived.

In many business applications, large amounts of information are managed by computers. For example, an airline reservation system keeps track of thousands of customer reservations, flight information for several airlines, airplane status and fare structures, etc. Travel information is accessed on a continuous basis by airline employees and travel agents. Although search and retrieval activity is very high, the computer is used sparingly for communicating the results of the search.

If a travel agent needs information about a travel promotion to Hawaii, information about fares and flights can be accessed on-line but promotional material about Hawaii, hotels, and recreational activity is only available in printed brochures. The reservations computer is not used to communicate anything but alphanumeric information. The process of enhancing reservation systems to include audio, image, and video information has begun. Over the next few years such systems will play a major role in communicating information on an interactive basis.

Expanding Communicating Capabilities of Computers

Television programs and movies use photorealistic images, high-quality audio, animation, and full-motion video to deliver powerful, persuasive, and entertaining messages. Computers that are capable of storing, retrieving, and manipulating images, audio, animation, and full-motion video represent a powerful force for the future of business communication.

In many cases, personal computers have been used as a controller for VCRs, laser disc players, or audio tape decks. All of these devices store information in analog form and are commonly used in the television and entertainment industries. It is not surprising that many of the early adopters of multimedia came from these industries. CBT and merchandising applications have been successfully deployed using the computer to control analog playback devices and providing adequate levels of interactivity. However, the level of success was not as great as originally envisioned, due in part to the mixed analog/digital environment.

However, as noted earlier, the world is shifting to an all-digital environment. The digitization of audio and video information allows dynamic, real world media to be fully integrated in the computing and networking environments. All multimedia applications can benefit from this shift.

Multimedia extensions are having a profound impact on the role of the personal computer and workstation. The shift in the role from a compute-intensive to a communications-intensive role will have almost as significant an impact on the lives of people as the invention of the computer itself. The extended capabilities enhance the usefulness and effectiveness of the computer as a communications tool. In this information age, communication is a major part of everyone's job. A tool that makes communication more effective will revolutionize the way that work itself is carried out by organizations.

Communication-Intensive Use of Computers

In communications-intensive applications such as presentations or CBT or hypermedia documentation, the goal is to present ideas in the most effective way. The effectiveness of these communication processes in CBT has been amply demonstrated in a number of intensive studies. Refer to Chapter 7 for more information.

CBT has become a very large industry because it has been shown to take less time to reach equivalent levels of achievement when compared to traditional lecture/laboratory training by the Institute for Defense Analysis. In addition, companies such as Steelcase, Inc., 3M Corporation, and American Airlines have achieved both cost savings and time savings. A study by *CBT Directions* magazine in October 1991 forecasted expenditures of

$2.68 billion on integrating multimedia into courseware in 1992, up from $1.96 billion in 1991 (Kemske 1991).

Personal computers have replaced the typewriter for word processing for memos, correspondence, and report preparation. Personal computers are used extensively in the preparation of presentation material such as slides and overhead transparencies. When compared to a television program, a movie, or a multimedia presentation prepared by a professional, it is evident that such slide presentations are relatively primitive. When the personal computer is able to handle audio and video as effectively and inexpensively as text and graphics, it will have come of age and will be ready to participate in the potentially huge and growing domain of personal communications in the information age.

Host Computers in Communications Intensive Environments

What role will the host or mainframe computers play in the multimedia environment? The traditional role of host computers, i.e., computing, transaction processing, and database systems, is not likely to disappear.

Many corporations have mission critical databases, which means that the core business of the company depends on the integrity and availability of the database. The databases are shared by many parts of the organization on a continuous basis. These databases will continue to be the major task of host computers. In addition, host computers will play a critical role for multimedia database and transaction processing systems.

Many large corporations generate massive quantities of information which is primarily for communication-intensive applications. The abilities of host computers to manage the large amounts of shared data will be used to manage digitized image, audio, and video information. The amount of storage needed for these new data types is one or more orders of magnitude greater than that needed for text and graphics. There will also be a need to operate on the content so the search process is efficient. Current database management technology will go through a major transformation to accommodate multimedia storage and management requirements.

Existing computer networks deal primarily with static information. As dynamic media such as audio and video are added, computer networks must be capable of delivering much larger quantities of data without any undue delays so as to preserve the integrity of these time-dependent media types. The addition of dynamic media requires fundamental changes in the design of network software and hardware. Host computers will play an important role as database management systems.

There are many challenges to be faced by the developers of host computers and networks as we shift into the communications-intensive world of personal computers.

The Emerging Personal Communicator

The personal computer brings something unique to the domain of communication-intensive applications—interactivity. Interactivity is the one of the keys to popularity of the personal computer. Books, magazines, movies, and radio and television programs offer very little opportunity for user interaction. Although a number of organizations intend to offer interactive television services, the level of interactivity will be limited compared to that available on personal computers.

Personal will become the operative word in personal computing. The personal computer will be able to make certain types of communication more personal by maintaining and using a profile of its user. The user profile will enable the personal computer to provide intelligent filtering of incoming information based on individual interests and preferences. For example, an expert system will sort incoming mail or broadcasted information to help solve the information overload problem.

The *personal computer* may be more appropriately called the *personal communicator*. As a personal communicator it will not only transform current prevalent communications processes but it will also transform the work environment. It will empower people to communicate ideas and concepts in new ways with an efficiency and effectiveness levels that were heretofore impractical if not impossible.

Evolution of the Personal Communicator

Broad acceptance of the communications-intensive role of the personal computer will come about over next 3 to 5 years. There does not seem to be a "killer application" that will instantly transform the computing machine into a communicating machine. In fact the killer application may simply be greatly improved communications in all aspects of business operations. The evolution will be a combination of social and technological changes. The personal computer has become an integral part of our society. Technological changes, such as the ones described in this book, will enable the personal computer to become a powerful communication machine. The changes will facilitate this evolution or they may even accelerate it.

In the next chapter we provide an outline of how technology and applications will evolve over the next few years.

SUMMARY OF THE BOOK

Chapter 1 introduces multimedia and defines the scope of the book. The movement to an all-digital environment for all communications-oriented media such as television, telephony, and photography is described as it reinforces the role of computers in the communication industry. The role of the computer is shifting from that of a computing machine to a communicating machine. By the middle of this decade multimedia technology will be fully integrated in computers and will be so affordable that the personal computer will be used to access a wide variety of information.

Chapter 2 covers the process of evolutionary growth of multimedia technology and its acceptance by industry and consumers. The technology push and market pull of multimedia computing is described. Multimedia technology, much like any other new technology, will be accepted and adopted in phases. The evolution begins as the technology is applied to *enable* existing and proven applications, then moves to the *enhance* phase where a broad range of popular applications use the technology as it becomes more cost effective, and finally the technology will *pervade* the computer industry. The use of multimedia in applications will be taken for granted. Multimedia capabilities will appear in the user interface and completely change the way that computers are perceived and used.

Chapter 3 presents a market structure based on customer type and application segment. Three types of information customers or users are introduced: information consumer, information presenter, and information/knowledge worker. Applications are categorized in four categories: (1) content-centric (2) interactive presentation-centric (3) office-centric and (4) business operations-centric. A description is given of the creators and users, products, economic factors, market size, and distribution channels for each application class.

Chapter 4 develops a conceptual model that starts with face-to-face communication and builds the need for communications machines as the communications process becomes more complex. The elements, attributes, and values of business applications are introduced and defined.

Chapter 5 describes the applications of interest to the information consumer, the information presenter, and the information/knowledge worker. Business applications are described and classified in accordance with the categories introduced in Chapter 3.

Chapter 6 introduces a structured way for characterizing the elements of an application and analyzing the requirements to determine if proposed solutions are viable.

Chapter 7 provides some insights into the studies that have proven the value of multimedia, discusses the issues surrounding the justification of multimedia applications and analyzes the ROI for three applications.

Chapter 8 introduces the computer-generated microworlds of graphics-based simulation and virtual reality. Leading edge graphics-based simulation products are discussed which enable "teaching by doing" as part of the paradigm shift from training events to learning as a process. It also explores virtual reality applications that will amuse, entertain, inform, and educate the consumer.

Chapter 9 is a comprehensive collection of information about the technologies that are required to implement multimedia solutions. It summarizes available and planned hardware and software platforms, authoring tools, storage systems, and local and wide area networking, compression techniques and tools for capturing and manipulating audio and video. It is written for managers who may be in the decision-making process and have no interest in developing an in-depth understanding of the field but must deal with application of multimedia computing in this new and rapidly evolving field.

Chapter 10 covers the authors' conclusions and projections of what to expect in the next decade in terms of the application of multimedia computing and the availability of technology.

REFERENCES

Johansen, Robert; Sibbet, David; Benson, Suzyn; Martin, Alexia; Mittman, Robert; Saffo, Paul. 1991. *Leading Business Teams*. Menlo Park, California: Addison-Wesley.

Kemske, Floyd. 1991. The CBT Directions Study of Multimedia Utilization in CBT. Boston, Massachusetts: Weingarten Publications.

Weddle, Peter D. 1990. Human Capital: Reality or Rhetoric? *Human Capital* 1(4):45–47.

2

Multimedia Evolution

GROWTH AND ACCEPTANCE

The word "computer" was not in common use until after the debut of the famous Electronic Numeric Integrator and Computer (ENIAC)—the first electronic computer—in the 1940s. ENIAC gave birth to the data processing industry. In the 1990s, computers have become part of almost every person's life, in the form of personal computers at home or in the office, or a "black box" that controls the timing and flow of fuel in an automobile. It took roughly four decades for mainframe computers and less than one decade for personal computers to become pervasive. Computers and especially the personal computer have revolutionized the way we live and work.

Multimedia technology is causing a minirevolution within the computer revolution. It is highly likely that it will take a few years before the use of multimedia capabilities is pervasive in the home or the office. However, it will not take decades for multimedia to become pervasive. The authors believe that all new personal computers will be equipped with full multimedia capabilities by the middle of this decade. The term "multimedia-capable" will be redundant by 1995. In the fast pace of today's world, it is useful to remember that the process is evolutionary and note that the computing and communications industries will have time to adapt products and services as multimedia capability becomes ubiquitous.

THE PULL AND PUSH OF MULTIMEDIA

The four major global problems listed below are providing the "pull" and "push" to move multimedia into the business marketplace.

The major personal computer and consumer electronics manufacturers face a common, life threatening problem: rapidly saturating markets for core products. They need to create more demand for increasingly full-featured devices with more and more power. Multimedia appears to be a significant potential solution to these manufacturers.

Multimedia computing has the potential to rejuvenate the computer and consumer electronics industries and solve major problems for businesses in the ways shown below.

• Rapidly saturating current technology markets

• Information overload and degradation of the quality of information

• Increasing importance of knowledge accompanied by the decreasing life

 cycle of "current knowledge"

• Changing societal work ethic paradigm

Personal computer vendors are incorporating the abilities to handle real-world media into their products and consumer electronics firms are adding interactivity to theirs.

At this point, most large businesses have evolved from *data-based* to *information-based* organizations (i.e., they require information that has been processed and analyzed). Information overload and the subsequent degradation of the quality of information content is a problem that is plaguing all industrial nations. The drive for success in the global marketplace creates a critical need for products that offer improved ways for finding, acquiring, presenting, and using relevant information.

Knowledge is even more important than information in today's highly competitive environment. The World Future Society predicts that a new corporate elite will emerge this decade: the highly educated "gold collar" knowledge worker. Ironically, it also notes that the life cycle of current knowledge is decreasing rapidly. It is estimated that the half-life of an engineer's knowledge will decline from 5 years today to 3 years by the year 2000.

This potential skill gap will trigger continuous on-the-job training in the business environment. Multimedia offers potential solutions for portions of the two preceding problems.

Advanced applications environments, such as Hewlett-Packard's NewWave, will be able to exploit the communications enhancement power afforded by multimedia. These environments will allow users to create, transmit, and receive compound documents composed of any digital media, including animation, audio, and video. Such environments can help alleviate information overload and improve the quality of the content of information by making it easier to find and retrieve relevant information.

Any consideration of the problem area of knowledge must address the rate of change issue. Change occurs so rapidly today that the content of many books is not current, valid, or relevant by the time the book is published. This fact, coupled with the increasing need for continuous on-the-job employee training, leads to the conclusion that multimedia offers a potential solution to the critical problem of the rapidly shrinking knowledge life cycle.

Knowledge stored in digital form can be easily and rapidly updated using a computer.

Sociologists have recently noted the occurrence of a significant paradigm shift related to the work ethic in leading industrial societies. Personal quality time is "in" and workaholism is "out." People want more leisure time for relaxation and for personal development outside their work environment.

Interactive multimedia players, coupled to the ubiquitous television set, will play a major role in this problem area as well by providing interactive access to information, television programs, home study courses, and entirely new forms of entertainment. The video game machine has already been described as the "home computer for the masses." In effect, the video games provided by Nintendo, Sega, and others have already prepared the home market for multimedia.

EVOLUTIONARY PHASES

There are three distinct phases in the evolution of multimedia computing technology:

• Enable

• Enhance

• Pervade

Each of the phases is described in detail including application areas, cost and justification, infrastructure, and standards.

Enable

The first phase of evolution, which covers the infancy of multimedia, can be appropriately called *Enable*. During this phase, the value of the application is so great that the cost of implementation can easily be justified or ignored. These applications use audio and video in spite of the high cost of incorporating dynamic media and the fact that effective tools are not available for use by the subject matter expert. The use of multimedia technology simply makes the solutions for these applications cheaper, faster, and/or better.

Application Areas

A number of application areas have depended on interactive use of multiple media albeit hybrid analog/digital for more than a decade. CBT is a good example. If the objective is to train an employee to repair a particular piece of equipment, it is very effective for the student to see the repair process. Currently the trainer might use a videotape to show how an expert would effect the repair. The trainer and the student can review the recorded material as often as necessary to ensure that a desired level of comprehension is achieved. Prior to the availability of videotape or laser disc, the trainer was forced to use "live" demonstrations which were repeated as often as necessary.

It is evident that the use of an audio and visual medium is critical to the success of this application. In the enable phase of evolution of multimedia, interactive multimedia capabilities are used to simply improve the solution. Applications are simply enabled on the multimedia-capable computing platforms. A multimedia computer provides the user with many levels of decision and control, on an interactive basis, thereby altering the way that information is conveyed.

It is generally agreed that the ability to interact with information in addition to seeing and hearing improves the retention of information. People retain about 20 percent of what they hear, 40 percent of what they see and hear, and up to 75 percent of what they see, hear, and do. Thus the interactivity provided by a multimedia computer significantly improves the effectiveness of the solution. Course materials can be prepared and distributed on CD-ROMs or removable disk cartridges so that large numbers of students can take the training course at their convenience. This results in incremental decreases in cost and improvements in learning that are typical of this phase.

The value of the improvements to applications in the enable phase is so great that the use of new and expensive technology can be justified. The cost and benefit of the use of video in training applications can be justified in spite of the fact that it might cost $100,000 to develop an hour of interactive video training. The increased development costs over more traditional methods is justified because more students can be trained in less time, travel expenses can be reduced, less time is spent off-the-job, etc. Trainers are able to handle more students. Training schedules can be much more flexible so that students can take the courses when it bests suits his or her work schedule. Each student is able to take the course at his or her own pace further which results in more effective learning.

Cost and Justification

The uses of multimedia in the enable phase are targeted at well-defined applications and sets of users. In training applications a selected group of students receive a well-defined set of information. Such applications are appropriately called vertical applications. Horizontal applications are those that can be used by a wide variety of users without regard to the nature of the business. For example, a spreadsheet is a horizontal application that is used by many different types of users in all kinds of businesses. In the enable phase, justification parameters are easy to understand and apply to traditional ROI analysis. Effectiveness measures can be classified as cost reductions, productivity improvements, or revenue increases within the scope of an existing application.

Applications developed during the enable phase do not have the opportunity to benefit from the economies derived from mass production of products. However, the applications that are enabled can absorb the high initial costs of multimedia technology since they result in incremental cost improvements over the current way of doing things. Multimedia technology and applications are emerging from this phase and will enter the enhance phase in 1993–1994.

Infrastructure

In addition to expensive equipment, applications developed in the enable phase must overcome the hurdles posed by a relatively immature set of tools and scarcity of skills. There are relatively few products and applications developers available during this phase. The multimedia authoring tools that have emerged are analogous to early word processors for text applications. For example, AuthorWare Professional by MacroMedia, Inc. is a well established multimedia authoring tool. AuthorWare Professional is targeted at business users that are interested in developing training material for use by large numbers of people (e.g., more than 200 or 300) and is priced at $8000 per copy. The availability of a simplified version of AuthorWare Professional called STAR at a much lower price and with reduced functionality and greater ease of use is evidence of the shift from the enable to the enhance phase. Several other tools that exhibit the same type of change are starting to appear in the market.

The skill set required to implement solutions involve the use of multiple media by subject matter experts. Auto repair mechanics know little about the use of multimedia but must participate in the development of training modules as subject matter experts. Current state-of-the-art authoring tools still require that multimedia professionals be involved in production and organization of material for use on computing platforms. As long as professional developers continue to be critical resources, their limited numbers constrain the growth of the technology. Unless multimedia professionals become more prolific or authoring tools mature so that subject matter experts are able to directly produce multimedia products, rapid growth remains impractical. The availability of authoring tools that minimize the skill requirements of the user combined with simultaneous growth in the number of multimedia professionals will drive the evolution of multimedia into the next phase.

Standards

Since the applications are specific to the needs of the targeted user, and cost justified by a very specific requirement, the actual implementations are very distinct. Very little of a given solution is adaptable for use in another. For example, an auto repair training course would be developed independently of a training course for car salespersons. Standards are not critical since applications are created and justified independently and there is no perceived need to exchange content and tools. This is appropriate for this phase since industry experts are still trying to determine which standards make sense in the longer term. The application of multimedia technology proceeds through the enable phase with little or no focus on standards.

In summary, multimedia technology simply enables existing applications to operate in a new environment during the enable phase. There is no fundamental change or shift in the application. Significant paradigm shifts aren't needed to realize the value of multimedia applications. Cost and value parameters are well understood. The use of the new technology makes applications feasible at lower cost and as a result, extends their applicability. The tools and infrastructure are under-developed. Product development must reach critical mass in the enable phase before multimedia technology can move into the next phase.

Most of the current multimedia applications during this enable phase are in the areas of training, education, and merchandising, all of which are primarily interactive presentations. It is natural that information presenters have been the early adoptersof multimedia technology during the enable phase.

Enhance

The second and most rapidly growing phase of multimedia technology is the enhance phase. During this phase the technology becomes significantly cheaper, faster, and easy to use. Applications implemented during the enable phase have prompted the development of an array of products and tools and an infrastructure capable of sustaining more growth. The cost of the technology has reduced to a point that many applications begin to take advantage of multimedia capabilities. Large numbers of applications (for which multimedia was not essential for their viability) begin to use these capabilities to enhance their functionality and competitiveness. The following list covers successful applications that will take advantage of multimedia capabilities:

• Spreadsheets

• Word processors

• Electronic mail (e-mail) systems

• Groupware

• Document imaging systems

• Database management systems

Multimedia has entered this phase of evolution.

Application Areas

Spreadsheets are good examples of products that are incorporating multimedia capabilities. Many spreadsheet products such as Microsoft Excel and Lotus 1-2-3 are available and their use is pervasive. Spreadsheets are horizontal applications since they serve a wide variety of users. Up until this point in time, the addition of voice, pictures, or music has not been viable. However, the availability of inexpensive audio capability on personal computers has motivated leading developers of spreadsheet products to add voice capabilities. This is what we mean by *enhancing* an existing product in a highly pervasive application area. Voice capabilities allow the user to annotate a cell or cells in a spreadsheet. Voice capability is also being used to provide the "help function" in a variety of applications in a way that is not intrusive to the user. Current "help functions" hide a portion of the screen and prevent the user from referring to the area in question. By using audio, the user continues to have full access to the screen while receiving help. Lotus Development Corporation introduced a new version of Lotus 1-2-3 with multimedia SmartHelp in March 1992.

SmartHelp contains all of the text documentation for Lotus 1-2-3 and a series of introductory lessons incorporating sound and animated sequences covering the use of the product. If a user chooses the "help" function while preparing a spreadsheet, an audio/video sequence is played that demonstrates how to use the function in question.

Vendors are motivated to enhance existing applications because of the availability of inexpensive new capabilities, to gain competitive advantage or to keep up with the competition. Several word processing and e-mail vendors are already adding voice capabilities to their products. Such solutions are not driven by a compelling need on the part of the user but by a "want to have" requirement. The developers of application products are inclined to add new functions when hardware ceases to be an impediment or the installed base is large enough to create visibility for the new features.

Significant reductions in the cost of multimedia functions will become feasible because of high volume deployment. The existing installed base and inventory of personal computers will be upgraded so they are multimedia capable. New products will ship with multimedia capabilities built-in. Hardware manufactures will also be driven to add functionality to their products because of competitive pressures.

Cost and Justification

Effectiveness measurements, value, and cost justification make a significant shift in the enhance phase. The cost of deploying new hardware will reach a point where a "whimsical, just let us try it attitude" becomes significant. Many users will say "I don't know if I really need it, but so and so is using it, so I'll give it a try." A form of "function envy" becomes prevalent. In addition, a shift in the quality of interaction will significantly change the way that people work. For example, when it becomes easy to annotate individual cells in a spreadsheet we can expect better communication between coworkers and faster interchange of information. Because it is dynamic and includes both tone and inflection, a voice clip can also carry a greater impact than written annotation alone. This will contribute to improved quality of work and reduce the cycle time.

Such changes are very fundamental and they make the process of evolution totally irreversible. People become addicted to the new technology because of the positive impact. Multimedia changes the job rather than just improving it. It is this shift that causes the movement to "you've got to have it" and launches the technology into the final evolutionary phase—pervade.

Infrastructure

In the *enhance* phase, the tools evolve to a point where a large numbers of people, who are not skilled in multimedia technologies, will be able to perform simple, necessary functions supported by the wide variety of horizontal applications. These tools will be offered at much lower cost to a wider variety of users. The development of additional skills will occur for a very wide number of users but these users never need to master multimedia technology as the early adopters were forced to do. For example, Lotus introduced a very simple program called Lotus Sound in March 1992 which allows any user to add sound to Windows applications that incorporate Object Linking and Embedding (OLE) capabilities.

OLE provides a standard mechanism for media integration so that developers can embed multimedia objects such as sound into their applications without writing any new code.

Lotus Sound can be used to add voice annotation to word processing documents, spreadsheets, and other text and data files. For example, voice annotation could be used to explain why an individual item on an expense report exceeds normal limits. By combining e-mail with the capabilities of voice mail voice clips can be included in electronic mail messages.

Many other similar tools have started to appear. Sound wave form editors provide simple "cut and paste" type editing functions that can be used by a nonsound expert.

Standards

In the enhance phase, it becomes very important to facilitate the exchange of information between users of similar or related products. Various product developers and user groups will voice their concerns about coexistence and interchange of data and documents. Standards become a significant issue so that agreement and adoption becomes important for the continued growth of the business.

Standards such as Pulse Code Modulation (PCM) for voice are already part of the Multimedia Personal Computer (MPC) standard. There has already been significant progress toward compression standards for audio such as Adaptive Delta Pulse Code Modulation (ADPCM) in the Compact Disc Read Only Memory Extended Architecture (CD-ROM XA) definition. In the areas of image and video compression, the standards debate has begun in earnest and includes proposals like Motion Picture Experts Group (MPEG), Joint Photographic Experts Group (JPEG), and others. Refer to Chapter 9 for more information on compression standards. The acceptance of a small number of standards by all of the major players is critical to the success of multimedia at the end of the enhance phase.

In summary, during the enhance phase the use of multimedia technology will spread to a large set of horizontal applications which large numbers of people use in the normal course of their work. Easy-to-use tools will be available and we can expect large numbers of users to be familiar with the technology and have access to multimedia-capable hardware. Widespread application of multimedia capabilities in this phase will lead us into the final phase of multimedia evolution.

Pervade

In the mature phase, every personal computer will be built with multimedia capabilities because both cost and usage will have reached the point that makes it feasible to do so.

The personal computer will have become the complete personal communicator. By 1995 or 1996, multimedia capabilities will be available to all applications in all machines. Usage will pervade applications on the personal communicator. A significant manifestation of this is likely to be the use of audio and video in the user interface of the systems and applications. Application developers will take the availability of multimedia capabilities for granted and users will expect it to be included as a standard offering.

Application Areas

The application of multimedia technology at his stage will not need to be justified based on specific results. Multimedia will be recognized as the most effective way to communicate information in all business environments. Operating systems, networks, and database management tools will incorporate multimedia technology so that other product developers can depend on fundamental, standard sets of capabilities. For example, Microsoft has already included modifications to its Windows operating system that are called Multimedia Extensions (MME). The purpose of these extensions is to make it easy for both product and application developers to add multimedia capabilities. For example, an operating system extension automatically maintains the data rate performance when reading from a CD-ROM drive so that audio is produced coherently. Similar extensions are being included in OS/2 by IBM. The extensions will be called OS/2 Multimedia Presentation Manager (PM).

Although these changes have begun to appear, we are still a few years away from having a complete set of multimedia enabling capabilities in standard operating systems. However, a beginning is apparent. Similar changes will be made to networking software. Today's popular computing networks are optimized for the "bursty" data traffic that is generated by the use of productivity and business software. The large, continuously flowing streams of information that are characteristic of digital video cause problems. Network operating system vendors will add capabilities to enable local area networks (LANs) to transport dynamic media. A small number of start-up companies are developing software products that will work with existing LAN operating systems and adapter boards and enable audio and video streaming. Starlight Networks, Inc. was established to enable the delivery of full motion video and audio, along with image, graphics, animation, and text to the desktop using LANs and wide area networks (WANs).

Cost and Justification

Cost justification of multimedia technology in this phase may be irrelevant. Every new computer will be equipped with the basic capabilities and software products will be using the functionality to create new applications that extend the value of multimedia and the computer itself. At this point, the paradigm shift related to the interactions between people that began in the second phase will be concluded. Totally new applications for multimedia will appear and prolific creativity will be unleashed.

Multimedia technology will become part of user interface much like the graphical user interface that is on the Macintosh and on personal computers under Microsoft Windows and IBM's OS/2. The productivity values are potentially so significant that they will not even be questioned. Today no one would even dream of buying a personal computer without a graphical user interface. Software products that do not fully support a graphical user interface will be the dinosaurs of the personal computer industry. Equally, personal computers and operating systems that do not have multimedia capabilities will be unable to compete.

Applications will use audio and video to deliver information when it is the most natural way to do so. Multiple media will be used, even if the use is redundant, to enhance the communication of information. Voice input will be used to interact with personal computers in addition to the keyboard and mouse. The help function in applications will demonstrate how to use the functionality using voice, full motion video, and animation as appropriate.

Infrastructure

Since multimedia capabilities will be built into system software the use of tools will be fully unobtrusive for most users. Improved user interfaces will offer extremely easy ways of using new technology. The skill question will be diffused by pervasive awareness, increased skills developed over the first two phases, and increased usability.

Standards

Concerns about standards will have been completely resolved. End users will be totally unaware of the issues involved in interchange between products and uses. This is no different from the environment today for text and graphics. For example, the PostScript standard makes it feasible to print documents from any source on any printer. A similar transparency will develop for all of the other media. Although the solution is not quite at hand, several standard bodies are at work and some solution will emerge during the final phase of multimedia evolution.

In summary, the technology will appeal to the masses in the pervade phase. Personal computers and workstations will be equipped with all of the necessary features to play a vast array of content or applications that may be created by a potentially very large cottage industry. The personal communicator will find its way into homes and businesses and applications will have usability that cannot even be imagined by users today.

MULTIMEDIA—ONE "BYTE" AT A TIME

In its fully mature form, the personal communicator will handle all forms of information—text, image, graphics, animation, full-motion video, and audio with equal ease. The user will be able to interact with all the media types because of built-in usability. Networks will be fully capable of transporting all of the media. Distance and bandwidth will not impede the development of networked multimedia applications. However, this grand vision requires that all the pieces of the technology be inexpensive and provide simultaneous ease of use and interactivity. It is a big step to move from the personal computer of today to the mature, inexpensive, and easy-to-use personal communicator of tomorrow, as is shown in Figure 2-1.

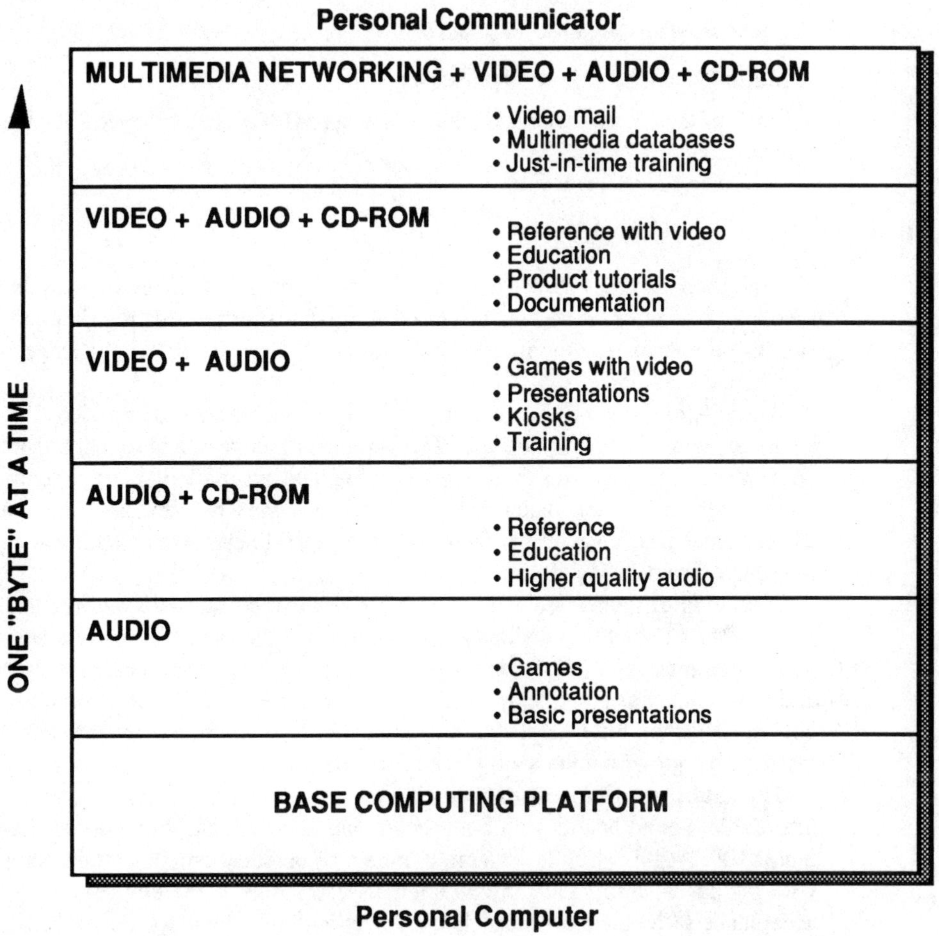

Personal Communicator

ONE "BYTE" AT A TIME →

MULTIMEDIA NETWORKING + VIDEO + AUDIO + CD-ROM
• Video mail • Multimedia databases • Just-in-time training

VIDEO + AUDIO + CD-ROM
• Reference with video • Education • Product tutorials • Documentation

VIDEO + AUDIO
• Games with video • Presentations • Kiosks • Training

AUDIO + CD-ROM
• Reference • Education • Higher quality audio

AUDIO
• Games • Annotation • Basic presentations

BASE COMPUTING PLATFORM

Personal Computer

Figure 2-1. Multimedia acceptance is occurring one "byte" at a time, paced by the availability of the pieces.

This complete solution can be broken into small, digestible pieces that will be acceptable from a cost and usability perspective that will lead to the personal communicator. The pieces required for transition to the personal communicator are

1. Audio

2. High-capacity removable storage—CD-ROM

3. Motion video

    a. Inexpensive software-based playback

    b. Hardware-based playback and capture

4. Multimedia networking—client servers

Each of the "bytes" are discussed briefly below. Refer to Chapter 9 for more detailed information.

Audio—The First "Byte"

The addition of audio means that the personal computer will need to handle a dynamic media type in addition to the current static media. It introduces the first additional cost step to be justified by the market and some of the key technical challenges for system design and usability.

Audio is easier for the computing industry to incorporate than video. Developers of personal computer games have found it easy and attractive to add sound. Existing personal computer games became more sophisticated and are part of market segment that is independent of the television games that are provided by Nintendo, Sega, and others. These games take advantage of the interactive capabilities of the computer to engage users in complex games.

Hundreds of games are available and several trade magazines cover this area. The availability of sound, including music synthesis, is a great way for making the games more entertaining. All of the developers of games have added sound already or they will add it as quickly as possible in order to remain competitive. Personal computer games are collectively the "killer application" for sound. It is important to note that the second factor in the growth of the acceptance of sound is cost.

The addition of sound capabilities to the existing personal computers is quite affordable. Sound boards with both record and playback capability are available for less than $100. At this price level large numbers of personal computers are being equipped with sound capability. In the computer industry one of the key reasons for the slow acceptance of a new technology is a chicken-and-egg situation. Developers of software products wait for hardware to become abundant and inexpensive while hardware costs remain high because too few software products are available. The circle has been broken by the introduction of one small "byte" called sound. Sound can be added at a price point where many users buy it to enhance computer games or to try it for emerging business applications. Sound is available now at a price where it can be a whimsical or an impulse purchase.

The authors estimate that approximately 2.5 million add-on sound boards will be shipped in 1993. An equal number of personal computers will be shipped with built-in sound capability.

The growth in the installed base of sound enticed other software developers in the business area to add sound to their products. Lotus Development Corp. was among the first with a software product called Lotus Sound which is shipped with sound products from Media Vision. This product combination enables users of office applications such as word processors, spreadsheets, and e-mail to annotate documents with sound. Audio has come to business software products. Products such as Lotus Sound make it very easy for an office worker to use sound even though he or she is not skilled in dealing with the sophisticated audio manipulation techniques common to the audio video industry. The addition of a single dynamic media type, rather than both audio and video, makes it easier for the user to absorb multimedia capabilities.

The technical challenge faced by the designers of operating systems is limited to synchronization and continuous streaming of one dynamic medium when sound is the only time critical data in the system. Microsoft was able to enhance Windows with sound even though Windows was not designed originally to deal with high sustained data rates. Microsoft is modifying Windows to ensure that it is fully capable of dealing with both audio and video. Both OS/2 and the Macintosh operating system have been modified to effectively support sound capabilities.

Most computer users buy products from the retail channel. In this channel, there is little opportunity for the salesperson to sell on a feature/benefit basis and justify the cost. As a result, only simple, low cost products are sold effectively by this channel. The introduction of multimedia in "byte"-size pieces allows this channel to deal with it gracefully. Sound products are already understood by the retail channel and it is ready for the next "byte."

The introduction of sound as the first step has broken the problem into manageable "byte-size"-pieces. Sound has been introduced as a first step that is an economically and technically feasible piece of the multimedia puzzle. This is responsible for strong acceptance at this early stage while the rest of the puzzle catches up.

CD-ROM—the Second "Byte"

As a result of relatively broad acceptance of sound technology, many products are starting to exploit sound capability. For example, Compton's Multimedia Encyclopedia for Windows from Britannica Software adds sound clips to the information that is based on the hard copy counterpart. The end result is document that contains text, images, and sound. The subject material becomes much more compelling when you hear Dylan Thomas recite his verses instead of simply reading the text on-screen yourself.

Digital sound consumes large quantities of data storage. Audio CD-quality stereo sound is sampled at 44.1 kHz with 16 bits per sample. At this level, audio devices must be capable of handling a transfer rate of 705,600 bits per second (bit/s) per channel. A 1.44 -Mbyte floppy disk can store 8 seconds of CD-quality sound. In some cases, audio is sampled at 22 kHz and at 8 bits per sample which lowers the transfer rate requirement to 176,000 bit/s per channel. Thus 22 kbytes are needed to store 1 second of digitized sound with modest frequency modulation (FM) radio quality. Thus a 1.44 -Mbyte floppy disk can store 65 seconds of modest-quality sound.

An hour of sound at 22 kHz and 8 bits per sample consumes roughly 80 Mbytes of storage. This leads to the second piece of the multimedia puzzle. CD-ROMtechnology provides inexpensive high-capacity (650 Mbytes) removable storage. CD-ROM allows large quantities of data to be published for use in multimedia applications.

CD-ROM technology has been around since 1986 when a group of computer experts standardized the data format used to write data on a CD audio disk. A number of well-known figureheads in the computer industry have hailed it as the new "papyrus." CD-ROM production costs are low because the music industry uses the same disk for the distribution of music. It takes approximately $1 to produce this disc, which makes it even cheaper than a newspaper. CD-ROM drives are generally more expensive than their audio counterparts since they are faster and more robust. Audio CDs can be played on most CD-ROM drives but the inverse is not true.

A single CD-ROM disk can store approximately 650 Mbytes of information which is more than is contained in 100 issues of the Sunday New York Times. The large storage capacity has made CD-ROM an interesting medium for distribution of large amounts of text information but it is even more important for distribution of multimedia data.

Kodak's Photo CD system was enabled by the availability of CD-ROM. The Photo CD system allows high-resolution 35 mm film images to be converted to digital form, stored on CDs, and used in desktop publishing and many other applications. A standard 35 mm camera can be used to capture the photographic images needed for multimedia applications. For more details, review Chapter 9.

The cost of CD-ROM drives has not yet reached the point where it is an impulse purchase. CD-ROM drives with sufficient performance for multimedia use cost around $500. In 1993, the costs are forecast to fall below $300 which is acceptable for mass appeal.

This second step toward completing the multimedia puzzle is needed for distribution of content such as Compton's Multimedia Encyclopedia for Windows from Britannica Software or Microsoft's Bookshelf. The important point is that software developers can treat sound and CD-ROM drives as two separate "bytes" and address their products to the relevant installed base of sound, CD-ROM and the combination of the two.

The first two "bytes" along with a set of performance requirements form the basis for the Level 1 specification developed by the MPC Marketing Council formed under the leadership of Microsoft. The MPC specifications are supported by a growing number of companies (refer to Chapter 9 for more information).

Motion Video—the Third "Byte"

The addition of full-motion video to the personal computer has received a good deal of attention. The promise of video on the screen seems to be most exciting to large numbers of people. Video capabilities have demonstrated the exciting potential of multimedia computing. Most people have been exposed to and recognize the powerful impact that audio and video have on the communication of information. The first live demonstration of DVI enticed the computer industry to consider the addition of full-motion video to the personal computer in 1987 at the CD-ROM and Multimedia Conference in San Francisco. This singular event accelerated the pace of research in this field. As a result, a large number of options are available today.

The early adopters of multimedia technology used analog sources such as laser disc players to add video to the interactive computing environment. These configurations were useful in an important but limited set of applications. The approach fell short because the video disc player could not be integrated with computer networks and required special boards and monitors. Full seamless integration demands digitized video. Reductions in cost and improvements in the usability of digital video hardware and software products will dictate the pace at which this dynamic medium grows in the 1990s.

Cost of Digital Motion Video

The cost of adding full-screen, full-motion video to a personal computer for both input and output is too high for broad acceptance. For example, the cost of adding the playback option-using DVI technology is approximately $1500. Although there are potential cost reductions, the price range is significantly higher than the price of an audio add-on or a CD-ROM drive. And $1500 does not cover the cost of video capture products. The high cost of equipping the personal computer to handle full-motion video has restricted the use of video to a few vertical applications where the cost is easily justified by the value. These applications are primarily in the areas of education, training, and merchandising.

The usability of motion video is another issue which is just beginning to be dealt with by system software and tools developers. The addition of video to the personal computer severely challenges the skill level of most personal computer users. Most people are not trained or prepared to use motion video in their daily work. The tools that will provide the ease of use needed for broad acceptance of the third byte of the multimedia puzzle will not be widely available until 1993 or 1994.

As an intermediate step that primarily addresses the cost issue, the major suppliers of operating systems are introducing software video playback.

Software Video Playback

By limiting the size of the playback window and limiting the number of frames per second to approximately 15 fps, it is feasible to use the personal computer processor to play "motion video" on personal computers now. Apple was the first platform provider to announce software playback for video at 15 fps in a window 160 by 120 pixels. Apple provided an extension to the operating system architecture called QuickTime™ which enabled this capability. Refer to Chapter 9 for more details. Similar capabilities are available for IBM-compatible personal computers using Microsoft's Video for Windows and Media Vision's MotiVE. IBM announced software-based motion video on their Ultimedia product line. Demonstration videos have been shown in 320 by 240-pixel window on a 256-color display at 16 fps. Refer to Chapter 9 for more information.

All of these approaches require additional hardware for video capture along with the attendant complexity of the current suite of tools. Several new products will ship in late 1992 or early 1993 that will reduce the cost of video hardware significantly.

What is the value of the software video step? The key observation is that millions of personal computers can be instantly enabled with video playback capability without the need for additional hardware. Thus it is feasible to develop and sell a class of products containing published information that includes motion video. This class of products will stimulate the growth of this medium even though most users do not need to capture video. The capturing and input tasks for these applications are of interest to video producers which represent a much smaller number of customers than the number of typical personal computer users. Video producers can afford to accept current prices and have the skills needed to use existing tools.

The complexity and usability issues will be resolved in the same time frame as video hardware costs are reduced.

Software video is a critical bridge to availability of hardware-based full-motion, full-screen digital video which is the next step. The reader is referred to Chapter 9 for more detailed information about Apple Computer's QuickTime and Microsoft's Video for Windows.

Full-Motion Digital Video

As the cost of adding full-motion, full-screen digital video is reduced to acceptable levels and the usability level matches the skill level of most users, the addition of video will be an incremental step for most product developers.

Multimedia Networking—The Fourth "Byte"

Many personal computers in business are connected to LANs to provide access to other personal computers, servers, or host computers. Users share information in work groups, access data from on-line services and handle transactions on corporate databases. These networks are built around static medium use and are optimized for use with the bursty traffic that business and productivity software create. They were never meant to handle dynamic media such as audio and video which require time-critical delivery to the receiver.

LAN networking software must be modified to provide efficient management of audio/video streams. Network-based servers must be capable of handling audio and video information along with typical business data. Both the performance and architecture of these networks need fundamental changes prior to broad acceptance of multimedia in the networks. This will of course happen as a piece of the multimedia puzzle and can proceed concurrently with the "bytes" described above. Solutions that need this "byte" will emerge as multimedia networking becomes affordable and usable.

Each of the separate pieces or "bytes" will evolve until it is feasible to add them to the personal computer. The "bytes" are evolving concurrently and are not sequential steps. Each "byte" enables a set of applications as shown in Figure 2-1. Any combination of "bytes" can be used to address a set of application requirements. When all of the pieces have been added, the result is the personal communicator as shown in Figure 2-2.

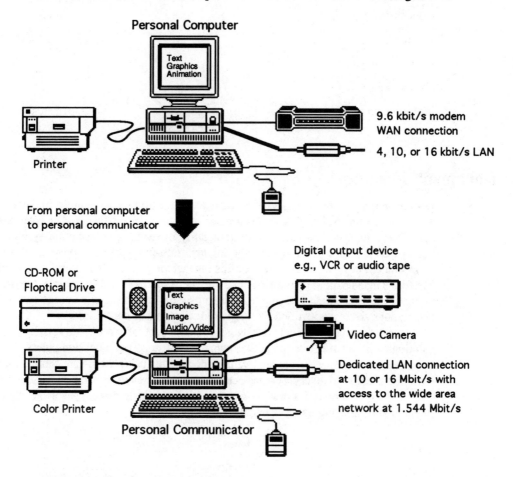

Figure 2-2. Multimedia evolution from personal computer to personal communicator.

RELATED TECHNOLOGIES

In the computing industry several technologies are evolving simultaneously that may have a positive or a negative impact on one another. In this section we will explore several related technologies, examine relationships, and discuss how they might accelerate or retard the growth and acceptance of multimedia applications. In the end it will be the convolution of all these technologies that will determine the pace at which the multimedia technology is accepted. The following technologies will be considered:

- Document imaging

- Facsimile

- Voice mail

- Networking

- Information storage

- Display

Document Imaging

Document imaging has emerged as a practical application for large archival databases. In 1990, the document imaging and computer industries joined forces. The relationship is symbiotic: imaging enhances the functionality of existing information systems while building on the same platforms and sharing the same components as other applications.

Document imaging is used for records management, records preservation, archiving, and forms management applications in a variety of industries. For example, the insurance industry uses document imaging to archive original insurance application forms. These applications are easily justified by simply reducing cost of paper storage.

As imaging hardware and software become part of every workstation, imaging solutions will be integrated into the mainstream use of personal computers. It will be quite practical for everyone to archive their documents using the image capture capability that will be part of every personal computer. As a result special document imaging database applications may not be needed. Multimedia technology will accelerate the integration of imaging systems into desktop applications.

Facsimile

Today facsimile or fax is very popular and is based on use of the telephone system. As a result it has been isolated from the personal computer. The addition of Group 3–compatible fax modems to the personal computer enable the user to both send and receive facsimile messages. However, the fax modem has no built-in printing or scanning capabilities of its own. It is very convenient for sending faxes as you need not work with hard copy documents. Documents created in almost any application can be converted to a fax document and sent.

Received faxes may need to be converted to a PICT or TIFF file before they can printed. Refer to the Glossary for more information about PICT and TIFF file formats. The process tends to be a bit cumbersome and is somewhat slow. The fax capability needs to be integrated seamlessly into the multimedia computing environment and it appears that this will happen in the near term. Once a personal computer is able to capture an image using a camera or a scanner, fax documents can be transported on computer networks. The required level of integration will be facilitated with a more mature personal communicator is available on every desktop.

Voice Mail

Large numbers of business and residential telephones are equipped with voice mail or phone mail systems. In all cases, except for answering machines, voice is digitized and stored on a special-purpose computer system. Both the caller and the receiver have access to a number of functions that allow them to compose, send, receive, and store messages. A caller may be given the opportunity to edit the message and to specify the time of delivery.

The receiver may have the ability to preview the list of incoming messages before listening to individual messages either in the order received or in a specified order. Voice messages can be forwarded to a colleague or broadcast to a group.

Voice messaging functions tend to be similar to those offered by e-mail systems. As more and more personal computers are connected to the public telephone network, it is more and more reasonable to expect that voice mail and e-mail could be combined to allow the user to enjoy a single interface to both types of communications.

Networking

Voice networks and data networks have been separate and are based on different technologies. The voice network is both analog and digital and uses circuit switching to provide the routing function. Data networks are based on LAN technology in local environments with bridges and routers to provide the routing function. In some cases, local networks are interconnected by packet switching networks. Neither LANs nor packet networks can accommodate time-dependent traffic such as audio and video without changes. On the other hand, the latency of circuit switched networks is not a problem but the bandwidth tends to be too low for most multimedia applications. The bandwidth is adequate for desktop videoconferencing applications.

The Integrated Services Digital Network or ISDN has the ability to handle both voice and data traffic simultaneously on the two circuit switched 64 kbit/s channels available with Basic Rate ISDN. Desktop applications such as videoconferencing and collaborative computing can take advantage of the 64 kbit/s bandwidth available to every desktop in an ISDN network. However, this bandwidth is not adequate for many types of multimedia applications. As noted earlier, the CD-ROM transfer rate for audio and video is 1.5 Mbit/s. Thus the public telephone network needs to provide at least 1.5 Mbit/s to the desktop to be able to transport full-motion video based on the CD-ROM standard.

A number of LAN vendors are offering hubs that can be configured to provide dedicated Ethernet segments to large numbers of desktops. These "superhubs" or switched hubs can handle audio and video information when equipped with audiovisual streaming hardware/software from companies such as Fluent, Inc. and Starlight Networks, Inc. The problem of cost-effective, wide area transport has yet to be solved except for videoconferencing applications.

A new switching technology called Asynchronous Transfer Mode (ATM) satisfies both the bandwidth and time-dependent requirements of full-motion video. When combined with fiber optic transmission systems based on the Synchronous Optical Network or SONET standard, ATM switches will be able to deliver 155 or 600 Mbit/s to the desktop. When this type of high-bandwidth access is available to all personal computers at an affordable price, multimedia applications will become available to all users.

The deployment of SONET transmission facilities across the nation may help speed up this process. However, there are still many technical and regulatory challenges to be met in the United States over next few years before high-bandwidth network access is available to all personal computers. The availability of multimedia-capable networks is a fundamental gating factor in the acceptance of networked multimedia applications.

Information Storage

The multimedia data types require database servers capable of handling large amounts of storage with significant input/output capacity. For example, Digital Equipment Corporationdemonstrated a disk storage tower at DECWORLD '92 than can store 100 full-length feature movies and play back all of the movies simultaneously.

Hard disk capacities are increasing rapidly and the cost of per unit of storage is decreasing. New personal computers are typically sold with more than 50 Mbytes of storage. Hard disk drive arrays are available with hundreds of Gigabytes in a single storage system. The availability of large-capacity, low-cost disk storage devices with fast input/output capability is critical for networked multimedia applications.

CD-ROM has already proven its worth for the distribution of multimedia information. However, the transfer rate and the access time are impediments to improving the quality of audio and video that can be offered on a personal computer. New standards efforts are aimed at increasing the data rates to improve the quality of audio and video. NEC Technologies and others and others offer dual-speed CD-ROM drives that are compatible with the current format and operate at twice the speed. This can be very important as the quality of video will improve significantly with the resultant increase in the data rate.

In addition there is significant progress in the area of erasable optical storage technology. This technology offers the potential for individuals to create massive multimedia files at every desktop and to distribute it on inexpensive "floptical disks." This will open up new application areas for multimedia by making it feasible to publish complex material in final form on an ordinary personal computer.

High speed, low cost storage technology is very important to the implementation of multimedia applications in business environments. Fortunately the technology is moving at a gratifying pace that will help multimedia technology gain acceptance.

Display

HDTV has received a lot of attention in the last few years as a technology that offer higher resolution, better quality images, and much larger pictures. If and when HDTV gains acceptance, it will impact the computing industry in general and multimedia computing in particular in two different ways.

First, HDTV technology should reduce the cost of high-resolution displays which will make it less expensive to offer improved picture quality on personal computers and workstations. Second, HDTV television will increase the picture quality expectations of the consumer and raise the quality expectations for computer displays. Higher-quality displays will drive the need for higher storage and bandwidth on desktop computing platforms.

A more interesting development in the short term is the advent of flat color displays. As this technology becomes less expensive it will help move multimedia computing from the desktop to portable computers. This will greatly enhance the use of the personal communicator since people will have multimedia computing with them where ever they go.

The growth and acceptance process of multimedia computing is evolutionary and inevitable. The process will be accomplished by enabling current multimedia applications on the personal computer, then by enhancing existing popular applications and finally by leading to pervasive use of the technology and incorporation multimedia technology in the user interface of the computer. Audio, CD-ROM, video, and multimedia networking are useful and practical as individual capabilities that can be added in turn. This piecewise acceptance of multimedia technology will continue to drive the evolution of multimedia computing.

3

Users and Market Structure

INFORMATION USERS

In this chapter, three kinds of information users are identified and a structure for the market based on the multimedia computing application segments is presented. The authors believe that the evolution of multimedia will lead to pervasive use of personal computers, or perhaps more appropriately, personal communicators, in the near future. Physically these devices may not even resemble current personal computers since multimedia functionality will be integrated into the processing units.

The information age which has its roots in the 1970s has spawned an information technology industry. Customers of the information technology industry can be broadly categorized into three groups. These groups are not mutually exclusive but they do establish the roles of the information customer. The customer may play one or more of the following roles at any particular point in time:

• Information consumer

• Information presenter

• Information knowledge worker

Information Consumer

Almost everyone consumes information in one form or another. We watch television, listen to the radio; read newspapers, books, and reports; listen to lectures and presentations; attend conferences, etc. As consumers of information we are entertained, informed, educated, asked to do something, promised something, and persuaded to buy products and services or to accept an idea. All of these activities represent applications of interest to the information consumer. In some cases we interact with the information that is presented to us. For example, when we play computer games or order products through shopping services available on the Home Shopping Network or Prodigy, we are interacting with information that is presented.

The information consumer; reviews the information as it is presented and based on the information, follows a particular course of action. An information consumer does not create new information (except for an order or a request for more information) or change it. The information consumer represents the largest set of prospective customers for multimedia products and applications. For the computer industry, the information consumer is potentially any individual who has access to a personal computer. It is highly likely that most information consumers in business environments will have access to personal computers that are capable of handling all of the media including audio or video, by 1995.

The information available to the information consumer is usually prepared by highly skilled teams of multimedia and content experts. Often the information is widely distributed so that many consumers are able to receive it concurrently. Multimedia content can be expensive to produce. Expensive and sophisticated equipment is used to develop quality information that has high value for large audiences. These content-oriented publications are often referred to as "titles."

A great deal of money has been invested in titles: IBM invested $400,000 in Ulysses and $1.2 million in Columbus; Philips Interactive Media of America (PIMA), formerly American Interactive Media, funded the development of more than 50 titles at $300,000 to $400,000 each; and Commodore has paid for 30 to 40 titles at $200,000 to $300,000 each. Fortunately the economics of the market are such that the expense can be justified.

As a result of the information age that began in the 1970s, information overload has become a significant problem for the information consumer. Information overload is a critical issue because of the large volumes of information available today and the difficulty in finding relevant information quickly and easily. What are the economic forces that lead to excessive information generation? Will multimedia technology be part of the problem or part of the solution? On one hand, hypermedia is of great assistance in dealing with large amounts of information. On the other hand, multimedia technology will significantly increase the quantity of information that is easily accessible.

Hypermedia delivers information in a format that provides multiple connected pathways through a body of information, allowing the user to jump easily from one topic to related or supplementary material, which may be text, graphics, audio, images, or video. However, audio, images, and video generate huge files which are too large to store and manipulate in the personal computer environment and too large to transmit in the current networking environment.

The key economic factor that contributes to the generation and delivery of excessive amounts of information is the phenomenon of delivering commercial advertising to the consumer as part of the "information package." Advertising appears at the beginning, the middle, and the end of magazines and television programs with the merciful exception of the Public Broadcasting System (PBS). Advertising is inserted next to useful and relevant information at every opportunity so it will get attention. However, advertising also serves a very useful function because it reduces the direct cost of information to the information consumer. As a result, most of us are willing to tolerate advertising. Multimedia will not be an exception to the commercial advertising phenomenon.

Multimedia technology will contribute to both the problem and the solution of information overload. Much more information will be available through on-line services in addition to current publishing channels. The capabilities of the personal computer will be used to selectively and intelligently filter information to suit the interests of the user. It is logical to assume that the personal computer ought to be capable of personalizing the information that is presented to the user. Multimedia computing offers the tools to help alleviate the information overload problem. The authors hope that the capabilities are used in the best interests of the information consumer.

There are tens of millions of information consumers, all of which are potential customers for multimedia products from the computer and consumer electronics industries.

Information Presenter

The second group of information customers is much smaller and consists of people who are subject matter experts. As such they present or present and create interactive presentations. In most cases the presenter uses some type of audio/visual equipment to make the presentation. A slide projector or overhead transparency project is often used. In the case of a multimedia presentation, the presenter would use a multimedia computer. The presentation itself with its interactivity and flexibility is a significant component of the communication process.

For CBT or point-of-information (POI) kiosks, the rate of flow of the information and the paths through the presentation are controlled by the user. Business presentations can be delivered by the information presenter or the user can interact directly with the presentation based on events and branches that are programmed by the subject matter expert.

The information presenter usually creates the information to be presented since he or she is the subject matter expert. In many business environments both creative and production assistance is available from audio/visual departments. In some cases the presentation is not prepared by the information presenter but by an individual or a group of experts who are more familiar with the information transfer process and the authoring tools.

Information content may be acquired from other sources to augment the presentation. For example, music may be added to enhance a product demonstration video. As a customer, the information presenter buys the tools that are used to prepare and present the content.

The information content is usually intended to be of specific interest to a target audience and is presented to small groups. The authoring tools that are needed for creating presentations need to be simple and inexpensive so that the information presenter need not be an authoring tool expert. Authoring software is the glue that binds together the multiple media in multimedia applications. The authoring version of an authoring software package is a tool that is used to create, integrate, and orchestrate interactive multimedia applications.

More than 60 business presentation authoring tools are available to address the needs of the information presenter and/or author. Presentation authoring tools with multimedia capabilities have been around for more than a decade and are being significantly improved at this time. Toolbook by Asymetrix, Action by Macromedia, Icon Author by AimTech Corp., and Animation Works Interactive by Gold Disk, Inc. are excellent examples.

Toolbook employs a book format to create presentations which the user may follow in an interactive manner using multiple connected pathways to go from a topic to related material. In addition, Toolbook comes with a library of more than 250 fully functional, prescripted objects that add cut and paste capability to application development.

Macromedia's Action is a highly simplified tool set based on an earlier product called Macromind Director. Action is used by business users who need to produce multimedia for internal use or for sales presentations covering their products and services using audio, animation, and full-motion digital video.

Animation Works Interactive is used for business presentation applications that require animation and interactivity.

Information presenters were early adopters of multimedia technology because of the impact that dynamic media has on presentations.

There are hundreds of thousands of information presenters who are candidates for multimedia computing products

Information Knowledge Worker

The third group of information customers is the information knowledge worker. Many office workers use computers in the normal course of their daily activities to complete work assignments and to communicate with co-workers. Information knowledge workers create their own information and receive information from others that is used to make decisions and take action.

In this group the individuals that create and send messages are most often the same individuals that receive messages from others. The primary skills of the individuals are different from the authors of multimedia documents or presentations. The use of multimedia capabilities is incidental to the main task of an information knowledge workers, in the same way that the use of word processors and spreadsheets is today. The number of individuals in this group exceeds the number of information presenters but is much less than the number of information consumers. There are millions of office workers with personal computers who are potential customers for multimedia products and services.

Nearly all of the information content is created by the information knowledge worker as part of the on-the-job process. Thus this group buys tools that are designed to assist in the communication of information or transfer of knowledge. The tools needed to facilitate the applications for this group must be simple to use and compatible with widely available personal computers and workstations. The tools must be available for use in the context of the tasks of the information knowledge workers.

Many of the developers of the software products that are being used by information knowledge workers are adding multimedia elements to their products. Electronic mail systems are evolving to include audio and full-motion video. Word processors are evolving to include multiple media to enable them to function as multimedia documentation processors. Spreadsheet programs are incorporating voice annotation to enhance their ability to communicate information.

MARKET STRUCTURE—MULTIMEDIA APPLICATIONS

For each of the four multimedia application segments that follow, the authors review the customers (creators and users), products of interest, economic factors, market size, and distribution channels.

1. Content-centric applications

2. Presentation-centric applications

3. Office-centric applications

4. Operations-centric applications

Table 3.1 shows the range of applications available in all four segments. End users and authors are identified for each segment. It is important to distinguish between the professional author and the "casual" business author since the requirements for each are different.

Interactive presentation-centric applications have been available for several years. Large number of content-centric applications are being developed due to the growing acceptance of CD-ROM technology. A few office-centric applications exist at this time. As the cost of adding dynamic media is reduced, the number of applications will increase. Operations-centric applications are few but represent the major thrust of multimedia computing into the business environment. The first three applications classes are often combined in the business operations environment since multimedia is being tailored to suit the needs of the work environment of the individual and the business.

Table 3-1. Four Applications Classes Cover All of the Multimedia Applications in the Business Environment

Application Type	Users	Creators
Content-centric	Information consumers	Subject matter expert
Reference material		
Documentation		
Information services		
Education		
Policies and procedures		
Presentation-centric	Information Consumers (uses the product to receive)	Subject matter expert
Business presentation		
Training	Information presenter (uses the product to present)	
Merchandising kiosks		
Office-centric	Information knowledge workers	Information knowledge worker
Word processing		
Desktop publishing		
Spreadsheet		
Mail		
Operations-centric	Integration of	Subject matter experts
Electronic Performance	Information consumers	Business operation
Support System (EPSS)	Information presenters	experts
Just-in-time training	Information knowledge workers	

Content-Centric Applications

Content-centric applications are primarily based on providing cost-effective access to information. These applications offer information that has been collected by the creators of content-centric products based on predefined user interest or on product specifications. The information consumer; does not interact with the information except for selecting portions of interest from the offered collection. Content-centric applications can also be called publishing or documentation applications.

Typical examples of content-centric applications based on text and graphics are newspapers, magazines, and books. Applications based on audio include radio programs, audio tapes, and compact discs for education and entertainment. Video applications include television programs and video tapes which are also used for training, education, and merchandising in addition to entertainment.

Multimedia content-centric applications are emerging from a number of sources. Compton's Multimedia Encyclopedia by Britannica Software is a very popular example. This CD-ROM–based product includes the contents of the complete 26-book encyclopedia as well as audio clips and images. The information consumer can listen to one of President Kennedy's speeches or the sound of an animal in the wild. Future versions of the encyclopedia or similar documents will undoubtedly include motion video to provide an even more realistic portrayal of the content.

Microsoft's Bookshelf for Windows is comprised of a dictionary, a thesaurus, and an atlas all on a single CD-ROM. The dictionary includes the proper pronunciation using audio in addition to the meanings of words. Hypermedia capability provides a convenient way of searching and relating words using the thesaurus without thumbing through the pages in multiple books.

Nautilus magazine is a third example of an early content-centric application. This monthly magazine which covers topics in the area of multimedia is delivered on a CD-ROM and contains product information with related audio and animation clips.

Customers: Creators and Users

Customers in this application segment are either the creators of content-centric products or the users of such products.

Users

The users of content-centric applications are the information consumers described above. As indicated, users are primarily interested in receiving the content in an effective and inexpensive manner. Currently these users receive information through newspapers, magazines, and television and radio programs. Most users are willing to tolerate the advertisements that are interspersed with the information of specific interest. Information is also available to the information consumer in the form of books which, of course, do not include advertisements at present.

Although content-centric applications will be delivered predominantly on CD-ROM, some information will be available on networks. The shift from CD-ROM-based distribution to storage, retrieval, and distribution using networked servers will occur when the information must be updated frequently and/or when the storage requirement exceeds the capacity and transfer rates of CD-ROM drives.

Creators

Creators develop products and solutions for the information consumer. They either create the content themselves or edit and assemble information obtained from another source. The job of the creator is similar to that of a movie producer. They are responsible for acquiring content and the right to use it, for obtaining the tools that are needed, and for coordinating the efforts of the individuals that produce the final product. For example, Compton's Multimedia Encyclopedia on CD-ROM reused major portions of the text version of the encyclopedia. In some cases the audio clips were probably obtained from news services or freelance journalists or naturalists, etc.

The creator organizes the content with the appropriate levels of interactivity, usability and access to the detail necessary for an effective use with multimedia platforms targeted for a given application. Creators of content-centric multimedia solutions need skills that are very different from the programming skills commonly found in the current software development industry. They need to be skilled in editing sound, animation, and video in addition to text and graphics.

Products

The key products for users in this segment are the content products themselves. Information consumers have demonstrated interest in the information (through their current buying habits) and will be able to choose from an array of content-centric products. It is safe to predict that a whole new publishing industry will flourish based on these content-centric publications.

Users will need an appropriately equipped personal computer or a workstation to be able to use the products. As a minimum they will need a CD-ROM drive to play the CD-ROM which is the most popular medium for publishing large amounts of content at this time. In addition, the personal computer needs to be capable of audio playback. In the near future, the availability of more video content on the CD-ROM will generate the need for video playback capability on the personal computer.

The system software must be able to support CD playback with sufficient audio quality now and video in the near future. The major personal computer and workstation architectures are already capable of providing this level of functionality. The Macintosh has had basic sound capabilities for a number of years. IBM personal computers or clones can be upgraded to meet the minimum acceptable configuration for multimedia playback as specified by the MPC Marketing Councilfor less than $1000 including a CD-ROM drive.

Creators also need various types of equipment for capturing content in digitized form or they need to digitize content from analog sources. For video they need cameras and scanners and adapter boards capable of capturing pictures. A suite of equipment is needed for audio. Software tools are required for editing and composing the content. The final product will be produced on the medium of choice, which is often a CD-ROM.

Creators need access to the infrastructure to be able to produce the CD-ROMs themselves. Fortunately, all of these products are available today. However, there is a great deal of room for improvement in terms of usability and ease of integration of the various elements of content. Network-based content-centric applications cannot be implemented until public networks support audio and video transport at high speeds for reasonable cost. The authors believe that these applications will become prevalent in the last half of this decade.

Economic Factors

Some of the economic factors that influence this segment of the multimedia applications market are the same as those in the current publishing industry. There is also growing concern about the copyright and licensing issues in the multimedia computing and networking environment.[1]

The content published in products such as Compton's Multimedia Encyclopedia and Microsoft's Bookshelf is paid for by the user since there is no advertising revenue to defray costs. This situation is similar to the book publishing industry.

The value of the information to the user needs to be such that it justifies the cost of the hardware and software needed to run it as well as the expenditure on individual content centric products. At the present time the cost of the user's hardware presents a significant initial barrier to the growth and acceptance of these applications. Once there is a large installed base of multimedia-capable user platforms, content-centric products will only need to be justified on their own merit.

For applications such as the Nautilusmagazine, the cost of content production and distribution is shared by the advertisers of the products featured in the magazine and the buyer of the magazine. This is very similar to the magazine publishing industry. The resultant CD-ROM product is less expensive because of advertising. Once again it is critical that a large number of multimedia-capable user platforms become available before such magazines will be viable.

This generates concerns about an apparent vicious circle. User platforms cannot become a viable market unless large numbers of content-centric products are available. Content-centric products can only be viable when large numbers of potential users acquire the appropriate playback platform. All of the leading computer and workstation companies are actively reducing the cost and increasing the capabilities and the performance of hardware platforms. The continual cost improvements and acceptance of multimedia one "byte" at a time will generate the critical mass needed for these applications to flourish.

A study by Mark Symons at the Summer Institute of Linguistics (Rettig 1992) was based on the amount of computer resource that can be purchased for $1000 as follows:

• Memory capacity (random access memory or RAM) is growing at 52.4 percent per year.

---

[1] This publishing process brings forth concerns about copyright and licensing rights. Once the information is available in digitized form and is compatible with personal computers, it is easy to duplicate and share this information with large numbers of people. Further, it is difficult to determine who is duplicating the information.

• Disk capacity is growing at 115.2 percent per year.

• Central processing unit (CPU) capacity is growing at 47 percent per year.

• Screen capacity is growing at 46.5 percent per year.

The study suggested a formal model for predicting total system price. Using that model, the price for a laptop computer with an Intel 80486SX running at 33 MHz with 16 Mbytes of RAM, a 400-Mbyte hard disk, and a 640 by 480 video graphics array (VGA) display with 16 levels of gray, will be $2000 in 1995.

When the annual growth rate of computer performance per dollar exceeds 60 percent, it only takes 2 years for a $4000 computer to come down in price to $2000.

Since many personal computers enjoy network connections and access to bulletin boards, the information could be proliferated quickly and indiscriminately. This potential lack of control is causing obvious concern for owners of intellectual property. Although there are few mechanisms to allow payment based on usage, the content-centric industry seems to be taking the problem in stride. There is caution and concern but this has not yet proven to be a major barrier to product introduction. However, this concern may lead to growth in the related legal industry for negotiating and litigating intellectual property rights.

Market Size

The potential number of users in this application segment is very large. According to The Peregrine Group there are almost 70 million personal computers worldwide as of 1992 based on the installed base for DOS, Windows, Macintosh, Sun Microsystems, and OS/2 systems (Harmon 1991). The number of personal computers (excluding Intel 286-based systems) that could be multimedia-capable through upgrades is approximately 34 million. Of the potential base of more than 120 million units, the authors believe that the number of multimedia-capable personal computers will exceed 15 million by 1995.

The number of creators in this content-centric segment is limited to a few players that are interested in leading the market and establishing a solid position. The creators need a range of skills ranging from audio/video production to editing to programming. A number of small enterprises have emerged that pool the required skill set and produce products. There will also be big players such as Disney and Sony. As the tools get simpler there will be significant growth for small businesses in this area. The authors estimate that there will be several thousand creators in 1992–1993 growing to tens of thousands in the latter part of the decade.

Distribution Channels

Will these content-centric products be sold in the computer stores, music stores where record and CDs are sold, or in the bookshops? Perhaps they will be available through videotext services like America Online, Prodigy or CompuServe. The answer is most likely all of the above. The age of the new personal communicator is likely to cause a major overhaul of the personal computer distribution channels in ways we cannot yet predict. The authors leave this area more as a question than an answer.

Presentation-Centric Applications

The next group of applications covers situations where information is presented to the user with either presenter or user interactivity. The dominant applications in this group are business presentations, training, education, and merchandising kiosks. The level of interactivity and the presentation of the information are more dominant factors than the content itself. The amount of information in a presentation-centric application is usually much smaller than in a content-centric application. Since flexibility, level of interactivity, and effectiveness of the presentation are critical to success, the presenter is often highly involved with the creation and organization of the content.

When the presentation is delivered on a personal computer and the flow is controlled by the user, very high emphasis is placed on the presentation element of the solution. The user controls the sequence or selection of the content based on his or her need or level of knowledge. In some cases the path through the material is based on the user's response to questions. This approach is very common in computer-based training applications.

Presentation-centric solutions were the first applications that took advantage of multimedia capabilities. In training and education, the combination of reading, hearing, and seeing information improves an individual's attention, concentration, comprehension, and retention.

Presentation-centric authoring software first appeared in the 1970s in the CBT industry. Today there are more than one hundred CBT authoring tools on the market. One of the more visible tools for preparing computer assisted training solutions is Authorware Professional by Macromedia. This type of tool allows the creator of a CBT solution to develop a flow of instructional material that allows declarative and procedural knowledge to be transferred electronically and validated and distributed in a controlled manner.

The solution may contain questions to test the users' progress. Based on the responses, the user may be asked to repeat the material or to speed up or slow down his or her pace through the content. There are a number of similar products such as Quest by Allen Communications, TourGuide by ATI, and many others.

Note that the products cited are examples of software tools that are used to create presentations. The end user solution is the final presentation which in most cases is very specific to the user and the company.

Customers: Creators and Users

Customers in the interactive presentation-centric segment are the users of presentations, the presenters, and the creators of presentations. Creators may be the same as presenters or they could be an audio/video production house working with the subject matter expert. For some businesses it has been cost-effective to develop presentation preparation facilities complete with appropriate software tools and multimedia subject matter available on-line, so that the presenters (e.g., sales personnel) can prepare customized, interactive presentations without the support of multimedia experts.

Users

When a business presentation is delivered by a person, the users influence the presentation by interacting with the presenter. The interactive presenter needs to be able to change the flow of the presentation based on input from the audience. Since the presenter is often the subject matter expert, the design of the user interface can be targeted at the presenter. Normally, the presenter will take a preplanned and well-understood path through the content. In this case this presenter is the user or customer of finished presentation. For example, business managers may need to prepare a multimedia presentation for the board of directors of their company. Although the board of directors are the users of the information, the customer or the user is the business manager who prepares and makes the presentation.

In training applications, the user usually controls the pace of the presentation. The users of a training presentation are totally dependent on the creator of the material to develop meaningful paths through the training course and to prepare questions and answers that determine the success of the training effort. The users interact directly with the presentation and influence the information flow by responding to the prompts that were provided by the people that created the course material. Thus the customers for training products are the end users themselves.

Creators

The creators of training courses are instructional designers, instructional technologists, instructors, teachers, and subject matter experts who know the subjects at hand. The creators are the customers for the software tools needed to prepare the content of presentation-centric products. Tools need to be targeted at such customers.

Products

There are product opportunities for all the customers of interactive presentation applications. Interactive presentation creators need tools to prepare the solution that will be played on a computer. There is need for presentation products for end users who are interested in training or education courses or product information obtained through a merchandising kiosk. When the public network is multimedia capable, users will be able to take training courses or obtain product information from the comfort of their homes and offices. Finally, content creators need tools to assist them in capture and editing of the material with greater ease and efficiency than is available today.

Many products are available for the solution developers. A few were mentioned in the previous section. Presentation solutions are often developed for very specific use and are not usually targeted at a broad audience. However, the market for general-purpose education and self-help products based on multimedia-interactive presentations is growing and could become very large.

The personal computer or workstation-based presentation platforms represent the largest hardware opportunity. The platforms must be more capable and expensive than the consumer platforms mentioned in the content-centric Applications segment. Presentation platforms must be capable of better quality audio and video and higher performance. Although presentation platforms cost more, the additional cost is justifiable because of the perceived value.

Economic Factors

Multimedia presentations are usually justified by businesses based on the perceived value and importance of the presentation in a given environment. The content is usually specific to the business and is often unique to the presentation. As a result, all of the content creation costs must be justified by the value of a presentation. Business managers may choose to have in-house facilities to create, capture, and edit content or to contract with outside firms. The business may also acquire the software tools needed to develop the presentations as well as the personal computers or workstations. The costs of developing an in-house infrastructure are usually acceptable if business presentations are developed regularly and there are concerns about the confidentiality of the content. Although the cost of the tools and equipment can be significant, it is acceptable since it is shared over a large number of presentations.

For training applications in business environments, there are usually many employees to be trained. As a rule of thumb, the cost of developing and delivering CBT courses is usually justified if more than 200 students are trained per year. The life cycle of current knowledge is decreasing at a time when the rate of change of business practices, competitive threats, and technology is increasing. This will trigger the need for continuous on-the-job training in many businesses.

Significant expense can be justified for the creation of effective training material. Once again the cost of tools, hardware, and course development is substantial but it can be justified based on potential savings in training time and increased course effectiveness. A complete ROI analysis is developed in Chapter 7.

Similarly, merchandising kiosks need to be very effective in presenting marketing and sales material, and higher costs for tools and making the presentation are justifiable.

Because the value obtained through the use of multimedia technology is tangible, measurable, and significant, training and presentation applications were the first to adapt in spite of the high cost of hardware, software, and development.

Although, higher costs are justifiable for production and creation, the cost of the user hardware platforms needs to be much lower than the creation hardware since hundreds or thousands of training platforms or merchandising kiosks need to be deployed for wide-spread use of the interactive presentations.

Market Size

The market forecast for presentation-centric applications should be estimated based on products and customers. The market size for presentation development tools depends on target users. If the users are subject matter experts who want to use the tools to enhance their presentations, then there is a broad market for these products. Not all of these professionals are personal computer or workstation users. The market for development tools for the casual business user is 1 or 2 million units over the next 5 years.

The expertise needed to develop employee training applications is seldom found in a single individual. A team of players including trainers, instructional designers, subject matter experts, project leaders, and others are required to develop such sophisticated applications. The market for tools that are targeted at sophisticated users is much smaller and numbers, perhaps, in the tens of thousands of units. In the 1990s, there will likely be too few individuals with the skills required to do this kind of work to satisfy the demands of business.

Content-based products such as training courses on how to tune your car or how to plant fruit trees in your garden represent a new and emerging market. This market is similar to the market for "how-to-do-it" books and could represent millions of units. This market has the potential to be as large as the market for content-centric products. In order for this to happen, the price of the user hardware platform for presentation-centric products must come down to the same level as content-centric playback platforms. Availability of presentation-centric products at this price level will probably lag behind content-centric platform prices by 12 to 18 months. This market will grow rapidly but it will be a year or more behind the content-centric applications market.

Hardware platforms for playback of presentations must have high-quality sound and the ability to playback animation and, in some cases, full-motion video. The market is defined as all of the playback stations to be used for training, merchandising, and business presentations. The numbers are modest compared to the information consumers but we estimate that 1 million units will be sold by 1994. Many of these will be upgrades of current high performance personal computers and workstations.

Distribution Channels

The hardware platforms for creators and users will be sold through the existing channels for current computer products. The software tools will also be marketed through the same channels. Training and merchandising solutions are usually customer-specific and marketed directly to customers by third parties or developed in-house. Generic training and "how-to do-it" content-based presentations may be sold through the channels that distribute books. Once again this area is difficult to predict and a great deal of change is likely.

Office-Centric Applications

Office-centric applications are used by office workers to communicate information internally and externally, as a matter of course in their daily tasks. Office or knowledge workers use word processors to prepare documents, spreadsheet programs to analyze financial information, charting programs to display information in graphical form, and e-mail to exchange information with peers or managers. The communications process is much more effective if audio and video are included in these applications. Audio and video capabilities must be easy to use so that knowledge workers need not develop special audio and video skills.

Lotus Corporation's Lotus Sound and Media Vision's Pocket Recorder are examples of tools that enable a number of business software products to include audio anywhere it is appropriate. Current business software products such as Lotus Corporation's Ami Pro word processor and Microsoft's Excel can use these tools because of an architectural capability known as Object Linking and Embedding (OLE). Users can annotate a cell in the spreadsheet or add sound to a document at any appropriate point. Multimedia applications will be centered on the office work in the information society of the 1990s. The video equivalent of these can't be too far behind.

Over time, all of the business software products will offer seamless integration of multimedia capabilities.

A key feature of office-centric applications is that the content is created and used on an impromptu basis. The focus on content preparation is not as extensive as it is for content-centric applications since it is usually part of the normal work flow in the office.

Customers

Customers or users of products in this case are information knowledge workers. They are computer literate and are accustomed to using computers to assist them in their jobs, however, they have no expertise in the audio and video domains. Knowledge workers don't have time to learn how to use complex tools. Thus it is critical that the tools be very easy to use for the functions needed by this group of customers. There is no distinction between creators and users in office-centric applications. The same person creates information at one point in time and receives it at another.

Products

Hardware platforms for this application segment need to be the same for both the creation and playback processes. The capability to capture and playback audio and video information must be supported on the desktop. The cost of these capabilities will be a key factor in the growth of these applications as it will be difficult to measure tangible benefits. Over time, businesses will realize that the resultant improvement in the effectiveness of communications is such that they cannot afford not to support audio and video at the desktop. Reasonably priced audio capabilities are available to meet these requirements now. Video capture and playback for this segment will become widely available at an attractive price by 1993.

Digital video cameras and digital VCRswill be needed in the office to capture video clips and to make "hard copies" of multimedia documents.

Almost all the software products used in the office today on the personal computer will need to provide multimedia functionality in the future. The leading candidates are word processor, spreadsheet, and e-mail products.

There is also a market opportunity for utilities that facilitate the interchange of multimedia information between application software developed by various companies based on different formats.

Economic Factors

The cost of personal computer hardware and software is justified at present by increased productivity of knowledge workers. Desktop computing has so fundamentally changed the workplace that traditional measures for cost savings or productivity improvements are not even relevant. The use of personal computers and workstations results in enhanced office communications which shortens the communication cycle between workers and leads to better and faster decision-making capability. The acceptance of multimedia applications will be determined by factors of usability and acceptable costs for broad deployment of the required hardware and software. Significant penetration of this market is not expected until late 1993.

Market Size

The customer base for these applications is all of the office workers that use the computers in their work environment. It has been estimated that most large companies are targeting one computer per employee. The market for office-centric products is definitely in the tens of millions of units.

Distribution Channels

Office-centric applications represent the main stream of the current computer business and will be served by the same channels that serve the business market today—retail computer stores.

Operations-Centric Applications

For most businesses the communication of information is critical to the support of their mainstream activities. Content-centric, presentation-centric and office-centric applications are loosely linked to mainstream activities. Multimedia applications where the communication of information is closely tied to core business activities are defined as operations-centric applications. Such applications deliver information where, when, and how it is needed, in the context of the tasks of the individual or workgroup.

For example, consider a travel agent who is connected to the American Airlines' Sabre system for reservations and ticketing. The Sabre system, which is an information processing application, is absolutely critical to the travel agent's operation. It is an operations-centric application. This section explores the role of multimedia in this application segment.

To continue with the travel agent example, assume that the Sabre system is capable of providing promotional material in multimedia format as the travel agent is interacting with the customer. The computer could show pictures of hotel rooms, or beaches of a holiday resort along with music and narration to persuade the customer to make the desired choice. This application would be defined as an operations-centric multimedia application.

Sales and technical support representatives and applications specialists at a leading information technology company are implementing an EPSS. Sales teams will have on-line access to industry-specific information, product information and configurations, services, and business information, as well as information specific to their accounts to help them prepare strategies and tactics for individual accounts. Field sales personnel will be able to prepare presentations using information from presentation resource centers, and will be able to present them using multimedia-capable laptop computers. The sales teams will also have access to learning modules to help them prepare for new products or markets. In addition, product descriptions, boilerplate[2] , and pricing will be available for preparing quotations.

The existing home shopping services on Prodigy's videotext service primarily uses text and graphics to describe the products it is trying to sell. Selling is a mainstream business for Prodigy. If and when Prodigy begins to offer multimedia-based services, home shopping could demonstrate a product, promote it, and answer questions using experts' voice clips and pictures during the sale process. While the transaction is being closed, the buyer's account will be debited, the shipment of goods will be scheduled, and the inventory will be updated. This would be classified as an operations-centric multimedia application.

Customers

In the 1990s, the health and wealth of organizations will be measured by how well they create, manage, distribute, and use information. Large and small corporations will form the customer base for these applications since their competitiveness will depend on timely on-line delivery of operational information to both employees and customers. Of course, the customers or users of the applications will be employees of these companies. The applications will be very specific to individual companies' requirements. Initially they will be one-of-a-kind projects that may evolve over time to become generic solutions for an industry group.

Products

The solutions in this segment are going to be unique to each company. The hardware products may be general-purpose multimedia computers but the content creation, and software to interact with the users will be unique to each customer or to industry groups. In many cases, there will be an ongoing need to ensure that the multimedia content of the database is current with business operations. The networking requirements are also going to be unique for each customers. Invariably, operations-centric applications will be complex. Consulting services may be needed to assist in the development of these solutions by many businesses.

---

[2] A standard passage of text and/or graphics that is used over and over again in letters, memos, reports, and proposals.

Economic Factors

These applications will be justified by operational efficiencies and improved competitiveness of the business. The justification process will be complex in nature and will involve fundamental strategic decisions on the part of the most senior management. However, this application segment could easily become fundamental to the survival of businesses as newer businesses use multimedia technologies to enhance the way they do business and gain a competitive edge.

Market Size

The size of this segment is very difficult to estimate at this time. All large companies are potential customers of operations-centric solutions. However, the market could take 5 to 10 years to mature because of the fundamental operational change required to make these solutions effective. The size of the data processing market, which is based on operations-centric use of computing, could not have been estimated 20 or 30 years ago. Multimedia applications have the potential of becoming equally or perhaps even more persuasive.

Distribution Channels

While hardware platform products will continue to be marketed to these through existing major channels, the software and system solutions will probably be developed in-house much like the operations-centric data processing applications have been developed.

REFERENCES

Harmon, Scott. 1991. Video Compression Analysis. Portola Valley, California, The Peregrine Group.

Rettig, Marc. 1992. A succotash of projections and insights. *Communications of the ACM* 35(5):25–30.

4

Conceptual Framework

TOOLS AND MACHINES IN HUMAN COMMUNICATION

In the previous chapters we noted that the personal computer is rapidly evolving into a personal communicator. In this chapter we analyze the human communication process to identify some basic elements and to establish a structure for human communication. The results of the analyses are used to develop a structured approach for assessing applications and solutions employing multimedia technology. It is our intention to equip managers and professionals in fields other than computing and multimedia with a way to assess when and how multimedia technology will be relevant to their businesses. We begin by showing how all personal computing applications are really centered on communication and then we get into the conceptual analysis of the communication process itself.

Individuals have been coordinating actions with others ever since humans started hunting in teams. The need to communicate ideas, thoughts, and feelings between individuals is a prerequisite for effective coordination. Communication between individuals and groups has become as basic as air and water for survival and living. And as our society grows, communication becomes more complex and prolific. Multimedia computing should be regarded as a set of tools and machines that aid and abet the communication process in the same way that automobiles, planes, and trains have assisted the transportation process.

We are all connected!

In the current work environment the personal computer has become a pervasive tool. Most, if not all, computer applications are directed at communicating with others.

Whether we use personal applications or productivity tools or access information services, database management systems or transaction processing systems, the results of our efforts are always communicated to others.

All of the applications shown in Figure 4-1 involve communications with others and will take advantage of multimedia tools and technology as cost, value, and other parameters make it feasible to do so.

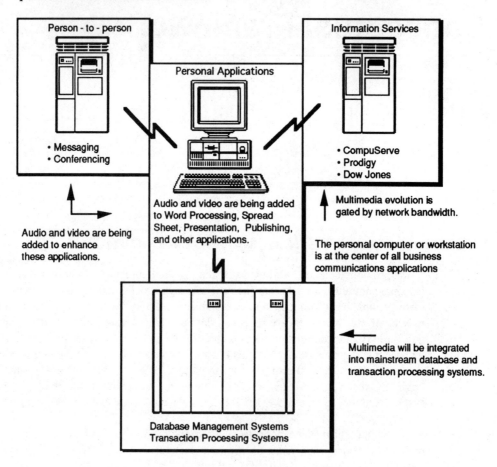

Figure 4-1. All of the categories—personal, person to person, information services, and shared database applications—require multimedia-capable networks because communication is central to business operations.

PERSONAL COMPUTER APPLICATIONS

Personal computer applications can be broadly classified in four categories. All of these applications will eventually include multimedia capabilities since all are centered on communication.

• Personal

• Person-to-person

• Information services

• Shared databases

Personal Applications

Personal applications are defined as a class of business applications in which an individual does a significant amount of work alone. Communication between workers is infrequent. Although communication is infrequent, the results of personal efforts are inevitably presented to other individuals or to groups in a typical business environment. The results are communicated using memos, e-mail, reports, or face-to-face presentations.

Word processors, spreadsheets, and presentation preparation tools are normally used in personal applications. Today only a few of these applications have been multimedia enabled. Presentation preparation tools are beginning to take advantage of multimedia. It is apparent that many of the other personal application tools will follow the lead of software products such as Lotus Sound and Pocket Recorder which were mentioned in the previous chapter.

Person-to-Person Applications

Applications that require frequent interpersonal communication include electronic messaging or e-mail, conferencing, and document transfer. It is clear that communication is the essence of these applications.

The addition of multimedia data types will significantly enhance the communication process in person-to-person applications.

Information Services Applications

Information services applications are defined as those where the personal computer is used to access information sources such as America Online, CompuServe, Dow Jones, Prodigy, The Source, or other videotext services. None of the current videotext services have been multimedia enabled. Several developments are needed before these services will be able to embrace multimedia. Sufficient network bandwidth must be available at affordable prices. Personal computer platforms must be multimedia capable, network servers must have massive storage capacity and input/output capability, and the information provider needs easy to use tools for adding multimedia information rapidly so it remains current. Multimedia offers significant opportunities for information service providers to enhance their products.

Shared Database Applications

The final set of applications covers the use of the personal computer to access a shared database, either to update the information or to process a transaction. Airline reservation systems, order entry systems or the shopping services on Prodigy are typical examples. Shared database applications are communications-intensive and will benefit from the use of multimedia technology.

Almost all business applications for the personal computer are communication based. As a result all of them will be effected by multimedia usage in positive sense since multimedia is primarily a communication technology.

INCREASING COMPLEXITY OF COMMUNICATIONS

The environment for business and in some cases even personal communication has evolved over time to a level of significant complexity. As a result various types of equipment and tools have been developed to assist with the process. Six factors that contribute to increasing complexity are

1. More interested people

2. Increasingly complex thoughts and ideas

3. Increasing complexity of tasks

4. Time synchronization

5. Timeliness of communication

6. Increased need for interactivity

More Interested People

In today's business environment actions or decisions made by one person impact many others both inside and outside the organization. A change in a product definition may have a significant impact on manufacturing, sales, engineering, and accounting. This mandates that such actions be communicated to all interested parties in a short period of time.

In the past a given task often involved only a few people so the communications task could be handled at a meeting. Today the number of people is much larger and the interested parties are not likely to be present at the same time and at the same place. The communication requirement demands that networks of one kind or another be used to meet the need for timeliness.

The need to access large audiences is very common in the entertainment business. The communications requirement is effectively handled by television and radio broadcasting systems. The broadcasting process is used to communicate to large groups of people simultaneously. Recently companies have started to use computers to automatically fax information to all interested parties concurrently.

Increasingly Complex Thoughts and Ideas

Pundits claim the information generated in the last decade exceeded the amount generated in the previous 2000 years. Because of increased amount of knowledge and information that is available, we are forced to deal with ideas that are very complex in our work environment. For example, if an design engineer wants to review an idea for improving a certain part of the body of an airplane, the engineer must examine a collection of drawings, discuss the concept with others, and conduct a detailed analysis to understand all of the implications of the change. This process requires that the engineer have access to state-of-the-art computing tools and high speed networks to make the process practical.

Increasing Complexity of Tasks

As tasks increase in complexity, more coordination and more precise communication is required. The tasks we are called upon to perform individually and as part of a team are becoming very complex. For example, the modern automobile is assembled using hundreds of parts that must work together. Even though parts may be designed independently, all of the interrelationships in a successful design need to be understood if the design team is to complete the task.

A great deal of information must be communicated to a large number of people with a level of accuracy that will enable all of the participants to perform their tasks in a coordinated and accurate fashion to ensure all of the pieces fit together perfectly. Networked computers and workstations today are used as machines and tools to assist in this process. We have come a long way in terms of complexity from the days of a coordinated hunt by a tribe of cave dwellers.

Time Synchronization

Many people need access to a wealth of information all at once so they can reach consensus on business issues. For example, medical specialists in a remote city will be able to monitor an operation using videoconferencing systems and consult with the surgeon performing the operation. All the doctors that are observing and consulting need access to patient records on demand. This requires a combination of computing and a networking tools with unprecedented ease of use to make the process really effective. The need for simultaneous, synchronized actions further increases complexity of the communications process and fuels the need for machines and tools.

Timeliness of Communications

The value of information decreases over time. In many instances, many people who are geographically dispersed need to receive relevant information in an expedient manner. For example, news about a company can impact the value of the firm's stock. All of the customers of an investment broker must be reached quickly so they can decide to buy, sell, or hold the stock. Any delay could result in a considerable loss or a lost opportunity. This is another example where appropriate computing and communicating equipment can satisfy the needs of all parties in this contemporary communication environment.

Increased Need for Interactivity

As the intricacy of the information to be communicated increase and the task at hand becomes complex and requires the cooperation of many people, it is critical that information be understood by all the people involved. The receivers must able to interact with the sender of information and with each other to ensure the clarity of the communication. This increased need for interactivity once again necessitates that the computers and networks involved provide the capability for such interactions.

The general increase in the complexity of the communication environment has naturally led to the invention of tools—telephones, fax machines, e-mail and voice mail systems and others—to assist in the process. The capabilities of multimedia computers are well suited to the task of assisting the communication process. The personal computer will have a dramatic impact and become more indispensable than it is today.

BASIC COMMUNICATIONS PROCESSES

The next section covers some observations about basic communication processes and the evolution of modern computer-assisted communications.

Face-to-Face Communications

The earliest communications were most likely "face-to-face" sessions between individuals or groups. The participants were close to one another, so they could hear and see one another quite easily. In the beginning people likely used gestures and sounds to express their thoughts and feelings. Each side would try to influence the behavior of the other party. Even in primitive times, communications involved multiple media.

Both audio and visual channels were involved concurrently in the exchange of information. The other senses—taste, touch, and smell—which are often involved when the parties are in close proximity, will not be included in our discussions. Perhaps virtual reality will eventually allow us include taste, touch, and smell in the future.

Face-to-face sessions remain the most popular mode of communication. Sight is our most dominant sense. Face-to-face is our earliest and most important form of communication, beginning in infancy. We feel that it is the most effective mode in most situations. It is also clear that there are circumstances where face-to-face communicationis not appropriate. We will look at the elements of the communications process and analyze why and how increasing complexity leads to development of alternative processes that complement and supplement face-to-face communications.

The key elements of the communications process will be identified in the context of contemporary processes that involve computers and networks.

The face-to-face communication process has five basic elements:

1. A sender

2. One or more receivers

3. A message or content[1]

4. The ability of the sender and receiver to interact

5. A transport mechanism between sender and receiver

The *sender* is the person who wishes to communicate something to the *receiver(s)*. The *sender* creates the *message* or *messages* that are to be transported to the *receiver(s)*. Sound and light waves are the transport mechanism in face-to-face communication. In most face-to-face communications the *sender* becomes a *receiver* when one of the *receivers* asks a question or redirects the flow of information by sending a message to the original *sender*. The exchange of messages is defined as *interactivity*.

The entire communication process is directed at some *content* that the sender wants to communicate to the receiver(s). Although there are temporary role reversals in extended sessions there is usually a primary *sender* who is attempting to relay information to the *receiver(s)*.

Typical communications sessions may involve many interactions between *sender* and *receiver*. The information exchanged in a session is defined as a *message*. The overall batch of *messages* that flows from sender to receiver is defined as *content*. The distinction between *message* and *content* will be observed where needed for clarity.

For example, consider Compton's Family Encyclopedia, which does not represent face-to-face communications. The *content* means all of the text, graphics, audio, and animation that is included on the CD-ROM disk. When the user or *receiver* interacts with this multimedia document, he or she selects the information that is of interest and receives only a portion of the content in a given session. The user receives portions of the *content* which are called *messages*. The commands or messages that are used by the receiver to select the *content*, only have relevance in influencing the portion of the content received by the user. They are not an intrinsic part of the communication. However, the computer commands or messages are very important since they allow the user to *interact* with the computer. Transport is accomplished by physically delivering the CD to the receiver.

---

[1] An abstraction of a thought or an idea, which is often encoded using symbols in one or more media such as voice, images, or gestures.

The interactions between sender and receiver in face-to-face sessions are a very effective mechanism for improving the communications process. Both sender and receiver have access to input from the other on an instantaneous basis. This is analogous to having a very high bandwidth communication channel between sender and receiver. As a result the receiver can influence the flow of content significantly and may even influence the content itself. This ability to influence information flow and content is the essence of interactivity.

Both sender and receiver have access to aural and visual information. The availability of multiple media significantly increases the number of symbols that senders and receivers can use to develop abstractions of the thoughts and ideas they want to communicate.

There is another item that is critical to effective communications. This is the language that is common to both sender and receiver(s). Language is used in the most general sense of the word which includes verbal and gestural coding of thoughts and ideas using both aural and visual media.

In face-to-face communications modern tools are used to enhance the use of aural and visual media. Devices such as slide projectors are used to add images and video tape players to add full-motion video and music for enhanced face-to-face communications.

Communications—Different Time and Place

In the contemporary business environment, senders and receivers may not be available at the same time and place. Messages need to be created, stored, transported, and retrieved on personal computers using tools to facilitate the process.

The Need for Sender and Receiver Platforms

At any given time in communications sessions, we may play the role of sender and/or receiver. If the communication is interactive, we are the sender in one instance and the receiver in another. This section examines the activities of senders and receivers which defines the need for sender and receiver platforms. Multimedia computing platforms are needed to facilitate these tasks.

Sender Tasks

Create a Message or Content

The communications process begins when the sender creates a message or content that is to be sent to one or more receivers.

The content in Compton's Multimedia Encyclopedia was created for use by a broad audience at a time of their choosing. In this case, an intermediary software program is needed to assist the receiver in receiving the content. The "intermediary program" acts on behalf of the sender. The program plays the part of the sender in the communication.

In some cases the message or content is created by someone other that the sender. However, the task of creating a content remains the responsibility of the sender. For our purposes, the sender may be a team of creator(s), actual sender(s), and any software programs that act on their behalf. All of these roles will be grouped under the term "sender" and will only be separated when it adds to clarity.

Send the Message or Content

In face-to-face communications sending is the act of uttering the message and/or making gestures. In a more contemporary environment, sending may take the form of publishing a document and sending it by mail or sending it electronically by the public network.

Receiver Tasks

Receive the Message

The receiver can read or listen or watch and listen to the message.

React to the Message

The receiver can make decisions and take some form of action based on the message. The receiver can ignore the message, act on it by performing a task, or forward it with changes and additions to someone else. The receiver can also respond to the message in which case the receiver assumes the role of a sender.

Both sender and receiver need tools and machines for multimedia communications. The requirements of the sender and receiver platforms can be satisfied by multimedia-capable personal computers or workstations.

Mapping Displacement in Communications

The ubiquitous telephone can be used to deal with spatial separation but other systems are needed when sender and receiver are separated in time and space concurrently. Communications at a different time and different place dictates that the content must be stored and transported.

Communication sessions take place under four different types of conditions:

• Same time, same place

• Same time, different place

• Different time, same place

• Different time, different place

Same Time, Same Place

In business environments, employees work together at the same time and place (e.g., in meetings) and at different times and places. Face-to-face communications dominates when employees are at the same time and place. Multimedia computing can and will serve all of the different environments as shown in Figure 4-2. In meetings, interactive presentations may be used. The role that the multimedia computer plays will change as time and place conditions change. Multimedia mail with voice and video in addition to text will be useful when the communication takes place at a different time and place.

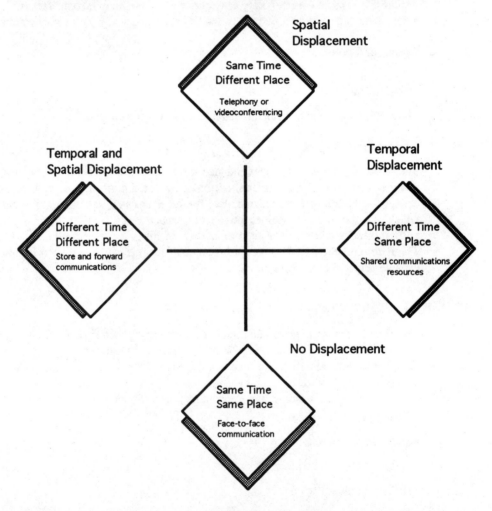

Figure 4-2. Different mechanisms are used for communications as time and place configurations change. R. Johansen/S. Sibbet/S. Benson/A. Martin/R. Mittman/P. Saffo. Leading Business Teams. © 1991 by Addison-Wesley Publishing Company. Reprinted with permission of the publisher.

Same Time, Different Place

As noted above, this condition is usually satisfied using the telephone. However, the effectiveness of the communications session is limited to the spoken word. In some instances, text or graphics information is sent in advance using fax or regular mail so that it can be discussed during the call. Changes to the content can be discussed but are not seen by both parties simultaneously.

In many instances, the sender and receiver need to be able to share a graphics space capable of accommodating text, graphics, images, and full-motion video information. The communication will be much more robust if sender and receiver are able to create, modify, and review messages in real time. More effective sessions will result when sender and receiver can see and hear one another, and share text, graphics, animation, audio, images and video clips in spite of being at different places.

The sender and receiver platforms and the transport mechanism must be capable of handling all of the media combinations in an interactive, real time mode.

Different Time , Same Place

When senders and receivers are separated in time it becomes essential that the message or content be preserved until the receiver is ready to receive it. This prompted the need for storage mechanisms that could store the message as it is created and allow the receiver to retrieve it at a later time.

The earliest storage mechanisms were probably the walls of caves. Paper is one of the most prolific storage mechanisms and is a relatively old way for storing information.

It is important that storage mechanisms allow us to view a message many times and to do so at different times. This eliminates the need to repeat or recreate the same message for multiple communication sessions. This is true for paper, magnetic, and optical storage mechanisms.

The written language is the second item that is important for preserving the content for communication at a later time. Written language is used in its more general form to include all forms of encoding including pictures, gestures, and symbols to describe the message or content. The development of written language was a turning point in the efforts of the human race to bring about effective communication in spite of temporal separation of the sender and receiver.

The invention of the printing press represented a major transformation because paper became an inexpensive and standard mechanism for storage.

Different Time , Different Place

Voice mail and e-mail are available to deal with concurrent time and spatial separation.

One of the challenges of time and spatial separation is the need to maintain an effective mechanism for interaction between the sender and the receiver. Computers and networks help with the problem but the level of interactivity is compromised. If each of the parties use the mail systems on a frequent basis, the communication can be effective even though interaction is always delayed.

MULTIMEDIA APPLICATIONS STRUCTURE

Multimedia Application Defined

Potentially, all of the communications processes covered to this point can be improved through the use of multiple media. A multimedia computing application is defined as a communication process that involves computers, networks, interactivity, and the use of multiple media. It has certain objectives and goals relating to the intended business benefit. The definition applies in the context of communication processes and the use of computing and networks in business today.

Based on this definition, all of the elements, tasks, and attributes identified for the communication process can be applied to multimedia computing applications. We will identify additional ones that apply to our contemporary business computing environment.

Application Elements

Table 4-1. Multiple Elements Are Needed to Effect the Communications Process Under All Time and Place Conditions

Element	Description
Content	• Made up of multiple messages
Sender platform	• To create message or content
Receiver platform	• To receive and review content
Storage mechanism	• To store content for use at a different time. The mechanism may be part of the sender or receiver platform or a separate platform.
Transport mechanism	• To transport content between sender and receiver
Interactivity	• To allow sender and receiver to interact

Table 4-1 summarizes the elements of the communications process that have been identified by examining the basic communications process. The application elements that are described below will be used in the analysis process in Chapter 6.

Content

The purpose of a communication application is to transport content from sender to the receiver. As discussed above, content can be made up of several messages.

Content makes use of "encoding languages" and may include static and/or dynamic media or may be synthesized in its entirety using words or symbols or captured from a real-world source. Applications tools are needed to create content for effective use in communications.

Sender and/or Creator Platform

The sender or creator platform consists of computer hardware and software used by the sender (and creator) to create messages or content and sends the message to the receiver.

If the communication is to be fully interactive, the receivers platform must have the same capabilities as the senders since they will reverse their roles.

Receiver Platform

The receiver platform consists of computer hardware and software that facilitate the task of the receiving messages or content. The receiver must be able to read, watch, or listen to a message and then act on it.

Storage Mechanism/Server Platform

As noted above, content must be stored in order to deal with temporal separation. The storage devices can be part of the sender or receiver platforms or a networked database server that is shared by many senders and receivers. Removable storage media such as compact discs or SyQuest magnetic disks can be used much like paper.

Transport Mechanisms

Transport mechanisms are needed to deal with communications when the sender and receiver are in different places. Multimedia content will be delivered by three media distribution mechanisms:

1. Stand-alone mode with content or messages delivered on CD-ROM, removable disks, or flopticals. Removable storage media can be sent via regular mail or courier or other forms of physical transport, including "sneaker net."

2. Closed networks in the near term, using high-speed local and wide area network technologies, to satisfy a community of interest. Intelligent superhubs that provide dedicated bandwidth to each sender or receiver platform are available for LAN transport.

3. Open networks support simultaneous desktop videoconferencing and collaborative computing now. After 1995 with the deployment of BISDN, the public network will support multimedia applications without distance or bandwidth considerations.

Interactivity

The infrastructure needed to support multimedia applications poses some interesting challenges for interactivity. Since interactivity is a basic element of multimedia applications, it must be analyzed across the elements mentioned above.

Each of the elements has attributes which in turn have a range of values. Interactivity can range from a situation where the receiver can only follow the path established by the sender to having complete control over the information flow with the ability to change the content itself. The effectiveness of a given application depends on the relationship of the attributes of these elements to the purpose of the communication.

To assist readers in their efforts to define and implement solutions to multimedia application requirements, the authors have developed a model for analyzing the elements. The model, which is covered in Chapter 6, provides a structured approach for determining how well alternative solutions satisfy the requirements of a given application. It may also help readers understand when and why certain applications are likely to succeed and others will fail.

5

Applications

INFORMATION AND ROLES

Multimedia will change the way that we inform, consume, communicate and learn because it delivers information in intuitive, multisensory ways that allow us to experience information rather than simply acquire it. Hypermedia adds the ability to experience the information in a non-linear fashion so we can navigate to suit our specific interests.

Before we examine applications, it is appropriate to review the significance of the multimedia phenomenon in communicating information or transferring knowledge. Multimedia computers allow us to create "knowledge structures" to represent information content. Humans use mental models to represent the same information as shown in Figure 5-1. No matter how sophisticated the computational representation becomes, it can never be equivalent to the internal or cognitive representation. However, multimedia allows us to get closer than was previously possible because we are able to use multiple media in our computational representation of our knowledge structures.

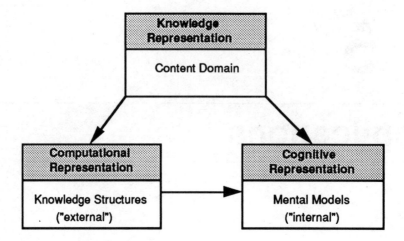

Figure 5-1. The difference between computational representations and mental models. Source: Authenticity Incorporated

When the external representation is text only, the gap between the computational and cognitive representations is large. When graphics are added, the gap is reduced. The current popularity of the Graphical User Interface (GUI) demonstrates the value of graphics.

As animation, audio, image, and video are added in turn, our ability to use the multimedia computer to develop knowledge structures that approach our mental models is greatly increased.

This is not to say that all six media types must be used in all multimedia applications but to provide a framework for understanding the value of a particular application.

For example, when a maintenance manual is converted from book form with text, graphics, and images to a hypermedia document with animation and video, the computational representation offers greater value. The user can see how individual elements or subsystems are assembled and how they operate using video clips. It is evident that the knowledge structures more closely represent the mental models in this instance.

As shown in Figure 5-2, the actions—"create, send, receive, and react"—taken by a sender or receiver can apply to all of the applications in four segments.

Different roles are played by sender and receiver in each of the application segments. In this chapter, we describe applications from two perspectives: first according to the roles played by the sender or receiver and second, according to the applications classes defined in Chapter 3.

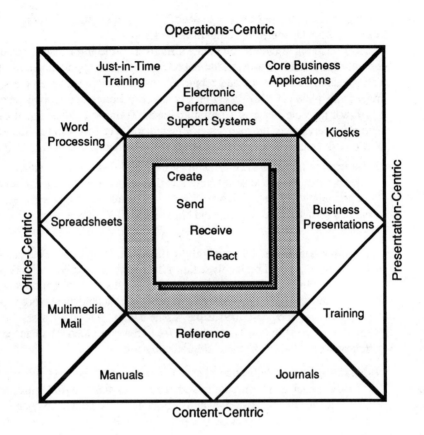

Figure 5-2. Multimedia enriches communications when used to inform, consume, communicate, or learn.

The user's interaction with the information or knowledge delivered by multimedia applications can be described as that of an information consumer, an information presenter or an information knowledge worker. For each of the roles, the key activities of the user are restated.

Information Consumer

The key role of the consumer is to absorb information and based on the information, to follow a particular course of action or behavior.

Most of the applications of greatest interest to the information consumer are in the content-centric class. However, the boundaries between application classes are blurred. A well-prepared maintenance and repair manual that includes video clips, animation and images to explain complex procedures is not only a reference tool but also a training tool. It will not take the place of Computer-Based Training courses but it can augment the learning experience of the maintenance technician. The following multimedia applications exist or will be available in the future for the information consumer.

• **Broadcast** of all types of entertainment in digital form will be available on request. The user will be able to select from a variety of sources. Interactive television programming will let the viewer "direct" the broadcast of sports games, "create" movies with multiple endings, and "produce" MTV titles with selected artists and songs.

• **Computer games** will be incredibly realistic and interactive. Fast-moving animation will be superimposed on highly detailed backgrounds complete with digitized sound effects. Multiple parties will be able to play at a distance in real time or in store-and-forward mode. The highly successful products of Nintendo and other videogame suppliers have been described as the "home computer for the masses." In effect, video games have prepared the home market for interactive video. Their success is another indicator of the power of the multimedia experience.

• **Education** has already begun to benefit from the availability of titles from ABC News Interactive such as *The Martin Luther King Story* and *The AIDS* disc, which are based on live news footage. Historical and current events in television documentary libraries and news footage will be available on an interactive basis to students. In addition, students will be able to search, acquire, and use the information available on personal computers in accordance with assignments prepared by teachers or third parties.

• **Maintenance manuals and software documentation** are being released on CD-ROM in hypermedia form and include animation, images, and video clips to explain complex procedures. Hypertext and hypermedia reference tools make it easier for users to look for information. Technicians need not search through multivolume manuals to find all of the relevant procedures needed to effect a repair. Key word, icon, or image-based searches and linking allows them to gain rapid access to the information they need.

In some cases the hypermedia documents are so effective at communicating information that they will decrease the amount of training required by technicians.

- **Reference** materials will be on-line at libraries, museums, and other archival facilities to allow individuals to browse, search, acquire, and use information. Newspapers, magazines, health care information, cookbooks, encyclopedias, and do-it-yourself information will be available in hypermedia formats. Materials that are inaccessible at this time, such as significant portions of collections at the Smithsonian, the Library of Congress, and other institutions, will be available on multimedia players or personal computers.

- **Telemarketing** will be more attractive when ISDN or other digital services are available to the home. Once the supplier has contacted a qualified prospect, collateral materials could delivered on-line or sent via fax or displayed on television sets.

- **Teleshopping** using interactive Yellow Pages will allow business and residential users to access product and service suppliers in any location. The consumer will be able to browse through full-color catalogs, look at consumer reports, interact with product experts, locate the nearest supplier, and complete the purchase on-line.

An interactive television service called TV Answer which is based on an electronic control unit in each home attached to a standard television set will allow the subscriber to access a variety of services. The user will be linked to a processing centers via satellite and will be able to pay bills, play along with game shows or sports events, respond to news polls or interactive commercials, participate in educational programming, and a number of other services.

- **Virtual reality** will submerge the user into selected artificial worlds. The user's senses will be stimulated by the sights, sounds, and touch of a "virtual" world. They may interface to this world of computer-generated stimuli via a "virtual reality suit" (special earphones, eye-pieces, and gloves). Users will experience activities that were not available previously. For example, armchair race car drivers will be able to drive exotic cars at Le Mans in competition with friends.

Information Presenter

The role of the presenter is to present information or knowledge using interactive media.

The information presenter is most concerned with interactive presentation-centric applications. The information presenter may or may not be present when the presentation is delivered since multimedia computing allows for delivery at any time or place. The fact that interactive presentations were one of the first application classes to exploit multimedia computing is a testament to the improvement that multimedia brings to the communication of information. The following generic applications are prepared by the information presenter:

- **Business presentations** include television-like images and stereo sound to fully engage the attention of the audience. More importantly, integrating video and audio make it possible to create interactive presentations that offer information on an as-you-need-it basis. Multimedia presentations generate a higher level of excitement in the audience and are a more effective way to communicate the right message than traditional presentations. Atlanta's successful bid for the 1996 Olympic Games was in no small part due to their use of interactive multimedia presentations to quickly show the important facts and to personally address the concerns of members of the selection committee.

- **Graphics-based device simulations** with audio and video enhancements will be used to learn about real-world equipment and processes through hands-on practice without the threat of damage to a real machine or system, or injury to the operator. The type of simulators used by the military (e.g., flight simulators) for many years will finally be used for learning purposes in business environments.

- **Retail kiosks** are already in use as information centers, electronic catalogs, product displays, and promotional devices. Retailers provide personal computers for interactive kitchen or landscape design to prospective clients. Kiosks can also be used to provide interactive "how to" information to do-it-yourself devotees. Public information access to local government programs, travel information and scenic highlights and other information of interest to general audiences.

- **Sales demonstrations** can be given which allow the potential customer to control animated sequences which demonstrate the capabilities of a product. For example, by clicking on the radio in an automobile, the user would hear music. The convertible top could be raised and lowered so the customer can see how it operates and what the car looks like in both situations.

- **Training** materials will be available at home and in the office. Multimedia is most powerful as a training tool because the user actually hears, sees, and uses the course content in an interactive environment. Computer-based training with interactive video courses will allow adults to be trained and retrained on the job. Home study materials will allow individuals to obtain self-help material

In some cases training materials prepared by companies for internal use will be passed onto clients, particularly to introduce new product concepts. In addition to the educational value, the client is certain to look favorably on the company's products. Thus training materials may also play a sales and marketing role. This will be particularly value in the computer and telecommunications fields because of the rapid rate of technological change, the new roles that products will play, and the consolidation and integration of previously separate products.

- **Transaction processing kiosks** are being used by state and local governments to provide new ways for agencies to transact business with the public to eliminate some application forms and interviews and to reduce the delays and input errors that characterize manual systems. The kiosks can also provide information, 24 hours a day, 7 days a week in multiple languages which reduces the number of telephone inquiries that need to be handled.

Information Knowledge Worker

The information knowledge worker creates and exchanges information with other individuals

- At the same time and place

- At the same time and different places

- At different times and the same place

- At different times and different places

The information knowledge worker is primarily concerned with business operations-centric applications which are comprised of content-, presentation-, and office-centric applications. Since the primary role of the information knowledge worker is to communicate, the tools and techniques are directed at making the communication effective regardless of the circumstance. Ideally the information must be delivered where it is needed, when it is needed, and how it is needed. Business operations-centric applications and the needs of the information knowledge worker are the driving force for the implementation of broadband networks that reduce current bandwidth and distance limitations.

- **Audiographics**, which combines voice-conferencing with interactive, shared graphics capabilities, is being used by a number of companies for training, remote problem solving sessions, and business meetings. Meeting participants can interact with text, still images, graphics, and data in addition to two-way voice communication.

- **Electronic Performance Support Systems (EPSS)** will be implemented on widespread basis in business organizations to improve competency through just-in-time training, easy access to information and support systems within the context of an individual's job. In effect, an electronic tutor/job aide is available 24 hours per day to coach/assist employees in the job environment. Learning takes place within the context of job tasks. Businesses will use EPSS to increase employees' competency levels and to achieve a competitive edge in the global marketplace.

- **Groupware** is an approach to using the computing and communications tools and infrastructure that already exists in organizations to better support the work of teams and groups. The basic tools are the telephone, including voice mail, the multimedia computer with attendant data network, and the conference room. Desktop videoconferencing with collaborative computing and multimedia capabilities play a role as does screen-based telephony. Networked multimedia computing contributes to the effectiveness of the groupware process by improving communications within the team or group.

- **Multimedia databases** will allow individuals to search and retrieve multimedia information and the database system will provide scalable audio and video to match the capabilities of the network and the personal computer or workstation.

Travel agents have access to a nationwide travel database containing maps to help pinpoint hotel locations in various cities and photographs of hotel lobbies and rooms in addition to descriptive information. All hotels that match the traveler's requirements can be found quickly and easily by completing a template.

Realtors and their clients can take color photo tours of homes from the comfort of the real estate office. All of the available homes that match the buyer's criteria can be selected from the database and "toured" so that the prospective buyers need visit only the most suitable properties.

- **Personal communications** will be extended beyond existing voice telephony, voice messaging, and e-mail to multimedia mail systems that include graphics, image and video. Screen sharing technology on personal computers is already being used to allow individuals to interact using graphics and text in addition to voice. Major voice messaging vendors are adding e-mail and fax to the systems with plans to add images and video in the future.

- **Videoconferencing** will be improved through the use of multiple live windows on the screen of personal computers so that participants can not only see and hear one another but they can interact using screen sharing for multimedia presentations. Desktop videoconferencing will become the norm for business communications.

APPLICATIONS CLASSES

Applications can be divided into four classes for definitional purposes as shown in Figure 5-3. The intent is to provide a framework for understanding the attributes that determine the degree of success of an application. Based on this understanding, the reader will be able to match the capabilities of the multimedia and networking platforms with the requirements of the applications. The judgments that can be made will not be black and white but they will be based on a solid base of information about the elements and attributes of applications.

Applications Classes	Applications
Content-Centric (Publishing or Documentation)	• Manuals/Documentation • Encyclopedias, Dictionaries/Thesaurus • Policies, Procedures, and Standards • Reference Books • Magazines
Presentation-Centric	• Computer-Based Training • Business Presentations • Merchandizing Kiosks • Point of Information Kiosks • DMV Testing Kiosks
Office-Centric	• Electronic Mail • Word Processing • Spreadsheets • Groupware
Operations-Centric	• Just-in-Time Training and Certification • Travel Reservations/ Information • Performance Support Systems • Simulations

Figure 5-3. Application classes provide a framework for determining attributes and technological requirements.

The process is more complex for applications that span multiple applications classes but an appreciation of the attributes of a given application in each relevant application class is important for defining the overall solution. Applications that span multiple classes result from a shift to the business operations-centric class. The shift occurs because multimedia and expert system capabilities are being applied to deliver information where, when, and how it is needed. The information knowledge worker will be the primary beneficiary of multimedia technology when it is provided within the context of the daily work environment.

For example, CBT provides an alternative training method that is cheaper, faster and better than traditional lecture/laboratory training for certain types of instruction. The fact that CBT results in reduced training time and better retention has been documented through numerous studies.

However, CBT, no matter how effective, only brings workers to a basic level of proficiency. It often does not prepare them to handle the variety of real-world situations they'll meet on the job. As a stand alone event, training is often too soon or too late. It usually deals only with a subset of the job and may contain large amounts of irrelevant material.

Hypermedia documentation makes it easier for the user to find and retrieve relevant information. The information itself has more impact because audio, animation and video can be included to make the material easier to understand and retain. However, hypermedia by itself does not satisfy all of the needs of the individual employee.

EPSS is directed specifically at making individuals and groups more competent. Training modules are one element of the system, not the reason for being. Hypermedia documentation is another element as are help systems and database access. The value of the EPSS derives from the premise that each employee is extraordinary, with unique work experience and ways of learning and constant changes in work requirements and information needs.

The elements of an EPSS provide access to information and to training modules in the context of an individual's job. EPSS represents a shift from interactive presentation- and content-centric applications to business operations-centric applications. EPSS applications are part of an organizations daily business operation whereas Computer-Based Training and hypermedia documentation tend to be stand alone events.

Applications have different attributes and may require different technologies for each major stage of use. For example, a resource center for use by sales personnel in preparing business presentations for clients will require a multimedia database server on a high speed network that is accessed using a personal computer. All of date content and the tools needed to develop a customized presentation will be available on the server. The company can ensure that the information used by the sales force is always up-to-date and accurate. However, delivery of the presentation at customer sites will require a multimedia-capable portable or laptop computer with CD-ROM for storage and retrieval of the customized presentation.

Content-Centric Applications

Content-centric applications can also be called publishing or documentation applications. Information is collected and published in hypermedia form by the developer based on pre-defined user interest or on product specifications. An information consumer interacts with the information by browsing or using keywords to select the sections that are of interest. Multiple connected pathways allow the user to jump from one topic to related or supplementary material.

A list of content-centric products is shown in Table 5-1 below:

Table 5-1. The Success of CD-ROM has Prompted the Development of an Array of Content-Centric Applications

Organization	Product	Description
3Com	3Com Laser Library	Product documentation including full-color data sheets, technical notes, and software patches on CD-ROM for use by resellers and distributors
Apple Computer	Service Source	CD-ROM that contains service tools and information for Apple-certified service providers
Arizona Department of Revenue	US West phone directories on CD-ROM	Tax enforcers search directories to track down delinquent taxpayers
CMC Research	New England Journal of Medicine on CD-ROM	Articles from the journal can be searched and retrieved using CMC's search and retrieval software
Britannica Software	Compton's Multimedia Encyclopedia	Multivolume encyclopedia on CD-ROM with images and audio
GeoSystems	Geolocate Plus	An electronic directory with worldwide map information that displays the most efficient route based on addresses or phone numbers
HyperLaw Inc.	Supreme Court on Disc	Hypertext book of U.S. Supreme Court opinions with full-text search and retrieval
International Computer Programs	Software listings	CD-ROM containing all business, educational, engineering, and scientific software for the Macintosh
Library of International Relations	Electronic library	On-line access for students, scholars, businesspeople, and others to international documents, treatises, serials, and periodicals
Price Waterhouse	Auditor database	40-volume set of information on CD-ROM used by 15,000 auditors to answer client questions
Social Security Agency (SSA)	POMS	30,000-page Procedures and Operations Manual System on CD-ROM for use by SSA field offices.
U.S. Geological Survey	Survey information	Satellite and other image databases are available on CD-ROM for worldwide distribution.
Verbum	Verbum Interactive	CD-ROM magazine that includes text, animation, music, and multimedia presentations

Most of the current content-centric applications are distributed on CD-ROM. It is likely that the CD-ROM will continue to be an extremely popular mechanism as it is inexpensive to reproduce and to distribute.

Presentation-Centric Applications

Table 5-2. Presentation-Centric Applications Were the First to Use Multimedia Computing

Company	Application	Description
American Airlines	Interactive multimedia training	Training courses for flight attendants, security, and cargo personnel as well as pilots as a means of accommodating growth, managing costs, and reducing training time
Allstate Insurance	Multimedia Plus	A system that is equal parts training and database, provides the capability to develop new employees, attract and retain employees, and inform field management of knowledge levels and requirements. Courses include customer relations, fundamentals of insurance, and management development.
Bethlehem Steel	Interactive video training	More than 60 courses, most of which are generic–hydraulics, electronics, rigging, etc.–while others cover Bethlehem's operating procedures
Digital Equipment Corporation	DECWORLD '92	Interactive full-motion video and audio application running on networked PCs with touch-sensitive screens that covered attractions, highlights of Boston, news and events, and an explanation of the system
Mannington Resilient Floors	Mannington Premiere Flooring Theatre	Used by consumers to select and view various floors in room settings similar to their homes
Oregon Department of Motor Vehicles (DMV)	RoadReady Driver's Test System	PC-based interactive testing system with video segments covering traffic situations. The system handles all DMV testing and paid for itself in less that 2 years
Tulare County, California	Tulare Touch	An interactive touchscreen system for processing welfare applications that will save $20 million per year by reducing input errors in applicant processing
Union Pacific Railroad	Lifeline	Teaches conductors how to use new on-board computers to track train movements

Abbreviations: DMV, Department of Motor Vehicles.

In an interactive presentation-centric application, information is presented on an interactive basis to the receiver. Typical applications are business presentations, Computer-Based Training, education, public information access, and merchandising kiosks. The information flow is controlled by the receiver when the presentation is on a personal computer.

Interactive presentation-centric applications have found widespread use in industry, education, health care, and government. The Armed Forces have been and continue to be a leader in exploiting multimedia capabilities for training. As a result, the value of Computer-Based Training in terms of content retention, consistency of learning, and training compression is well understood and documented. Severe shortages in employee skills have forced businesses to look for better, less expensive training methods. Training is big business as corporate America spends tens of billions of dollars per year on it. Table 5-2 lists a number of presentation-centric applications.

Office-Centric Applications

Office-Centric applications are used by office workers to communicate information internally and externally, as a matter of course in their daily tasks. Knowledge workers will have the ability to include audio and/or video clips at any point in a spreadsheet, a chart or graph, or a document. This does not imply that office workers must become audio and video experts. Audio and video must be simple to add in the context of the basic application. The issue is not the development of professional audio and video clips but the ability to include dynamic media because they improve our ability to communicate information.

Multimedia capabilities will be fundamental upgrades of the standard office computing environment and a component that is essential to business productivity. The types of communications possible between individuals and among workgroups will be expanded. Information will be presented in richer, more compelling ways with the addition of audio and video.

Lotus Corp. plans to integrate multimedia software capabilities into its core Windows products. Initially multimedia files will appear in Lotus applications as annotation, housed in container applications. The container applications will appear and function consistently across applications, and will enable users to link, embed, or attach messages to files as needed. Annotation will allow users to stick multimedia information—text, sound, pictures, and movies—into the middle of a file to exchange information with coworkers.

Office-centric applications are very new and there are few examples available at present. As multimedia enriches and empowers the standard tools of the work force, it will be included in all business productivity tools in the future.

Table 5-3. Although There Are Relatively Few Examples, it is Evident that Most Office-Centric Applications Tools Will Add Multimedia Capabilities

Company	Product	Description
Apple Computer	QuickTime	An architecture for time-based media that allows application tools such as word processors, spreadsheets, and databases to incorporate audio and video clips, animation, or images
Lotus Corp.	Lotus Sound	OLE server that allows recorded sound to be embedded in OLE-compatible Windows applications
Media Vision	Pocket Recorder	OLE server that allows recorded sound to be embedded in OLE-compatible Windows applications

Office-centric applications are not new applications but an extension of existing applications. Three examples are shown in Table 5-3.

Over time, all of the business software products will offer seamless integration of multimedia capabilities.

A key feature of office-centric applications is that the content is created and used on an impromptu basis. The focus on content is not as extensive as it is for content-centric applications since it is usually part of the normal work flow in the office.

Operation-Centric Applications

Operations-centric applications improve the communication of information in support of the mainstream activities of a business organization. Such applications deliver information where, when, and how it is needed, in the context of the tasks of the individual or work group.

They represent a shift in the use of multimedia computing from stand alone events to daily business operations that are central to the tasks of individuals, groups, and organizations.

Operations-centric applications delineate the ultimate business use of multimedia computing and there are many large companies making investments in this area as shown in Table 5-4.

Table 5-4.   Operations-Centric Applications Deliver Greatly Improved Communications

Company	Project	Description
AT&T	Training Delivery Consultant	A performance support tool for improving the performance of training test developers that consists of interactive documentation, interactive learning modules, and an expert system covering testing issues and test evaluation.
Caterpillar, Inc.	EPSS	Applications training in manufacturing processes, support system, and technical reference on shop floor workstations
Digital Equipment Corporation	Account Business Unit	Sales teams will have access to industry, product, services, and business information, as well as information specific to accounts on a laptop or notebook computer. In addition, sales reps can prepare presentations, take learning modules, and use product descriptions and pricing to prepare a quotation.
Massachusetts General Hospital & NYNEX	Telemedicine	Patient files consisting of medical images, video, text, and diagnostic annotations are available for medical consulting using videoconferencing facilities to hospitals and medical clinics
IBM	EPSS at Poughkeepsie	Employees have access to manufacturing procedures and will have access to learning modules that use video clips to capture the knowledge of experienced operators.
Northern Telecom	SkillPath	An interactive application that presents information about the company and its products
Prime Computer	Sales Source	An EPSS contains product descriptions, marketing and selling strategies and competitive information that allows sales personnel to access relevant information, obtain answers to task-specific questions, and provides just-in-time training

The following more detailed descriptions of business operations-centric applications are included to further illuminate the value and importance of applying multimedia computing in the business environment. Multimedia capabilities offer the most significant opportunity to increase competency and improve productivity through enhanced communications in the context of the work environment. All of the other types of application classes may be embodied in a business operations-centric application. Such applications signify that the application of multimedia computing is a strategic imperative and not just a training or business presentation event.

Further, business operations-centric applications will apply to all establishments in an enterprise which generate pull for broadband wide area networks. Multimedia applications will move from stand-alone ("sneaker net") through closed ("private net") to open network environments, where applications will not be limited by distance or bandwidth considerations.

EPSS at Caterpillar, Inc.

The manufacture of a variety of tractors, engines, lift trucks, pipe layers, and log skidders at Caterpillar, Inc. requires special skills and training (Caterpillar 1992). Caterpillar invested in multimedia training using DVI technology and IBM's ActionMedia II products because of problems they had with traditional training methods.

The change from one-person, one-machine stand alone operation to manufacturing cell and integrated manufacturing systems meant that better training was needed. With the new manufacturing situation it is not possible to conduct traditional training sessions with groups of employees. Caterpillar needed a solution that delivered one-on-one training in the shop environment and served as a reference tool as well.

Shop personnel can practice and learn with computer training and simulation without risk of harming manufacturing systems that cost millions of dollars. The new system acts as an Electronic Performance Support System with learning modules and a technical reference materials. The new system has become part of day-to-day operations in the manufacturing facility and not a stand alone training session.

Traditional training offered no convenient way for the student to review the material. It did not allow Caterpillar to handle unique situations or applications. DVI multimedia allows them to create their own applications or change them at will. Caterpillar will store all training applications on a mainframe for distribution to networked workstations.

Downtime at multimillion dollar complexes is very expensive and the objective of the specialized training is to reduce downtime. Management notes that shop floor operators and maintenance people have become more effective. They believe they've made a wise investment for the long run.

Telemedicine—Massachusetts General Hospital and Nynex

The Massachusetts General Hospital (MGH) is Boston's largest medical center and one of the highest-volume users of medical images in the world. The main hospital is in Boston, there is a medical imaging center in Charleston, the computing offices are in Cambridge, and there is a records library in Somerville. MGH provides diagnostic services to more than 80 referring hospitals in New England.

Nynex developed the Media Broadband Services (MBS) to provide a better way to deliver medical images over broadband networking facilities using a sophisticated switching and signal processing system and MEDOS™ software. MEDOS launches calls into the network so doctors can have voice communication and multiple active windows on their workstations. It establishes the needs of the user and the capabilities of the transport and switching systems to establish multimedia, multiuser conversational sessions. MBS provides much more than high-resolution transfer services for medical images. It is changing the way that the medical community operates.

Although the network consists of leased lines, high-speed switched digital services will be used where it is economically prudent to do so. With switched services, medical diagnosticians could have access to patient files whether at their homes or offices.

Medical diagnosticians must have access to the right high-resolution image at the right time because the patient's life may depend on the correct interpretation of tiny details in the image. Only lossless compression technologies can be used since the loss of a single bit could obscure important details. Sophisticated technologies such as computer-aided tomography (CAT) scans, magnetic resonance imaging (MRI), and video images taken inside the body provide a wealth of information in addition to traditional x-rays. In the past the images were delivered using delivery trucks, courier services, and even bicycles so that doctors could collaborate on diagnosis and treatment. With telemedicine, the images are delivered over high-speed lines to doctors and/or specialists.

Referring physicians are able to review the medical images, read the diagnostic report, and listen to an audio interpretation or communicate directly with the radiologist. Medical specialists can be included in conferencing sessions and all participants have access to all relevant information on their workstations, regardless of location. MBS ensures that transmitted images are as sharp as the originals and that patient files and diagnostic voice annotations accompany the images.

The digitization of all medical records, including images and video with voice annotation, improves record keeping capabilities in addition to allowing doctors to share information for collaborative health care at any time. No longer do they need to wait until medical images are physically transported from the Somerville warehouse.

MBS helps MGH and the referring hospitals reduce expenses by

• Containing liabilities through the use of expert consultation

• Increasing professional productivity (information is provided to doctors when, where and how they need it

• Decreasing the number of lost records and the cost of recreating the records

• Decreasing the consumables associated with the traditional medical records

In the long term, the benefits of MBS can be extended to remote locations including rural hospitals, health maintenance organizations (HMOs), group practices, physician's homes, research and teaching hospitals, etc. Medical insurers want to be able to handle insurance claims right at the hospital. MBS is good news at a time when health care costs are escalating beyond our ability to pay.

International Medical Research

Medtronic Inc., is a medical electronics company that does business in more than 80 countries and sells more than 10,000 pacemakers a month (Rudyk 1992). The company is also a major provider of prosthetic heart valves, membrane oxygenators, centrifugal pumps, therapeutic catheters, nerve and muscle stimulation devices, and drug delivery systems.

Medronic is using Group TeleCommunications Software (GTCS) to simultaneously share voice, text, data, still images, and video over the worldwide public switched network. GTCS allows participants to annotate the information they share on their respective personal computers in real time. GTCS was developed by Bell Northern Research and is marketed by WorldLinx Telecommunications Inc. (formerly IIS Technologies), a subsidiary of Bell Canada Enterprises.

Engineers at Medtronic's head office in Minneapolis, Minnesota can share multimedia information and discuss it with other researchers at the Bakken Research Center in Maastricht, The Netherlands, or at six other locations in Europe and the United States.

When engineers in Minneapolis want to review a new hybrid pacemaker design with colleagues in The Netherlands, they put a video feed of the design through GTCS. The scientists share a magnified image of the circuit layout and troubleshoot design problems in real time. Product designs benefit from the feedback received by the design team and time-to-market is reduced. The costs of meeting and travel expenses have been reduced.

At each location, users of GTCS have a personal computer, a scanner to capture documents and diagrams, a modem, a tablet and stylus to allow participants to annotate the shared screen, a speaker-phone, and a video camera.

REFERENCES

Caterpillar, Inc. 1992. East Peoria Systems, Manufacturing Operations and the Education and Training Divisions of Caterpillar, Inc., Peoria, IL.

Rudyk, Nathan. 1992. Canadian-Produced Software Package Improves International Medical Research. WorldLinx Telecommunications Inc.

6

Application Attributes

THE COMMUNICATION PROCESS

In this chapter we investigate the communications process as it relates to the business environment using multimedia computers and software tools. In these communications processes, messages are sent and received using a variety of transport mechanisms. Most of the processes represent current or potential applications for multimedia and may represent product opportunities. It is our objective to identify the key attributes of each element of a multimedia application based on the

• Tasks performed by the sender (creator) and receiver (user)

• Computing and networking platforms used

• Nature and form of the content and message to be communicated

Applications and Products

A *multimedia application* is defined as the specific use or application of the communication process using multimedia capabilities to meet relevant objectives and goals.

The term "multimedia application" is often used in reference to software products that help in implementing a solution for an application. This causes considerable confusion. For example, products such as authoring tools or encyclopedias are referred to as multimedia applications. To avoid confusion, we will not refer to these or any other software products as applications.

An *authoring tool* is a software product that can be used to create a solution for multimedia applications that incorporate animation, audio, and/or video. The complete implementation consists of one or more hardware and software products.

Similarly, the CD-ROM based encyclopedia is one of several component products that are needed to address a reference application based on the use of Compton's Multimedia Encyclopedia. The complete playback application requires a CD-ROM drive and a compatible computer system with appropriate features.

In this book we will distinguish between multimedia applications and products. We intend to develop a structured approach for analyzing an application so we can be more precise in the specification of goals and objectives and the definition of the significant attributes of the key elements of the application. The purpose of the analysis is to enable the reader to assess the viability of an application based on products and technology that are currently available or will be available in the near future.

An application can be characterized in terms of the requirements, objectives, goals, and costs quite independently of the products that may be used to address the solution. Table 6-1 identifies the considerations that characterize both applications and solutions. For example, a training application that is used to teach auto mechanics how to replace the fuel pump on a specific automobile may be specified by indicating that a video clip of the procedure is to be shown followed by a quiz to determine levels of comprehension. There may be cost and other organizational considerations that are independent of the technical implementation. The application can be characterized without discussing specific multimedia products.

Table 6-1. Application Considerations Are Independent of Both Solutions and Products

Application Considerations	Solution Considerations
Requirements	Computing platform
Objectives	Operating system
Goals	Application software
Organizational issues	Storage
Cost/value issues	Other peripherals
Installed equipment	Networking

However, the proposed solution may involve the use of one or more multimedia products. For example, the training program for mechanics mentioned above may involve networked multimedia computers at each service location so that training modules can be transmitted to the mechanics at their convenience. Our goal is to develop a structured and comprehensive process for assessing applications and proposed solutions that will allow the reader to make informed decisions about the implementation of multimedia applications.

Applications are often specified based on predetermined perspectives about the potential solution. Thus a complete set of application elements includes the specifications for some of the solutions components. This chapter identifies all of the elements of an application that need to be considered as part of the structured analysis approach that follows. The characterization of an application with a predefined solution set in mind usually limits the number solutions that need to be explored and is often an expedient way to proceed.

STRUCTURED ANALYSIS APPROACH

Multimedia applications are often described in the context of the computing and networking environments. We will use these environments to develop the attributes of the application. An application can be broken into six elements as follows:

• Content

• Interactivity

• Sender/creator computing platform

• Receiver/player computing platform

• Server computing platform and storage mechanisms

• Transport or communication network

The structured analysis approach provides the context used to develop and examine the values of attributes of each element that comprises an application. The analysis enables the user to approach the ideal solution through successive iterations. In some instances it may be necessary to change the characterization of the application to accommodate available technologies or business issues.

Step 1: Application Definition

Characterize the application in terms of the key attributes of each of the six elements of the application. This is not a precise or inflexible exercise. The requirements should be considered as having a range of values that will be weighed from a qualitative perspective later in the process.

For example, although full-screen, full-motion video is highly desirable, cost considerations may change the requirement to partial motion in a window based on the evaluation in step 3.

Step 2: Solution Definition

Formulate an initial solution based on availability of appropriate technologies.

Chapter 9 provides detailed information about the technologies that should be considered for the initial solution. Readers who understand their requirements but are not familiar with the technology should refer to product and service providers for help in formulating the solutions. The menu of available technologies is very complex. It is both appropriate and necessary to remain flexible so the options are not too narrowly defined in the early part of the analysis.

Step 3: Evaluation

Evaluate how well the proposed solution fits the attributes specified. Make qualitative tradeoffs for value versus cost. Examine procedural and operational considerations in order to reach one of the following conclusions:

• The solution is acceptable and the analysis is completed

• The application is not feasible at this time

• The application or the solution or both the application and solution must be modified.

Step 4: Modify Solution and/or Application

Make appropriate modifications and go back to step 3.

Step 5: Other Considerations

Review operational, policy, organizational, cost, and value issues. Examine implementation, training, support, and acceptance requirements for the application.

The procedure outlined in Figure 6-1 is most effective, particularly for complex applications, when it is applied to individual elements and attributes. The authors suggest that the steps be applied as many times as necessary. Successive iterations will help refine all of the elements of both the application and the solution.

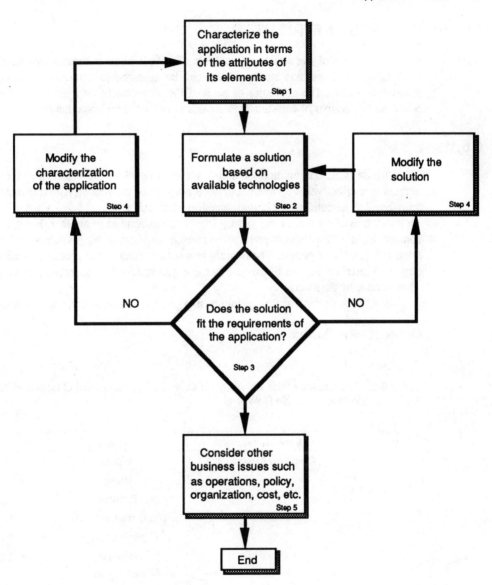

Figure 6-1. A structured analysis approach for multimedia applications ensures that the solution matches the requirements.

ELEMENTS AND ATTRIBUTES

For the purposes of the structured analysis, the application is broken into six elements. Each of the elements has attributes that can be assessed to determine if the proposed solution is viable. The attributes of each of the elements of an application are defined below and the values of each attribute are described in the sections that follow.

Content

The purpose of all communication is to transfer information from sender to receiver in a manner that effectively serves the intended purpose of the sender. The information to be transferred is the content of a communication application.

The nature of content varies greatly from one application to another. For example, the content in a multimedia mail application consists of short messages that are of interest to a limited number of people. The content in a set of policies and procedures may be very large and intended for use by anyone in the organization. It is accessed a piece at a time when needed by the receiver.

Content is comprised of text, graphics, images, animation, audio, and video media.

Content Attributes

Table 6-2. The Values of the Attributes of Content Determine the Quality and Impact of the Messages that Are to Be Delivered

Attributes	Values
Coding/language	Words
	Music
	Pictures
Source	Synthetic/artificial
	Captured/natural
Dynamics	Visual–static
	Visual–dynamic
	Audio–dynamic
Specificity	Specific
	General purpose
Useful life	Short
	Long
Quantity	Ranges from small to large

Content has six attributes which are summarized along with their values for multimedia applications in Table 6-2.

Coding/Language

The information that a sender intends to transfer to a receiver needs to be encoded as is appropriate for the transport mechanism and so that the receiver will be able to decode and understand it. For example, the words used and the rules governing their use in a letter or e-mail message must be understood both by sender and receiver. The language itself is the encoding mechanism.

In face-to-face communications, the spoken word is augmented by gestures, body language, and other sounds. The combination is an expanded language that includes dynamic audio and visual media which is quite acceptable for use in face-to-face communications.

The communication process can be improved using sketches or drawings and by pointing at existing objects in the area. Television makes extensive use of static and dynamic pictures that are recorded as part of the content encoding process.

Thus the specification for coding or language has three potential values.

- **Words** All or part of the content for an application may be made up of words. Words can be written or spoken and it may be necessary to consider the specific language. Languages such as Chinese, Japanese, or Arabic must also be considered in this analysis because they impose special graphic requirements for the computing platform.

- **Music** Content can include music in written or audio form. Written music is similar to the written word. When music is played it creates special requirements to accommodate the fact that it is a time-dependent or dynamic media.

If the music is synthesized as it is in video games, the solution must support an appropriate method of synthesis. For example, the FM synthesis techniques that are commonly used for personal computer games require special hardware components. Higher-quality music requirements force the implementer to determine if available technology will meet the goals of the application.

- **Pictures** Computer displays can be used to display moving, animated, or still pictures. It is important to specify the resolution, color depth, and appropriate standards for the source material.

Attribute values are not mutually exclusive and content will likely be comprised of a blend of values. The collective importance of the values must be considered when assessing the solution that is to be implemented.

Source

Content is either created through synthesis using an available encoding language or by capturing it directly from the environment. For example, an article in a newspaper may contain a verbatim statement made by an individual. When the statement is printed in a newspaper, it is artificial or synthesized content. When the same statement is recorded on tape for a radio broadcast it is natural or captured content. Similarly, a drawing is artificial while a photograph is natural. The *source* attribute has two values.

Synthetic or artificial content includes text, graphics, and animation. The media of the artificial or synthesized world are those of the traditional digital domain of the personal computer. This is usually an efficient way of representing content in terms of storage and bandwidth requirements. The coding language serves as a compression mechanism.

Captured or natural content includes recorded voice, music, photographs, and motion video. The natural forms of content existed historically only in the analog domain of the real world. They must be digitized and compressed to operate in the computer environment.

Source attribute values are often mixed with both artificial and natural content in the same application. It is important to specify which value dominates the application as it can determine whether the overall solution will be effective.

(Note: Although application requirements do not specify compression, the solution will need to use compression technology to satisfy cost, performance, and usability issues. This applies to all of the other types of technology.)

Dynamics

Content is either static, meaning that it is frozen in time as in printed material, or dynamic as in audio and motion video. Multimedia applications usually include at least one dynamic media. There are three values for this attribute.

Static-visual content includes everything in printed form including text, music, and graphics and photographs.

Audio is time-dependent content such as voice, sound effects, and live or recorded music. Dynamic-visual or motion video content is also time dependent content such as motion video and animated pictures or graphics. Continuously flowing streams of data are necessary to playback audio or dynamic visual content across a network. The time interrelationship between dynamic media is critical since audio and video must be synchronized.

Specificity

Content may be very focused and intended for a very limited group of receivers or general for a very broad audience. As shown in Figure 6-2, a video mail message that is targeted to a limited number of receivers is specific. However, a television broadcast that is intended for as large an audience as possible is general purpose.

Similarly, a business presentation is usually prepared for a limited number of people within a particular field of interest while a multimedia encyclopedia is intended for the general public. The design of the solution can vary a great deal based on the specificity of the content. This attribute has a range of values from specific to general purpose.

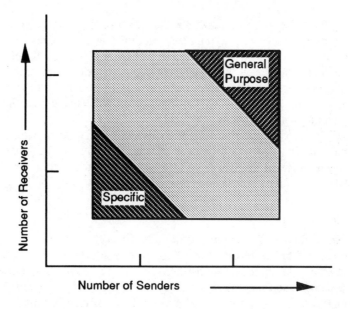

Figure 6-2. The specificity varies with the number of senders and receivers.

Specific content is directed to and focused on a very limited audience. If the presentation is to hit the mark, the interests of the receiver(s) directly influence the content.

General-purpose content is prepared for large audiences and targeted to suit the broad interests of various groups. Individual items may have little interest to members of the audience but overall, the audience in interested in the overall content.

In this case as well the attributes values range from very specific for small audiences to very general for large audiences. Both cost and production methods vary accordingly.

Useful Life

In some cases, the value or half-life of content exists for a short time and in others it may retain its value for a significant period of time. A video mail message may be meaningful for a few hours or days and a television news broadcast may be less valuable the next day. Some books or music or movies retain significant value over the years while others have limited value.

The life cycle of current knowledge is decreasing rapidly. In business environments, information must be updated on a continuous basis as it is the lifeblood of decision making activity. In any technical endeavor, a book covering the latest advances in most disciplines is likely to be obsolete before it is published. This suggests that such books must move to a "publication on-demand" format. Volatile material can be stored on magnetic or optical material and updated as often as is appropriate. Such "books" will become living documents that change in accordance with the evolution of the technology.

There is a range of values for this attribute that vary from short to long. Once again there are shades of gray and the solution that is selected can depend greatly on this attribute. For example, CD-ROM technology is a good solution for distributing a maintenance manual that is updated one per month. Information about customer orders that changes during the build-cycle needs to be distributed to workers on the factory floor as soon as it is available. On-line access will ensure that the product isn't built to yesterday's specifications.

The time-value of information dictates the type of storage and the distribution mechanisms that will provide a satisfactory solution. In general, the cost of creating specific content that has a short life is less than the cost of general-purpose content that has a long life.

Quantity

The inclusion of dynamic media significantly increases the quantity of information compared to traditional personal computer applications. The number of video and audio clips to be included in manuals, reference materials, encyclopedias, and other documentation may be restricted by the capacity of the storage mechanism. The floppy disk is the most universal mechanism for exchanging information but the capacity is too low for many applications. The capacity of CD-ROM is adequate for many applications and will prove to be a popular mechanism for distribution since it is included in the base MPC specification.

The amount of information to be stored by media type must be estimated for the life of the project. If the quantity of information increases and the update frequency increases, it may be practical to move from CD-ROM to networked file server during the life of the project.

Office- and business operations-centric applications will probably use network servers since networks are central to the movement of information in business operations. Content- and presentation-centric applications can exist very effectively using CD-ROM or removable disks provided that their storage capacity is sufficient.

Interactivity

In a complete communication session the receiver often needs to be able to influence the flow of information and even the content of the message itself. Interactivity describes the ability of the receiver to influence the message. In face-to-face communications, the interaction takes the form of frequent interruptions and questions. This represents the ultimate in interaction which is the *participative* level of interactivity. When we watch broadcast television, our ability to interact is limited to changing the channel which is the *passive* level of interactivity.

Multimedia computing applications afford the receiver varying degrees of freedom to choose and influence the flow of the content. Collaborative computing by its very nature must offer a high level of interactivity. Hypermedia documents offer less interactivity but interactivity remains very important to the success of the solution. CBT experts consistently note that students learn faster and retain more information because they are able to interact with the course material. All multimedia application require a certain level of interactivity to be effective—the issue is how much?

The most basic or atomic part of a communication session is the message that is being sent from sender to receiver. The message may be short or long. The level of interactivity may vary from passive to participative. The receiver or receivers may choose not to interact with the sender. It is important to determine the level of interactivity that is needed to ensure that the solution is successful.

When a speaker asks the audience to hold all questions until the end of the speech, the audience has no opportunity to change the flow of information or the content. There is no interaction between the receivers and the sender except for the question and answer period at the end of the speech. Obviously, the audience has no opportunity to influence the content. In the business operations environment, receivers often direct the sender's presentation by asking questions or making comments. Seasoned presenters redirect the flow of information based on verbal and nonverbal feedback from the audience.

Multimedia computing applications provide relatively high levels of interactivity as the receiver is able to select various options at many different points in the solution. *Interactivity* is the ability of the receiver to influence the flow of information from the sender. In general, interactivity is the essence of effective communications.

Interactivity has four levels as depicted in Figure 6-3, with the participative level providing the most effective communications between individuals and groups. In general, the level of interactivity will increase as we move from content-centric to business operations-centric applications.

Increasing Levels of Interactivity ———————▶

Level of Interactivity	Passive	Active-Serial	Active-Parallel	Participative
Interface Type	Buttons and Dials	Menus, One Context at a Time	Graphical Icons Multiple Contexts	User Controlled Links
Example	Television	Standard Personal Computer	Personal Computer with GUI	Multimedia Computer with Hypermedia

Figure 6-3. The sophistication of products and tools increases from the passive to the participative level of interactivity.

- **Passive** In many communication sessions the receiver is unable to influence what is being received. Communication takes place in a single context with a limited number of choices. Broadcast television does not allow us to influence the flow of information except for our ability to change channels or the sound level (or turn it off!). Very simple receiver platforms can be used if the receiver has no control over the flow of information. A storefront merchandising display that uses multimedia computing to promote products but offers no ability for the receiver to interact with the information is an example of a passive solution. The merchant decides which products to display and what to say about them.

- **Active-Serial** The receiver is presented with a predetermined selection of choices that were dictated by the sender. Multiple contexts are available but only one is available at any time and the choices are limited. Context changes are relatively difficult. The receiver follows paths through the content by choosing from a menu.

The options available to the receiver were preselected by the sender to suit the objectives established for the application. In the merchandising display example cited above, prospective customers would be allowed to select the products or product line that they want to review. Subsequent menus would allow the receiver to select finer and finer levels of detail or to return to the main menu so that the whole process could begin again. The shopper's ability to influence the information flow is restricted to the choices provided by the merchant.

- **Active-Parallel** Apple's Macintosh computer popularized the GUI in the mid-80s by offering a more intuitive interface using icons rather than text menus or text commands. Apple's success with the point-and-click capability using a desktop metaphor prompted the development of similar capabilities on personal computers with Windows, OS/2, and Unix. Multiple contexts are available at a time and it is easy to move from one to another. Many choices are available in each context. The user makes choices by selecting icons to move freely from one context to another. The GUI empowers users to explore and discover what is available in their own style, at their own pace, and in accordance with their preferences.

- **Participative** Hypermedia provides a method for delivering information using multiple connected pathways, which allow the user to easily jump from one topic to related or supplementary material. As a result users are able to interact freely with the content. The user can create specific contextual relationships and explore them in any order. Hypermedia capabilities allow the communication process to proceed in a nonlinear fashion.

The Computer maintenance manual mentioned in Chapter 5 is a good example of participative interactivity. The technician can select the product and area of interest and follow the suggested procedures. Icons signal that a QuickTime™ movie is available to illustrate a procedure or operation. The technician is free to move to other sections to find more information about the product or a potential problem or procedure by pointing and clicking.

The receiver has access to a significant level of flexibility in exploring the content. Although it is not the same as being able to ask questions in a face-to-face environment, hypermedia achieves a high level of interactivity. For the moment, the highest level of interactivity occurs when the sender and receiver are face-to-face.

The ability to ask questions and direct the information flow will be realized in the future because of advances being made in artificial intelligence and speech recognition and synthesis. Within the next 10 years, it is likely that we will enjoy a fully participative level of interactivity using multimedia computing capabilities.

The participative level of interactivity fosters very effective communications between individuals and groups. The level of interactivity has a great impact on the tools selected for use in multimedia solutions. The passive level can be satisfied with relatively unsophisticated tools and the participative level challenges the limits of current technology.

Computing and Networking Platforms

The next four elements of an application are the computing and transport platforms (i.e., sender, receiver, server, and transport). The following items combine to form the solution and must be considered when the application is being characterized.

• Multimedia computing platform

• Operating system software

• Application software

• Storage mechanism

• Audio/video components

• Other peripherals

• Networking

It is clear that by controlling the lion's share of the desktops, IBM's PC (and clones) and Apple's Macintosh will be the platforms of choice for playback in the business environment. For example, when a corporation decides to implement a training application on the desktop of every employee they are unlikely to replace existing PCs or Macintosh computers unless the cost of upgrades is higher than the cost of the replacement platforms.

If the existing personal computer base can meet the minimum capabilities needed for multimedia computing, the organization will simply upgrade to satisfy the requirements of the application. Thus in some cases, the solution must be developed around the existing installed base of personal computers.

In general, it makes good business sense to preserve the value of existing network infrastructure investments. Thus a networking solution that allows a business to continue to use the current wiring system, network operating system, and network interface cards will be preferred over a solution that demands wholesale change. For example, the new switched hubs can provide dedicated Ethernet bandwidth to individual desktops. When combined with the video networking solutions offered by Starlight Networks or other suppliers, existing LANs can provide video services to large number of users without impacting applications that currently run on the LAN. The solution preserves the investments in network interface cards, the network operating system, and application software.

The authors don't mean to imply that one should adopt a wait and see attitude but recognize that it is a nontrivial exercise to make changes to networks. Fortunately the evolution path for LANs and WANs is converging on the same technology. The technology is both compatible with existing networks and extensible to future networks that operate at much higher speeds (e.g., 155 and 600 Mbit/s). Refer to Chapter 9 for more information.

Multimedia Computing Platforms

A sender (or in turn the receiver) needs to be able to perform five tasks.

• Create or modify a message

• Store a message

• Send a message

• Retrieve messages for modification

• Play a message for verification prior to sending it

Each of these tasks must be considered when characterizing attributes of the computing platform. Sender/creator, receiver/player, and server elements have similar attributes since all are computing platforms. The specific values of the attributes of each element may be different in a particular application.[1] The attributes that apply to all three computing platforms are described below. Attributes that are unique to each platform are identified as appropriate.

A receiver needs to be able to hear an audio message and see a visual message whether it is text, image, graphics, animation, or motion video. If the receiver has little need to interact with the message, the receiver/player platform may be simpler than that of the sender. However, in a business environment, an individual is a receiver in one instant and a sender in another, so the sender and receiver platforms must be the same or similar.

A server platform may be connected to a LAN or WAN. It does not need to be capable of creating messages because it is only used as a storage and playback mechanism. The server (1) must be capable of simultaneous, real-time management of dynamic media

---

[1] A platform is not explicit in a face-to-face communication. Written communication uses a paper and pencil or a typewriter and the paper serves as a storage mechanism for the content. The platform for multimedia applications consists of a computer with a storage mechanism and a transport mechanism. The sender usually uses "authoring tools" to assist in the preparation of the message.

types; and (2) must be able to manage protocols and sessions; and (3) must be able to handle the large files needed to store audio, images, and video. Performance, storage capacity, and input/output characteristics are important as it must serve a large number of users. It may not be even explicitly identified except as a resource to store and forward data or messages.

The authors leave it to the reader to consider the general requirements of the display, keyboard, mouse, and other common components of computing platforms. Each of the dominant vendors has the base computing platform needed for multimedia applications. The focus in this section is on selected significant attributes.

Processor Attributes

Architectural compatibility: Intel and Apple.

Performance

Performance requirements of an application should be specified in the terms relevant to the users and tasks. There is no single measure that applies to all multimedia applications.

For example, it may be appropriate to specify that an image must appear on the screen less than 0.25 seconds, after a response from the user for a business operations-centric application. It is generally accepted that 0.25 seconds is an effective instantaneous response rate for browsing. Studies show that worker productivity improves with faster response times.

Similarly, it may be necessary to capture and process voice information in real time for an office-centric application. Processing after capture would be unacceptable.

Performance is a very broad and complex attribute. Its importance and emphasis vary from application to application.

Operating System Software

As is the case with processor architecture, the system software may be determined before multimedia applications are to be implemented. There are a number of operating systems to choose from and in some cases, more than one operating system may need to be supported. For example, an equipment manufacturer may select Apple's Macintosh with System 7 for use by employees but may find that distributors and system integrators have selected IBM-compatible personal computers with Windows 3.1. The attributes of the processor and system software may need to be specified for both architectures to provide for interchangeability or coexistence in an application.

The operating systems are DOS, Windows, Macintosh, and OS/2, with attendant multimedia extensions.

Application Software

The attributes of application software are very different for the sender/creator, receiver/player, and server platforms.

Sender/Creator Application Software

Functions and usability levels must be specified based on the target user. In office-centric and business operations-centric applications the sender and receiver may be the same person, which means that the application software characteristics may need to be specified as a combination.

Receiver/Player Application Software

Application software may be simple and very specific when the targeted receiver is focused on receiving information. For example, the application software for an instructional workstation may only need to deal with presenting the course material and not be capable of editing or designing user interfaces.

Server Application Software

The amount of data to be stored over given periods of time and the number of clients that need to be connected to one or more servers must be specified. The application software will need to handle time-dependent data and may need to serve multiples types of sender/creator and receiver/player platforms. Server application software must be capable of simultaneous, real-time data management for audio and video.

Multimedia database management systems will be available for networked multimedia applications.

Storage Platforms

It is important to understand how the content will be distributed and how often it will be updated and by whom. Will distribution on a CD-ROM or removable hard disk satisfy the requirements of the application or is remote on-line access needed?

Read/Write Storage

Storage capacity must be established based on typical usage of data by the end users of the application. For example, 1 hour of audio, 1000 pictures, and 10 minutes of motion video could be specified for storage on a fixed hard disk for an interactive presentation-centric application. Smaller application requirements can be served by removable hard disk storage.

Optical Storage

For applications that only need to support read-only storage capability, the requirement can be met by a CD-ROM. For example, read-only capability can be specified for reference material applications published on CD-ROM.

Read/Write Optical Storage

In applications where extremely large quantities of read/write content must be stored, magneto-optical storage devices may be required.

Note that almost all of the optical storage technologies are moving from read only to read/write capabilities. For example, the CD-Recordable (CD-R) consortium is extending the CD-ROM specifications to include read/write capability. Although distinctions based on read-only versus read/write are important in the near term, they will be meaningless in the future.

Audio/Video Components

Audio

The application should specify audio quality. This may be specified by indicating the sampling rate as 22 kHz monaural or 44 kHz stereo or by indicating that the quality must be equivalent that provided by audiotape or CD respectively. In addition, the specification should cover the need to

• Capture as well as playback audio

• Mix audio signals from various sources.

Video

The application must specify the

• Image resolution in quantitative terms by specifying the number of pixels on the screen or in qualitative terms as being photorealistic or newsprint-like

• Animation requirements and the number of frames per second

• Size of the picture on the screen (partial or full screen)

• Ability to capture video, both stills, and full motion with screen size and frame rate

Other Peripherals

Other equipment may be needed to meet the requirements of the application as follows
• VCRs to provide "hard copy" output or interim storage for editing

• Videodiscs for read-only analog video sources[2]

• Cameras for digital still or motion video input

• Microphones for audio input; and

---

[2] Although videodiscs continue to be used, the authors believe that digital alternatives offer a richer environment for the development of multimedia solutions.

• Speakers for audio output

Transport Platforms or Networks

The options will vary according to the community of interest and the nature of the content to be transported. If the application is for a local environment, the specification will need to cover the LAN and interconnection alternatives. If the application is for desktop-to-desktop communications in an enterprise, then all of the network types shown below must be considered. If audio and video files are to be transferred on a regular basis, the network must have both the bandwidth and latency characteristics appropriate for dynamic media.

Local Area Networks

The number of users, the nature, frequency, and type of traffic, the geographic dispersion of the target users and the other types of traffic that need to be carried by the LAN must be specified. In addition, decisions about the amount of data to be stored and the location of servers must be included. The bandwidth requirements of existing business applications represent a small fraction of the needs of dynamic data. In addition, dynamic media such as audio and video are very sensitive to network delays. A substantive change in the local requirements will impact internetworking and WAN requirements as well.

Wide Area Networks

The application may be served by a private network or the public network or both. In all cases the solution must be capable of transporting dynamic media with the quality and fidelity needed by the application. In the 1990s a wide variety of dedicated and switched services will be available to satisfy multimedia networking requirements with bandwidths ranging from multiples of 64 kbit/s to 600 Mbit/s. The tariffs established for broadband network services will be the key issue. New models will be needed since a tariff for 600 Mbit/s service that is 10,000 times the tariff for 64 kbit/s will be unacceptable to business users.

Office-centric and business operations-centric applications will drive the need for bandwidth along with computer-aided design/computer-aided manufacturing (CAD/CAM) and other high bandwidth applications. A network solution capable of handling full-motion video will be capable of handling all other media up to the point where the aggregate bandwidth is exceeded by the number of simultaneous users.

The number of users, the nature, frequency and type of traffic, the geographic dispersion of the target users, and the other types of traffic that need to be carried by the WAN must be specified. Generally the traffic levels on a LAN are far greater than those on a WAN. However, this will not be the case for workgroup applications that depend on networks that cross departmental and establishment boundaries.

ATTRIBUTE STRUCTURED ANALYSIS

A solution is simply a specification of the various products that will satisfy the requirements of a given application. An assessment of the attributes provides a perspective of how well the proposed solution meets the objectives and goals of the application. The developer of a solution or the prospective user or the customer must have some way of evaluating its effectiveness. Effectiveness can be matched against value to determine if the application can be justified.

Three examples follow which show how the structured analysis approach introduced at the beginning of the chapter is applied based on the attributes of an application. The applications selected are not complex and were specifically selected to demonstrate the use of the approach.

Content-Centric Application

Application Objective

Develop a hypermedia document to replace a 20- volume set of maintenance and repair manuals for a family of personal computer products. The objectives are to make it easier for technicians to find relevant information, to improve the quality and timeliness of service, and to reduce the cost of updating the manual. Thirty minutes of video clips and animation will be included to serve as learning modules for complex diagnostic and repair procedures. The pace of changes and new product introductions dictate that the manual will be updated once per month.

The Proposed Solution

Publish the manual using a CD-ROM player that is compatible with the MPC specifications. Refer to Chapter 9 for a detailed description of the MPC specifications. Use a GUI to ensure that the manual is easy to use.

Note that detailed information about the application and solution will be added as the analysis proceeds.

Content Attribute Analysis

The individual attributes of each element will be considered separately. All of the elements that make up the application will be reviewed below as necessary.

Coding and Language

Step 1. The content is largely text, with pictures and audio to embellish the presentation.

Step 2. The proposed solution will be published on CD-ROM discs.

Step 3. The playback platform will be based on the MPC specification which meets all of the requirements of the application except for full-motion video. The target MPC platform supports both audio and animation content.

Step 4. Modify the application requirements since available technologies only support animation or video clips in small windows at 15 fps.

Although the Macintosh or Ultimedia personal computers meet the requirements they are not suitable since most of the field service groups already have IBM-compatible PCs operating under Windows 3.0. Macintosh and Ultimedia platforms are described in detail in Chapter 9.

A disk operating system (DOS) solution will require additional development effort to provide support for audio and video content. The DOS user interface may be not attractive since the field service team are not computer literate.

Step 5. Up to this point, the application definition can be satisfied by the proposed solution.

Source

Step 1. Most of the content is artificial and is based on the text files used for the paper edition. Audio, video, and pictures are captured from various sources and are natural.

Step 2. The selected MPC platform supports audio, video, pictures, and text.

Step 3. Both artificial and natural content can be handled by the proposed solution.

Step 4. The quality of photographs is limited by the VGA display to a color depth of 8 bits and the sound quality is limited by the 22 kHz, 8-bit sampling rate available on the selected MPC platform. Video clips are limited to 15 fps in a 160 by 120 pixel window.

Step 5. Appropriate trade-offs have been made to keep the solution inexpensive to satisfy management and to provide acceptable quality to field service personnel.

Dynamics

Step 1. Static and dynamic visual and dynamic audio content are included. Animation is considered to be partially dynamic.

Step 2. MPC platform.

Step 3. The MPC playback environment can support all of the dynamic requirements but is not capable of handling full-motion video.

Step 4. A solution that delivers video at 15 fps in a small window is acceptable and it can be handled by the specified MPC platform.

Iteration: The solution restricts dynamic media to the types that can be handled by the specified MPC platform.

Steps 3 through 5. The solution is adequate provided that the restriction on content is observed.

Specificity

Step 1. Content is specific to the maintenance and repair of PC products.

Step 3. CD-ROM is a good medium for both the initial publication and periodic updates of the manual.

Steps 4 and 5. The proposed solution continues to be fine.

Useful Life

The content consists of information about products that have been in the field more than 5 years with attendant updates and improvements and new product information. The half-life varies from short to long.

Step 3. CD-ROM is appropriate for publishing information that needs to be updated on a periodic basis.

Step 4. Other considerations: It is important to investigate the updates. Information can be published and distributed easily on CD-ROMs. Further, the technicians will not need to manually update the document since each new edition arrives in an updated condition.

Step 5. Monthly updates are easier to manage and much cheaper to publish, store, and ship when using CD-ROM.

Steps 3, 4 and 5. Iteration: Upon consideration this solution still holds valid.

Quantity

Step 1. The content is largely text. The 20-volume set is estimated to be about 5000 pages of text which is equivalent to 10 to 15 million characters. This will take about 20 Mbytes of storage or about 3 percent of the capacity of a CD-ROM disc.

An hour of audio at 22 kHz with 8-bit samples will require 80 Mbytes of storage.

Thirty minutes of video clips at 15 fps in a 160 by 120 pixel window with 8-bit color depth takes approximately 320 Mbytes.

Thus entire content will consume roughly 420 Mbytes which leaves adequate room for future additions.

Step 2. A single CD-ROM will be used for the entire publication.

Step 3. A single CD-ROM is sufficient to contain all of the content of the 20-volume manual.

The proposed solution appears to meet the objectives established for the application.

Interactivity

Step 1. The application specifies the need to search based on key words and context. Unstructured access is also desirable to allow for browsing. The *active-serial* level of interactivity will be satisfactory.

Step 2. The software needed for playback must satisfy the *active-serial* level of interactivity.

Steps 3, 4, and 5 need to be reconsidered when a detailed description of the playback software is available to ensure that it complies with the requirements.

Computing Platforms

The only platform of interest in this case is the receiver/player platform. The user will not create new content and a networked server is not needed since local CD-ROM players will be employed in all cases.
   The receiver/player platform is defined the Level 1 MPC platform.

Processor Architecture

Step 1. Intel 386 compatible.

Steps 2, 3, 4, and 5 need not be considered since there is no need to change the specification.

Processor Performance

Step 1. The access to content and response to an input key should be less than 1 second or on the slowest 386SX machine that meets the MPC specifications.

Step 2. Specify the performance requirement when analyzing the playback software.

Step 3. Perform this evaluation on the hardware and software combination.

Steps 4 and 5. The solution satisfies the requirements of this element of the application.

System Software Architecture

Step 1. DOS/Windows 3.1 as part of the MPC specification.

Steps 2, 3, 4, and 5. No new insights or changes.

Application Software

The application software is the playback software referred to in the section on Interactivity, above. The application software requires unique development activity to meet the usability and performance requirements.

Storage

Step 1. The solution must provide approximately 425 Mbytes of removable storage (CD-ROM).

Step 2. MPC platform includes a CD-ROM drive.

Step 3. CD-ROM drive can meet the requirements.

Step 4. There are other storage alternatives. A networked server could be used in locations that have several technicians. Updates could be delivered over the WAN or distributed on CD-ROM. In this instance, it is assumed that each technician will have a workstation that includes a CD-ROM player.

Step 5. The proposed solution continues to meet the requirements.

Audio /Video

Step 1. The platform needs to be able to play back audio and video.

Step 2. MPC platforms minimum specifications.

Step 3. Adequate for this requirement.

Steps 4 and 5. OK. Continue.

Other Peripherals

None are required.

Conclusions

The specified MPC platform meets all of the requirements. The application software needs to be developed to meet requirements. The proposed solution is practical for the application.

This example was chosen to demonstrate the approach. The approach is structured but it is not precise. The example was broken down into small steps to keep it tractable. As the reader becomes more familiar with the approach, it will not be necessary to explicitly identify all of the steps. Some of the attributes will be obvious so the analysis can be handled more simply.

Presentation-Centric Application

The second example is a CBT application. The analysis covers the application and solution for the receiver (or student) and not the creation, selection, or use of the authoring tool or the sender/creator computing platform.

Brief Description of the Application

The objective is to train all new employees in the clothing section of a chain of large department stores. The employees are responsible for keeping the shelves fully stocked with every item stacked neatly in the appropriate place.

The turnover of employees is high and new employees are hired on a daily basis. Currently, an experienced employee must spend 2 hours showing each new employee how to do the job. The objective is to have the new employee spend 1 hour at a CBT station and then start the job.

Brief Description of the Proposed Solution

Install 1 or 2 CBT stations in the store to satisfy the training requirement specified above. It is assumed that the stations will also be available for other tasks. New employees will complete the training program before they report for work. The training solution must demonstrate realistic situations and show the proper way of performing each task. Each trainee is to be tested for comprehension and asked to repeat parts, as necessary, to ensure that all tasks are understood. The user interface should be graphical and intuitive.

The solution consists of a PC-based work station which uses a CD-ROM drive to store the content and DVI technology for full-motion video playback. DVI is described in detail in Chapter 9. The company is a nationwide chain that has many stores. Once the training material has been developed and tested, it will be used by all of the stores.

Content

Coding and Language

Step 1. Most of the content consists of realistic demonstrations of each task using motion video with narration. Music is used in the introduction and conclusion.

Source

Step 1. The motion video clips are captured by taping an experienced employee who demonstrates how to do the job properly. Menus guide the student through the instructional information and tests. The tests may ask the employee to respond by entering an answer or by selecting one of several choices following a video clip covering selected tasks.

Dynamics

Step 1. Most of the content is dynamic with some static content for text display and questions and answers.

Specificity

Step 1 The content is highly specific to the task and the customer (i.e., the department store chain). It must be unique and inexpensive to create.

Useful Life

Step 1. The useful life of the content is 3 to 4 months since each store changes both layout and space organization on a seasonal basis. The cost of capturing the video clips must not be too high since they may need to be replaced two or three times per year.

Quantity

Step 1. Approximately 20 minutes of motion video is required in 30- to 40-second segments. Voice narration, music, text, graphics, and testing software is also needed.

Step 2. The proposed solution supports motion video stored on a CD-ROM drive. A compact disc can store slightly more that 1 hour of motion video.

Step 3. All three attributes of content can be supported in the solution proposed.

The content can be updated by adding small changes to the hard disk on the PC or by creating a new CD.

Step 4. DVI offers two levels of video quality. Production Level Video (PLV) must be processed and compressed by service bureaus since it requires special equipment. The quality provided by Real-Time Video (RTV) compression will be acceptable for this application. It will be much less expensive and more convenient since it can be handled by the store using a PC equipped with ActionMedia hardware and software provided by IBM and Intel.

Step 5. RTV is an acceptable tradeoff because of operational considerations.

The solution seems to be acceptable so far.

Note: A Macintosh-based solution could have been selected for this application since it is fully capable of satisfying the requirement. The PC may be preferred simply because it is the computing platform of choice for this particular organization.

Interactivity

Step 1. The application requires that the user follow a structured path through the training sequence. However, the user should also be able to move from one sequence to another as needed. This is the *active-parallel* level of interactivity.

Step 2. The course material is to be developed using one of the tools that support the DVI-based products. Any of these tools can provide the required level of interactivity.

Step 3. The level of interactivity should be evaluated when the final course material is available to ensure that it complies with the specification.

Step 4. No modifications are needed at this point.

Step 5. Proceed since the proposed solution is okay so far.

Computing Platform

Only the training station or the receiver platform needs to be considered for this application.

Step 1. Processor architecture: Each store currently uses personal computers based on Intel's architecture for other applications so this architecture is preferred.

Step 2. The proposed solution will be based on DVI products running on the Intel processors. The hardware and software required are available from IBM and Intel.

Step 3. Available ActionMedia II products meet the requirements.

Steps 4 and 5. The solution seems acceptable so far.

Performance

Step 1. The response time for the interaction with the trainee must be less than 1 second.

Step 2. The training material will be distributed on CD-ROM and all of the processors will be 33 MHz 386s as a minimum.

Step 3. The performance requirements can be met with the hardware that is selected.

Steps 4 and 5. Proceed as there is no need to modify the proposed solution.

System Software

Step 1. The training station will be used for a variety of other applications in addition to this specific training task. The other applications run under DOS or Windows.

Step 2. The solution is built around Microsoft Windows

Step 3. Microsoft windows will allow the addition of this training application without disrupting the current set of applications.

Steps 4 and 5. Continue, since everything is still okay.

Application Software

The application software is specific to the needs of the department store. As a result, it is important to select appropriate tools for developing the application software. Since the required expertise is not available in-house, a developer that has demonstrated expertise in training program development must be found. *The analysis steps need to be applied to the specifications of the requirements and the solution.*

Storage Requirements

Step 1. Although CD-ROMs will be used for the course material, the hard disk at each training station must be able to accommodate interim updates. Such updates will not contain more than 5 minutes of video clips.

Step 2. At least 50 Mbytes of disk space needs to be available at each training station.

Step 3. Additional disk capacity can easily be added where it is required.

Steps 4 and 5. The solution continues to be feasible.

Other Peripherals

No other peripherals are required for the training application.

Transport Mechanism or Network

Step 1. All training stations should be able receive updates electronically.

Step 2. Each training station needs to have a 9600-bit/s modem as interim updates will be transmitted overnight and training statistics will be sent to an administrative server.

Step 3. At 9600 bit/s, it will take about an hour to send a 30-second video clip. Updates containing up to 5 Mbytes need to be sent to 200 stores. This solution is not practical.

Step 4. The proposed solution must be modified. The updates could be sent using an update CD. Each training station could transfer the update to the hard disk. The update material would need to be deleted when a completely new CD is provided. It may be easier to provide fully updated CDs instead of using interim updates.

Steps 4 and 5. The revised solution is practical and satisfies step 3 of the analysis. The solution meets the requirements. Continue.

There are no other considerations so the analysis is complete.

The structured analysis approach allowed us to develop and examine the values of attributes of each element of the sample application. Through successive iterations we were able to approach the ideal solution. As was demonstrated in the analysis, it was necessary to change the characterization of the application to accommodate available technologies or business issues.

7

Effectiveness Measures

COST AND VALUE

In the 1990s, the health and wealth of organizations will be measured by how well they create, manage, distribute and use information. Information is the heart of competitive advantage and must be communicated effectively to work groups. The communication must be in context so that individuals and groups are not buried in a sea of irrelevant information.

Information overload is an undesirable consequence of the Information Age created in the 1970s and 1980s. Organizations realize that information must be presented so it can be understood by individuals and groups. Employees must have easy access to up-to-date, job-related information when they need it, where they need it, and how they need it. The resultant improvement in the communication of information yields improved productivity, reduced costs, and increased revenue.

Scottish scientist James Burke has referred to the start of multimedia computing as a "radical information surge."(Burke 1991) Burke notes that similar surges in the past—for example, the definition of the first alphabet and the development of the printing press—introduced a change of nature that revolutionized the communication of information. He says that "the next surge will tie multimedia computing with high speed global networks" which will change the way that we look at national boundaries and interests (i.e., "the democratization of knowledge").

The profound difference between the way that computers are being used now and in the future, is that multimedia computing will provide the user with the capabilities needed to aid and abet the communications process in all aspects of business. People will have all of the tools needed for personal multimedia applications, for effective communications with others, for access to information services, and for storing and retrieving information from shared databases.

The application of multimedia computing in the work environment will finally lend truth to an old cliché—"our people are our most important asset." Currently, our systems and procedures assess equipment, machinery, and furniture as assets. We find it difficult to place value on improvements in productivity and competency partly because we don't have measures that are based on human assets. The following analysis demonstrates that multimedia applications can be justified based on "hard dollars" and that the "soft dollar" benefits may be even greater.

THE BUSINESS ENVIRONMENT OF THE 1990s

According to Peter W. Trachtenberg, the following factors cause major concern for U.S. businesses (Trachtenberg 1990)

• Financial pressures for short-term results

• Foreign competition compounded by public and governmental indifference to policies that could reinvigorate U.S. business

• The distraction of hostile takeover threats

• Glaring deficiencies in the American educational system.

In addition, far-reaching changes also affect U.S. businesses:

• Customers demand better service and switch to firms that provide it.

• Management instability has increased, as downsizing and other trends cause extensive turnover.

• Continued technological changes provide challenges and opportunities. As a result of the information explosion, one of the challenges is the increasing need of employees to have greater, more rapid access to information so they can make business decisions.

• The demographics of the workforce are changing. Employers need to recruit members of their workforce from groups with which they have little experience. Many of these new workers are even less prepared than current employees to contribute to the success of their companies.

The problem cannot be solved by more aggressive recruiting as the scarcity of trained, demographically familiar potential employees is increasing. Businesses may be "painting themselves into a corner" by failing to develop sufficient numbers of competent employees at a time when they face unprecedented challenges.

Training needs to be well-planned and intimately related to the needs of the business and employee. Training must be delivered using systems that efficiently and effectively deliver the needed knowledge and skills when they are needed. Further, the learning experience should be part of a system that integrates the work, information, and training environments of individuals, groups, and enterprises.

MULTIMEDIA EVOLUTION AND VALUE

The evolutionary stages of multimedia applications are defined in Chapter 2 as enable, enhance and pervade. When multimedia capabilities enable an application, the activity or process becomes cheaper, faster, and/or better. The effectiveness of the application can be measured by increased productivity, reduced cost, and increased sales. For example, CBT can reduce the cost of development, maintenance, and delivery of courses. Normally, however, development costs for CBT are greater than those for lecture/laboratory training. This points to the need for improved authoring tools to reduce the development cost. Organizations such as the Institute for Defense Analysis have documented average cost savings of 64 percent and reduced the amount of time needed to reach equivalent levels of achievement by 36 percent (Fletcher 1990) as shown in Figure 7-1.

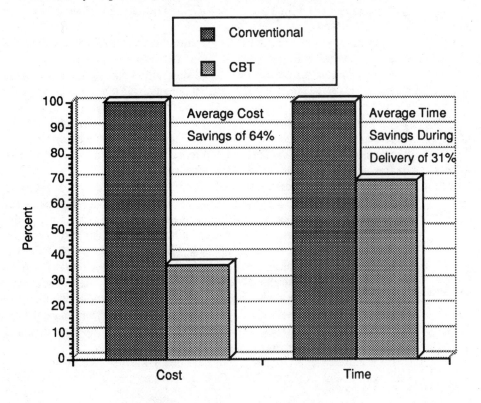

Figure 7-1. Efficiencies using interactive multimedia for training—both time and money are saved. Source: J.D. Fletcher, Institute for Defense Analysis.

The document image processing industry has demonstrated that cost savings and productivity improvements can be realized by capturing paper documents electronically and indexing them with key words so they are easier to file and retrieve. Multimedia applications can take advantage of the lessons learned by making it easier to find and retrieve relevant information.

Most Fortune 1000 companies consider that they must have document imaging technology to maintain their competitive advantage. Significant productivity savings have been documented. BIS CAP International, a market research firm, estimates that the average time to complete document-related transactions is reduced by 50 percent and transaction volume is cut by 50 percent. Reductions in staff of 30 percent can be achieved by replacing a manual, paper-based system with a document image processing systemIn the legal profession, document management savings of 50 percent have been recorded. Such examples prove that significant saving are realized when information is easy to store, retrieve, and process.

Applications that are enabled by multimedia capabilities are justified based on cost/value analysis with a suitable ROI.

As stated above, enhance means that a shift occurs and the nature of the application is changed. This stage represents the greatest potential value to the user or consumer and the greatest opportunity for vendors, developers, and service providers. The dilemma is that it may be difficult or impossible to measure the change. For example, the addition of a voice clip to a text document enhances the document. The voice clip may provide critical information needed by the receiver and reduce the time and expense of another form of communication, but how would the savings be measured?

Enhance means that we move beyond measurable or "hard dollar" savings and improvements to intuitive or "soft dollar" savings. The measurable savings are still valid but they may be exceeded by the value gained through the shift in the business process. The shift results in improvements to the abilities of individuals and work groups.

As is noted by Tom Peters in *Thriving on Chaos*, most organizations do not view their human resources as assets (Peters 1991). They are unable to measure the impact of improvements on organizational performance. Well-trained, highly motivated individuals are not viewed as assets by the generally accepted rules of accounting. Measurement necessitates a paradigm shift in which workers are viewed and managed as assets. The human capital concept is based on a new vision of the role of people in organizations and the goal of human resources management.

In the enhance phase, organizations must determine the investments needed to optimize the asset value of workers. Money must be allocated among investment options to obtain the best ROI.

In 1990, Aetna Life and Casualty Company completed a program to improve worker morale and performance. The goal was not unusual but the approach was unorthodox. Aetna invested in its workers by creating a better workplace environment. The payoff was a 67 percent improvement in productivity and a 14 percent decline in absenteeism. Spending money on people makes good business sense if it is invested wisely (Weddle 1990).

Pervade means that multimedia capability will be available on every personal computer or workstation and that it is taken for granted. Multimedia capabilities will be fully integrated into personal workstations and included in standard applications. Justification will not be required because multimedia will be essential to the conduct of business.

None of the current multimedia applications fall into the pervade category. Most are in the enable category where it is possible to validate that multimedia made the applications cheaper, faster, and/or better. Effectiveness measures for enhance can be addressed partially by extension to the enable category. However, measurement of the full value requires that the organization embrace the human capital concept.

Multimedia empowers interactive communication of all information types. Networking is going to be a significant factor because multimedia is a revolutionary way to communicate more effectively. In addition, the act of consuming, manipulating, and producing information is a group activity and it must be done within the standard work environment of the group.

Stand alone applications will migrate initially to closed networks using high speed local and wide area network technologies. In the long term, applications will move to open networks based on BISDN. Distance and bandwidth will cease to be constraining factors in the deployment of multimedia applications. Thus the business case for multimedia applications must include the cost and value of networking.

We will consider two applications—CBT and documentation—that are in the enable phase to demonstrate the cost and value of multimedia. Then we will explore the implications of the paradigm shift that occurs when we implement an EPSS. By definition, an EPSS is a computer-based system that delivers task-specific information, tools, and training when, where, and how they are needed by individuals. Note that an EPSS is a business operations-centric application. Finally, we will conclude the chapter with a look at the holistic approach to organizational planning and development espoused by The National Society for Performance and Instruction (Coscarelli, Geiss, Harless, Shrock, and Smith 1986).

THE BOTTOM LINE FOR MULTIMEDIA

Business organizations use ROI analysis to compare the dollars invested in a project to the dollars returned. In the final analysis, the evaluation must deal with the impact of multimedia solutions on the operation of the business. Business is impacted in three ways: cost reduction, productivity increase, and revenue gain. In order to develop an ROI model, we need to able to measure some of the areas where a change is made because of the successful implementation of a multimedia solution.

Multilevel evaluation and ROI models must be available for use with a variety of multimedia solutions in a variety of industries. Over the past decade, models and techniques have been developed for the application of multimedia capabilities in the training environment. The models are simple and easy to understand as it is important to verify that they are valid for the particular analysis. The models can be extended to include documentation, EPSS, and other multimedia applications.

ROI models can be used for cost/benefit analysis to support decision-making activities (e.g., spending money on training programs or on some other activities) or for cost-effectiveness analysis which compares different ways to carry out a single objective (e.g., continuing the current training program versus implementing a CBT program). When the program has been implemented, the ROI model can be used to evaluate the effectiveness of the implementation.

ROI models are based on bottom line issues. A 10 percent improvement in productivity for an employee who makes $75,000 per year cannot be shown as a $7500 gain on the company's balance sheet. However, if the 10 percent improvement means that fewer employees need to be hired to satisfy company goals, then the salaries and the cost of hiring and training the individuals that would have been hired, can flow to the bottom line. When training is decentralized or moved to the desktop, the reduction in travel expenses provides a direct contribution to the bottom line.

Many of the benefits of multimedia capabilities can be quantified, but some are more direct—and therefore more creditable—than others. The reduction in travel expenses that results when a distributed CBT program replaces training at a central site is easy to see. Similarly a reduction in mailing costs following a move from a paper-based to electronic-based documentation system can be measured. However, a 10 percent increase in sales revenue may be difficult to attribute to the training program because so many other factors may be involved.

The following areas must be examined with a critical eye to ensure that the application of multimedia capabilities will improve the bottom line of the organization.

The potential value of multimedia solutions and suggestions for tracking and measuring productivity improvements, cost reductions, and increased revenue are shown below. Specific examples with research results are shown for CBT, documentation, and EPSS in the sections that follow.

Increased Productivity

Improved training methods, hypermedia documentation, on-line access to information, EPSS, and other multimedia solutions can contribute to improvements in productivity as follows:

• Average time to reach equivalent levels of achievement can be reduced through CBT, interactive video training, and EPSS.

• Lost opportunity costs are reduced since employees spend less time away from the job.

• Less time is used to acquire the information needed to make decisions.

• More students achieve mastery of learning materials.

• New products, concepts, processes, procedures, etc. can be introduced and integrated into operations more rapidly.

• Customer queries can be responded to more quickly and accurately . The use of an EPSS allowed employees of a leading manufacturer of telecommunications equipment to reduce the time and effort to respond to customer inquiries by 50 percent.

• Document management and transaction time can be reduced by 30 to 50 percent according to studies by the Association for Information and Image Management (AIIM).

Reduced Cost

Cost reductions tend to be easy to measure and flow through to the bottom line because accounting practices and measures allow us to demonstrate savings as follows:

• The cost of development, maintenance, and delivery of interactive multimedia can be less than conventional training courses.

• Cost reductions in creation, maintenance, production, and physical distribution of paper-based reference materials and manuals.

• Reduced costs because of fewer delays and lower negative consequences because of delays.

• Reductions in the amount of overtime at peak periods because of improved operations.

• Decreased direct expenditures for training and learning, such as reduced student and instructor per diem cost, decreased learning time, ability to handle more students at a reduced rate per student, and improved facilities utilization.

• Reduced customer support costs using on-line support, desktop conferencing, and collaborative computing.

• Space reduction for electronic versus manual storage.

• Reduced travel costs through CBT, EPSS, and desktop videoconferencing with collaborative computing.

Increased Revenue

Although it is often difficult to measure improvements in this area that can be shown to directly impact the bottom line, it is clear that the revenue contribution of sales and sales support personnel will improve. Many managers disregard the benefits because they believe they would have received the order anyway. A paradigm shift may be needed before measures based on the items below can be included in ROI analysis. However, all successful sales organizations operate on the principle that sales revenues increase when more time is spent making sales calls.

• Increased sales since more productive time is spent in front of the customer.

- More effective portrayal of the company products and services in the context of the prospect's business.

- More employees operating at the level of the top performers (the performance gap between top and middle level performers can be reduced using EPSS).

- Improved service, credibility with customers, and responsiveness leads to fewer canceled orders, more referrals, and better customer loyalty.

- Distribution channels are more effective sooner because of more rapid and effective product introductions.

Investment Expense

It is important to consider both recurring and nonrecurring costs. Recurring costs include hardware maintenance, application software support, and revisions. In many cases, companies contract for development of specific solutions with multimedia developers.

Nonrecurring costs include the purchase of sender and receiver platforms, servers, networking products, and software development or authoring tools.

Costs are also categorized as either operating expenses or capital expenses Operating expenses vary year by year and are reported for accounting and tax purposes in the year they occur. Capital expenses are fixed, nonrecurring costs that can be depreciated over time. Usually both the hardware and software development expenses are depreciated.

COMPUTER-BASED TRAINING

At IBM, it costs around $350 for a 1-day workshop at a central facility (including travel expenses), $150 for an on-site workshop, and $75 for self-paced training, such as CBT (Ives and Foreman, 1991). It is estimated that 20 percent of business training in the United States is delivered using self-paced methods.

CBT lowers the overall cost of delivering training and learning modules, but requires investments in personal computers and workstations. As a result, initial startup costs are higher than conventional means and CBT programs must be cost justified.

Over the past 6 years, a number of organizations have studied the benefits that can be realized using interactive training solutions as an alternative to traditional training methods. Figure 7-2 provides a summary of key data from six organizations—Federal Express, IBM, United Technologies, U.S. Army, Wicat Systems, and Xerox (Adams 1992). In each case, a given course was developed in both CBT and classroom formats so that comparisons were relevant.

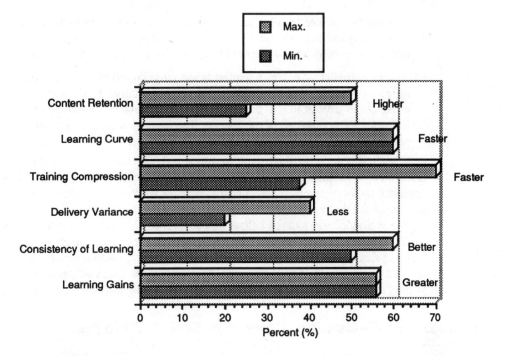

Figure 7-2. When compared with traditional training, interactive training delivered better results on six different measures. Source: MULTIMEDIA & VIDEODISC MONITOR.

The results of the studies are as follows

- **Learning gains.** The interactive versions of the courseware increased the understanding and retention of the content up to 56 percent compared to the classroom versions.

- **Consistency of learning.** The consistency of the understanding of content by individuals was determined to be 50 to 60 percent greater for interactive courseware.

- **Delivery variance.** The consistency of the delivery of the content from individual to individual and from class to class was measured for both the CBT version and the instructor. Even though some CBT allows students to take different paths through the course material, the studies determined that there was 20 to 40 percent less variance for the interactive training courseware.

- **Training compression.** Students were able to complete the interactive version of the course in much less time than the classroom version. On average, training time was compressed by 38 to 70 percent.

- **Learning curve.** The learning curve is similar to training compression as it measures how quickly students were able to master the content of the courses. The curve for interactive learners was 60 percent faster than that of the classroom courses.

- **Content retention.** Content retention is the most important measure since it is a reflection of the level of competency that will be sustained by the student. Retention provides the greatest ROI to the organization. Retention was tested 30 days or less following the completion of the courses. The results indicated that it was 25 to 50 percent higher for the interactive courses.

With training, it is important to place ROI in the larger context of training effectiveness to ensure that the numbers will be meaningful. Although a particular approach might appear to generate cost savings, it will be meaningless if the students do not learn from the experience.

The methodology outlined below was developed by Applied Learning-Spectrum of Bedford, Massachusetts and has been used to evaluate the use of multimedia capabilities in learning situations. It is a structured evaluation model that works with all delivery media and is especially useful for evaluating CBT projects. The ROI calculation is the final step in the process. The methodology is reprinted with permission of CBT Directions, 1991.

Methods for Evaluating Computer-Based Training

Table 7-1. Methods for Evaluating Multimedia Training. Source: CBT Directions

Level	Method	Evaluates
1. Use	Observation sign-up sheets	Process
2 Course reactions	Questionnaire	Process
3. Relevance/attitudes	Attitude survey	Outcome
4. Knowledge: facts	Criterion tests (multiple choice)	Outcome
5. Knowledge: intellectual skills	Criterion test (simulations)	Outcome
6. Performance	Observation	Outcome
7. Transfer to job	All of the above - attitudes, knowledge, intellectual skills, performance	Impact
8. Business results	Systems that track time, cost savings, productivity increase, revenue increase	Impact, money and quantity

An overall evaluation of CBT is important because it can explain why predicted improvements and hence, the ROI did not materialize. CBT could fail because learning objectives were unsound, or key points were not retained and used on the job, or the training simply was not used. The evaluation of training effectiveness in Table 7-1 provides a framework for understanding ROI (Ives and Foreman. 1991).

1. Use. With self-paced programs, it is essential to determine that the course material is actually used by the target population for the intended purpose. A system must be established to track overall usage and to compile individual results.

It is equally important to review learning practices. If students go through the course and do not take advantage of the on-the-job exercises, the course may not be effective.

2. Course reactions. The infamous "smile sheet" is used by many corporations to obtain course reactions. In many instances, the "smile sheets" have not been developed systematically to include open-ended and forced-response and a set of core questions that are used for all courses.

3. Relevance/attitude. Many evaluations overlook the affective domain. Although the relevance of course content and the attitude of the students may be difficult to measure, they are necessary for success. In most environments, people fail to perform for three reasons

• They don't know how to perform a task

• They don't want to do a particular task

• The policies, procedures, and reward system doesn't allow them to perform.

In many instances, the second reason is the most important. If people don't see a reason to change their behavior, they won't change it. Both the intended and unintended affective outcomes of CBT courses must be evaluated.

4. Knowledge/facts. Factual knowledge is easy to test with CBT and the results can be accumulated automatically. The test questions must be tied to specific training objectives to determine what each student has mastered.

8. Business results. The final evaluation level deals with the impact of CBT on the operation of the business. As noted above, business is impacted in three ways: cost reduction, productivity increase, and revenue gain. In order to proceed with the ROI model, we need to able to measure some of the areas where a change is made because of the successful implementation of CBT.

MULTILEVEL ROI MODEL

The multilevel evaluation and ROI models discussed below were developed for use in variety of industries for the application of multimedia capabilities in the training environment.

As noted above, ROI models must address contributions to the bottom line. The model shown in Table 7-1 can be used to identify the benefits to be gained through an improved training program.

Determining Benefits

All of the possible benefits of the CBT program should be listed under the appropriate headings—cost reduction, increased productivity, and revenue gain—and quantified where possible. All of the quantifiable benefits should be ranked according to contribution to the overall objectives and the ease with which they can be attributed to the training program.

At this point, the ROI analysis can be made using the top-ranked benefits to determine if the return will justify the proposed training program. The initial ROI model is used to demonstrate return based on top-ranked benefits. If a larger ROI is needed, other benefits can be added if necessary. It is best to justify the program by showing a return that is appropriate to the nature of the business of the company. Decision makers look for a break-even point of 2 to 3 years for cash flow and a positive profit-and-loss in the first or second year.

A return of 50 percent is desirable and anything over 500 percent is questionable unless all of the evidence is extremely solid.

Note that even though all of the benefits are not included in the model, it is important to track all of the benefits that can be quantified as the CBT program is implemented. This provides a complete picture of the actual return on investment as the program is implemented.

Determining Costs

All of the costs associated with the development of the CBT program must be considered. It is important to distinguish between recurring costs, which occur every time the program is offered, and nonrecurring costs, which are one-time costs, such as hardware purchases.

CBT programs generally have higher nonrecurring costs and lower recurring costs than the lecture-laboratory approaches they displace. The break-even point is in favor of lecture-laboratory for fewer students and in favor of CBT for larger numbers of students. Generally, the break-even point is between 200 to 300 students per year for current cost structures. The break-even point moves downward as the cost of multimedia-capable personal computers and course development expenses decreases.

In the ROI model, operating expenses are variable, recurring costs that are reported for accounting and tax purposes in the year they occur. Capital expenses are depreciated over time. Both hardware and course development costs can be depreciated which has a major impact on the ROI of CBT.

Constructing the Financial Model

Once the benefits and costs have been determined, the financial model can be developed to show the potential return on investment for the CBT program. The following is based on the analysis by a financial services company that was considering the use of CBT to replace the current workshop method of training service representatives.

Although there were many potential benefits, only two were needed to support the implementation of the CBT program. The benefits selected were consistent with the company's objectives for extensive growth while limiting expenses and the number of new hires. First, it was determined that CBT could save training time as has been supported by numerous studies. The new program was designed to take 30 percent less time for new hires and 50 percent less time for existing employees than the current instructor led programs. This meant that employees would spend more time on the job so that fewer new hires were needed to meet company goals.

Second, the training program provided automated practice on customer service skills, so that supervisors spent less time observing and critiquing employees. As a result, the number of employees per supervisor could be increased from increased from 10:1 to 12:1. Thus the company could grow with fewer supervisors.

The financial benefits were derived from reductions in salaries, benefits, and support for employees and supervisors because fewer new hires were needed and from the amount spent on the workshop training method. Program costs were based on capital expenses for CBT courseware and hardware including installation and maintenance, other implementation expenses, and the cost annual course updates.

It was entirely possible to quantify other benefits, but they would have been more difficult to attribute directly to the change to CBT and they were not needed to justify the program.

Table 7-2 shows the projected 6-year cash flow for the program. All figures are in thousands of dollars. The total benefits or cash inflow for the first year are $411,000 against an expense or cash outflow of $1,113,000. Much of the expense can be depreciated so that the profit-and-loss and the ROI are positive as shown in the following ROI chart. Negative numbers are shown in parentheses.

Table 7-2. Detailed Cash Inflow Showing the Source of Each Cash Inflow or Benefit [a]
Source: CBT Directions

	Year						Total
	1	2	3	4	5	6	
Cash inflow							
Reduced training time							
Headcount reduction	539	547	756	865	973	1,082	4,862
Training cost reduction	30	35	40	45	51	56	256
Better employee/supervisor ratio	1076	1347	1618	1889	2161	2432	10,522
Utilization factor (%)	25	50	100	100	100	100	
Projected cash inflow	411	1015	2414	2799	3185	3570	13,393
Cash outflow							
Hardware	200	300	0	0	0	0	500
Basic courseware	863	1147	0	0	0	0	2,010
Recurrent courseware	0	0	350	350	350	0	1,050
Maintenance	0	50	50	50	50	50	250
Updates	0	0	149	149	149	149	596
Implementation	50	100	50	0	0	0	200
Cash outflow	1113	1598	599	549	549	198	4,606
Net cash flow	(702)	(583)	1815	2250	2636	3372	8,787
Cumulative cash flow	(702)	(1286)	530	2780	5416	8787	

[a] Figures in thousands of dollars.

To account for the time it would take to develop and implement the program, the benefits were calculated based on utilization rates of 25 percent and 50 percent in the first and second years. In the third year, the program would be in full use so that 100 percent of the benefits could be realized.

The total savings of $539,000 shown for the first year in Table 7-3 were calculated as follows. The person-weeks saved are 30 percent of 2043 or 613 for training 916 new hires and 50 percent of 1404 or 702 for recurring training of existing employees. By dividing by the number of weeks an employee works per year, the head count reduction is 613/48 or 13 and 702/48 or 14 because CBT takes less time for new hires and existing employees, respectively. The total saved for salaries in the first year of the program is $539,000.

The reduction in supervisor costs for the first year is calculated by multiplying the current supervisory count (156) by the reduction in supervisor/employee ratio (16.7 percent) and by multiplying this figure (26) by the annual cost including support for a supervisor ($41,368) will results in a savings of $1,076,000.

Table 7-3. The Impact of Reducing the Number of New Hires per Year [a] Source: CBT Directions

	Year						
	1	2	3	4	5	6	Total
New hire training							
New hires per year	916	1048	1180	1311	1443	1575	
Total training weeks	2043	2337	2631	2935	3219	3513	
Reduced weeks (minus 30%)	613	701	789	878	966	1054	
Headcount reduction	13	15	16	18	20	22	
Recurring training							
Employee base	1560	1953	2347	2740	3134	3527	
Total training weeks	1404	1758	2112	2466	2820	3174	
Reduced weeks (minus 50%)	702	879	1056	1233	1410	1587	
Headcount reduction	14	18	22	26	30	33	
Total headcount reduction	27	33	38	44	50	55	
Average employee cost ($20,000)							
Total savings	539	647	756	865	973	1082	4,862
Improved employee/ supervisor ratio							
Current supervisors	156	195	235	274	313	353	
Reduction (minus 16.7%)	26	33	39	46	52	59	
Costs per supervisor ($41,368)							
Total savings	1076	1347	1618	1889	2161	2432	10,522

[a] Figures in thousands of dollars.

Much of the cost of implementing CBT can be considered capital expenses and spread out over a period of years—5 years in this case study. The effect of depreciating hardware and software costs is shown in Table 7-4. The costs to be depreciated over the 5-year period are shown in parentheses. The effect of depreciating the capital expenses over 5 years reduces the overall costs on the balance sheet from $1,113,000 to $263,000.

Table 7-4. Effect of Depreciation Spreads the Up-front Capital Costs over 5 Years [a]
Source: CBT Directions

Capital expenses depreciated (Hardware, courseware)							
Year 1	(1063)	213	213	213	213	213	0
Year 2	(1447)		289	289	289	289	289
Year 3	(350)			70	70	70	70
Year 4	(350)				70	70	70
Year 5	(350)					70	70
Year 6							0
Other Expenses (Not depreciated) (Maintenance, updates, implementation)		50	150	249	199	199	199
Total Cost (Depreciated)		263	652	821	841	911	698

[a] Figures in thousands of dollars.

The ROI shown in Table 7-5 is calculated as follows. The annual profit-and-loss impact of $148,000 is determined by subtracting the depreciated cost of $263,000 from the benefits or cash inflow of $411,000. The ROI of 57 percent for the first year is determined by dividing the first year profit-and-loss impact of $148,000 by the total cost for the first year of $263,000.

Table 7-5. The Cumulative Rate of Return over 6 Years, Which is Pre-tax, Is Impressive Even When Based on Conservative Assumptions [a] Source: CBT Directions

	Year						
	1	2	3	4	5	6	Total
Return on investment							
Projected cash inflow	411	1015	2414	2799	3185	3570	13,393
Projected cost (depreciated)	263	652	821	841	911	698	4,186
Annual P&L impact	148	362	1594	1959	2274	2872	9,208
Cumulative P&L impact	148	510	2104	4063	6337	9208	
Cumulative ROI (%) (P&L Cost)	57	56	121	157	181	220	

[a] Figures in thousands of dollars.

This case study is based on a real program and the numbers have been changed to preserve confidentiality. The ROI for the first year is 57 percent and the cumulative return on investment over the 6-year period is 220 percent.

These impressive results are all pretax and are extremely conservative. The study assumed no salary growth and no reduction in equipment costs over time and did not consider the time value of money (or what would happen if the savings were invested). In addition, only two of the quantifiable benefits were used to justify the CBT program.

All of the assumptions used in the model were developed through discussions with appropriate decision makers. Company field sources were used to document all of the assumptions and agreement was reached at each stage. Conservative assumptions were made to ensure that the figures were creditable.

The multilevel evaluation and ROI models have been used in a number of different industries, for profit and nonprofit organizations, and with and without cost depreciation. The models work as a pair: the evaluation model enables you to see what happens; and the ROI model enables you to project the financial impact of the new program.

DOCUMENTATION

Information is corporate America's "gold" but managing information quickly and easily is a intimidating task. Information overload and the subsequent degradation of the quality of information content is a problem that is plaguing all industrial nations. The drive for success in the global marketplace creates a critical need for products that offer improved ways for finding, acquiring, presenting, and using information.

Multimedia capabilities have allowed a number of organizations to move away from paper-based to hypertext or hypermedia documentation. Such moves reduce physical storage requirements and improve productivity. Document imaging improves productivity by reducing the time spent filing, indexing, and retrieving documents.

In addition to the improvements made possible by document imaging, hypermedia provides multiple connected pathways through information, which may be text, images, graphics, animation, audio, and video. Thus a maintenance manual could include video clips of a difficult procedure which can be replayed until the technician is completely familiar.

The sheer bulk of the documentation needed for complex systems poses enormous problems for distributing, storing, finding, and using information. An Air Force study noted that 80 percent of a maintenance technician's tasks are performed only once or twice a year. Often it takes longer to find the information about the procedure than it takes to carry it out. When information is so difficult to find, technicians may not follow procedures and simply swap components until the unit is repaired.

The documentation problem exists for all employees. Enormous amounts of time are spent looking for the information needed to make decisions and complete tasks. In 1989, U.S. companies produced 1 trillion, 267 billion pages of paper. On average, 20 percent or 253.4 billion pages were misfiled, lost, stolen, discarded, or accidentally destroyed.

Although the paperless office may not be achievable, it is clear that hypermedia offers a viable alternative for many applications.

The CD-ROM Users Group notes that it costs anywhere from $10 to $20 per copy to produce a book with a four-color cover in quantities of 1000. A CD-ROM can be duplicated for as little as little as $3.50 each for 1000 copies. The cost structure is such that most organizations can take advantage of the potential savings.

Some 15,000 auditors at Price-Waterhouse access information on a CD-ROM rather than the 40-volume set of printed material used previously. Often client requests required the auditor to extract information from all 40 volumes. With CD-ROM, the relevant information is accessed using keywords. Lower distribution costs and improved productivity have saved the firm millions of dollars. In addition, the threat of litigation has been reduced because the search technique results in fewer errors. The conversion to CD-ROM was cost-justified in 1 year.

Although the examples and the following analysis are based on the use of CD-ROM, all of the issues apply to other forms of storage such as hard disk and optical storage devices. The extensive use of CD-ROM is a reflection of both the applicability of CD-ROM technology for particular solutions and the current evolutionary stage of multimedia computing.

Both Sun Microsystems and Silicon Graphics, Inc. are loaning CD-ROM players to major customers because it is so much cheaper to publish documentation and to distribute software on CD-ROM.

Maintenance and Repair Manual

The following example is based on the experiences of a leading personal computer supplier. The actual numbers have been modified to preserve confidentiality. Twenty technical service procedure manuals contained troubleshooting and repair information and maintenance programs. The service organization with support from the finance department determined that the cost of preparing, printing, handling, storing, and shipping updates to the manuals was excessive.

Updates were prepared and shipped once per month to 6000 technicians. Each update consisted of 250 pages on average which meant that the technician was forced to remove outdated pages and insert new ones in the affected volumes.

While it was relatively easy to select CD-ROMs as the distribution medium, the selection of the user interface was a task that was the subject of much investigation and trial. Several prototypes with different types of navigational capability were trialed. The company chose a highly interactive software tool with a user friendly interface that provided rapid access to the volumes of technical information on the CD-ROM disk. The new service document is intended for service technicians and contains more than 75 Mbytes of repair, pricing, and program information that was previously available in binders and booklets.

Existing text, graphics, and image information was converted to hypermedia and animation and video clips were added to better explain difficult procedures.

The personal computers used by the technicians had to be upgraded with more memory and a CD-ROM drive for a total cost of $500 per technician. Since the user interface resembled the paper-based technical procedures, the new service document was immediately familiar to the technician. No additional training was required. The number of updates per year remained unchanged. However, as we will see, the cost of preparing and shipping the updates changed dramatically.

ROI Analysis

The impact of the CD-ROM maintenance manuals on the business was determined by listing all of the possible benefits of making the change.

Decreased Expenses

• Reduced cost of materials, production, storage, and shipping and handling

• Reduced maintenance manual update costs (technicians need not spend time removing and inserting 200 to 300 pages per update)

• Technicians no longer resort to component swapping as a repair procedure because it is easy to find the right procedure in the manuals

• Fewer "no fault found" components are returned to the factory for repair

• Less time is needed for training since animation and video clips can provide, in effect, "just-in-time training"

Improved Productivity

• Appropriate procedures can be found more quickly using key word searches

• Complex procedures are easier to understand and implement so repair is effected more quickly

• Speed of service will be increased so employees can handle a higher volume. Backlogs will be reduced

Cash Inflow

The cost of materials and production is currently $105,000 per update. This was reduced to $10,250 per update for the CD-ROM version. Shipping costs per update were reduced from $50,000 to $6475 per update. The net savings per update were $138,275. On an annual basis, the savings amount to $1,659,300.

Cash Outflow

The computers used by the technicians had to be upgraded with more memory and a CD-ROM drive for a total of $500 per computer. The total expenditure for 6000 technicians is $3,000,000.

The cost of converting the material from paper to digital form and of rewriting the manuals to take full advantage of the multimedia environment was $1,500,000.

The hardware and conversion costs were depreciated over a 5 year period.

The ongoing costs for maintenance and enhancements is $150,000 per year.

Return on Investment

Return on investment shown in Table 7-6 was calculated using the same procedures outlined above for CBT.

Table 7-6. Even Though the Capital Investment is High, the ROI is Positive in the First Year and the Cumulative ROI is Excellent over the 6-Year Period [a]

Return on Investment	Years						
	1	2	3	4	5	6	Total
Projected cash inflow	830	1,659	1659	1659	1659	1659	9125
Projected cost (Depreciated)	600	950	1050	1050	1050	450	5150
Annual P&L impact	230	709	609	609	609	1209	3975
Cumulative P&L impact	230	939	1548	2157	2766	3975	
Cumulative ROI (%)	38	61	60	59	59	77	

[a] Figures in thousands of dollars.

The ROI for the first year is 38 percent and the cumulative return on investment over the 6-year period is 77 percent, which is impressive since the figures are pretax. In addition, the figures are conservative since the hardware upgrades, which is the major cost item, were included at retail rather than internal transfer cost. No attempt was made to factor in other savings or productivity improvements that will result through the use of the new maintenance and repair manual.

It is conceivable that the amount of training required by the technicians may decrease because the hypermedia manual can deliver the equivalent of "just-in-time" training for some of the repair and maintenance procedures. It is clear that the groups responsible for training and documentation have an opportunity to develop courses and manuals that are mutually supportive to reduced costs and improve productivity further.

If the technicians were employees of third-party organizations, the personal computer company would not be obliged to pay for the cost of the hardware upgrades and the ROI would be so obvious that a detailed analysis would not be required.

ELECTRONIC PERFORMANCE SUPPORT SYSTEMS

There is a phenomenon that accompanies applications in the enable category. Such applications represent the use of multimedia capabilities to make an existing process cheaper, faster, and/or better and do not represent a shift or change in the nature of the applications.

For example, CBT satisfies the need to make training cheaper, faster, and/or better but it does not fully address the need to improve the overall competency of an organization. As a stand alone event, training is often too soon or too late (Ziegler 1990). It deals only with a subset of the job and may contain large amounts of irrelevant material.

Similarly, hypermedia solves problems of information search, retrieval, and presentation and reduces documentation costs but doesn't ensure improved competency. A coordinated effort on the part of the groups responsible for training and documentation can extend both cost reduction and performance improvements. However, even when they are combined, training and documentation only deal with a subset of the employee's job.

EPSS are directed specifically at making individuals and groups more competent as shown in Figure 7-3. Training modules are one element of the system and hypermedia databases are another. Proponents note that EPSS requires a shift in perspective on the overall problems of achieving competency. It changes the roles and responsibilities of the training, systems development, and documentation groups. An EPSS is an example of a business operations-centric application since we are using the capabilities of a multimedia computer in support of the operation of the business.

Traditional straightforward training, no matter how effective, only brings workers to a basic level of proficiency. It does not prepare them to handle the variety of real-world situations they will meet on the job. The EPSS integrates all of an employees tasks and it can be integrated with the larger systems of the organization.

The value of the EPSS derives from the premise that each employee is extraordinary, with unique work experience and ways of learning and constant changes in work requirements and information needs. With an EPSS the focus is on individuals and groups. The elements of an EPSS provide access to information and training modules in the context of an individual's job (Gery 1990).

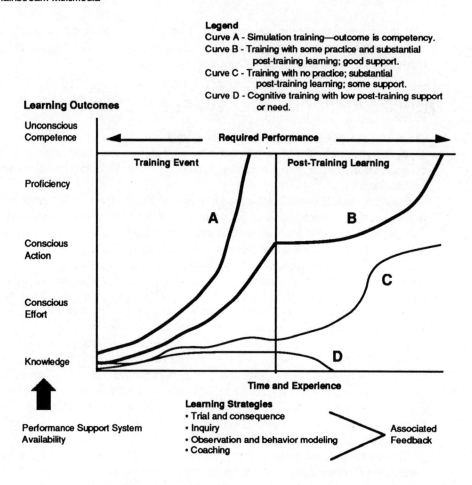

Legend
Curve A - Simulation training—outcome is competency.
Curve B - Training with some practice and substantial
          post-training learning; good support.
Curve C - Training with no practice; substantial
          post-training learning; some support.
Curve D - Cognitive training with low post-training support
          or need.

Learning Outcomes

Unconscious
Competence

Proficiency

Conscious
Action

Conscious
Effort

Knowledge

Required Performance

Training Event   **Post-Training Learning**

A   B

C

D

Time and Experience

Performance Support System
Availability

Learning Strategies
• Trial and consequence
• Inquiry
• Observation and behavior modeling
• Coaching

Associated
Feedback

Figure 7-3. Skill proficiency model shows the outcome of different training approaches and the relative time and experience needed to achieved the required level of performance. Source: Gloria J. Gery.

By definition, an EPSS is a computer-based system that delivers *task-specific or job-specific* information, tools and training when, where, and how they are needed by an individual (Raybould 1990. Building an Electronic Performance Support System). An EPSS such as the one shown in Figure 7-4 allows the user to navigate, retrieve, and display information contained in

• Help systems

• Expert systems

• Interactive learning modules

• Multimedia databases

On-line job aids or help systems provide answers to questions as and when needed. On-line access to multimedia databases provides all of the documentation and back-up information needed by the individual in the context of the tasks he or she is performing. Expert systems provide help and decision-support by retrieving information and diagnosing problems based on input from the employee. Training occurs as and when needed by the employee, instead of in environments away from the immediacy of the job itself.

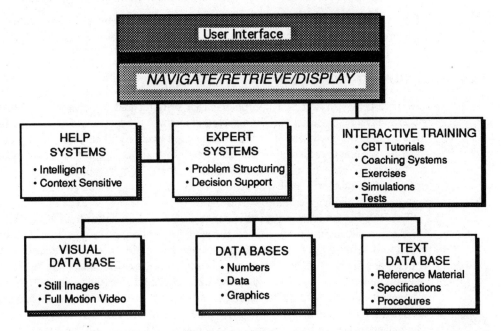

Figure 7-4. A single human machine interface provides access to all of the elements of an EPSS.

Electronic performance support systems offer improved performance through increased competence and problem solving capabilities, decreased errors and omissions, reductions in the amount of supervision and peer support, and improved communications with and response to customers.

The evaluation and ROI models outlined for CBT and for documentation are both relevant in modified form for EPSS solutions. For example, learning modules are available to the employee as and when they are needed. There is no need to leave the work environment to take a course. Instead a learning module is used when it is needed in the context of the employee's tasks. Similarly, documentation is available on-line and can be referenced, sent to another employee, or printed for distribution when needed by a customer.

EPSS provides benefits that are <u>not</u> available in other systems as follows (Raybould 1990. A New Approach to Using Computers to Improve Productivity in the Workplace):

• Expert assistance is available 24 hours per day, 7 days per week, and 52 weeks per year

• On-the-job support and training develop competency sooner and help maintain it

• Support costs are lower since much of the required support is available on-line

• Quality and consistency of decision-making by less experienced employees is improved. This closes the performance gap between less capable and most capable employees

• Company knowledge and expertise is captured and retained by an EPSS even though employees leave the company

ROI Analysis for an EPSS

We have demonstrated that computer-based training and hypermedia documentation systems have the potential to reduce costs and increase productivity. In addition, document imaging systems have been shown to reduce costs by 30 to 50 percent because they make it easier for employees to find and process information. It follows that a system that combines the benefits of computer-based training, hypermedia documentation, and document imaging systems will reduce costs, increase productivity, and improve the competency individuals and the organization.

The ROI for the learning modules of an EPSS will be better than are achieved with CBT since the learning experience happens in the context of the job. The time and expense of being away from the job can be reduced significantly, particularly if the CBT courses are given at a central facility. Retention and performance will be better since relevant material can be reviewed as and when needed. Increased sales and other benefits also result but are difficult to estimate since our measurement systems are geared to accounting principles that count furniture and equipment as assets rather than employees. The business case for business operations-centric applications will be based on the return on investment for providing the information and support when, where, and how it is needed in day-to-day activities.

EPSS for a Sales Organization

The financial analysis that follows is based on an analysis prepared by MAST[1] for a data networking company and incorporates computer-based training and hypermedia documentation elements. The networking company is proceeding with an EPSS system based in part on the analysis.

---

[1] MAST is a San Jose, California–based market research and consulting firm founded by Roger Fetterman in 1989.

The numbers have been modified to preserve the confidentiality of the company but are indicative of the tradeoffs that need to be examined when considering training, hypermedia documentation, and EPSS alternatives.

The company was experiencing a period of rapid growth in a market that had become more dynamic and competitive. Traditional training courses were missing the mark with both sales and support people as they seemed to be either too technical for sales or too general for sales support. Training costs were rising rapidly and the company wanted to find a training method that would change the relationship between training cost and the numbers of individuals trained.

The cost of delivering product documentation and presentation materials to a growing sales force appeared to be increasing at an alarming rate and it was always difficult to determine if field sales personnel were using the most up-to-date materials.

The following objectives were to be satisfied by the recommended EPSS solution:

• Reduce training and document distribution costs and change the linear relationship between training costs and number of students

• Increase overall competency of sales, marketing, and support personnel and improve employee performance

• Provide access to relevant information (reduce information overload)

• Accommodate target audiences with different levels of knowledge, experience, and areas of interest

• Ensure that users have access to the most up-to-date information

• Make it easy for employees to find answers to specific task-related questions

• Provide access to information when it is needed

The initial EPSS implementation was to include training modules and an information base of marketing documentation. Other items such as information about industries, competition, and applications and advisory and help systems were to follow.

Cost Analysis

The analysis that follows is based on a training cost model developed by Instructional Communications, Inc. (ICOM) of Denver, Colorado. The model was designed to identify the costs of existing training programs, to project the costs of new programs, and to contrast the costs of the two methods of delivering training courses (Head 1985).

In this case, the model was used to contrast the costs of current lecture/laboratory with both CBT and EPSS for selected courses. It was not assumed that all courses would move to CBT or EPSS in the short term.

The first step was to determine the basic cost factors shown in Table 7-7 which were used throughout the analysis.

Table 7-7. The Basic Cost Factors Are Used Throughout the Financial Analysis So It Is Important to Gather All of the Information Needed. Source: Glenn E. Head

---

Basic Cost Factors

Expected course life

Course length

Number of students in each class

Number of times the course is held

Geographic location of the course

Average annual salaries

Fringe benefits percentage

Annual productive days

Average travel and per diem expenses

Number of instructors per class

Lost opportunity costs

Production and materials cost

Development and evaluation time

The analysis was based on moving from 15 days of lecture/laboratory training to 8 days of lecture/laboratory training plus 5 hours of CBT and 4 hours of EPSS. Four days of lecture/laboratory were to be converted to 5 hours of CBT and an additional 3 days to 4 hours of EPSS learning modules.

The CBT courses were to be taken at the employee's work place as prerequisites to lecture/laboratory courses. The EPSS learning modules were to be used on an "as required" basis.

When CBT is used to develop a common comprehension level as a prerequisite to lecture/laboratory training, 1 hour of CBT can replace 6 to 8 hours of lecture/laboratory training. Similar ratios were applied to EPSS learning modules.

Each of the cost factors listed in Table 7-8 was established using the basic costs assuming that 300 students would be trained each year.

Table 7-8. All of the Cost Factors Associated with the Development and Delivery of the Learning Modules is Important to the Analysis. Source: Glenn E. Head

Item	Factors
• Student costs	Salaries + fringe benefits + productive days + per diem + travel + lost opportunity
• Instructor costs	Salaries + fringe benefits + productive days + per diem + travel + lost opportunity
• Instructional development costs	Personnel + production + materials + evaluation
• Facilities costs	Annual facilities costs multiplied by course allocation
• Maintenance costs	Administrative + consumable materials + revision factor

Table 7-9. Student Costs are the Most Significant Costs in a Comparative Analysis

Cost Element	Lecture/Lab Only	Lecture/Lab + CBT + EPSS		
		Lecture/Lab	CBT	EPSS
Student annual salary	$80,000	$80,000	$80,000	$80,000
Fringe benefits factor	1.35	1.35	1.35	1.35
Annual productive days	234	234	234	234
Student daily salary	$462	$462	$462	$462
Student per diem	$200	$200	$200	$200
Class length (days)	15	8	.75	.5
Salary per student per class	$9,923	$5,292	$496	$331
Student travel costs	$4,000	$2,000	$0	$0
Lost opportunity cost	$32,051	$17,094	$1,603	$1,068
Total number of students	300	300	300	300
Student costs subtotal	$13,792,308	$7,315,897	$629,615	$419,744
Miscellaneous costs	$120,000	$120,000	$0	$0
Total annual costs	$13,912,308	$7,435,897	$626,615	$419,744

Abbreviations: Lab, Laboratory

Often student costs are more than 80 percent of the cost of a training program so that changes in course length or location affect overall training costs significantly. The lost opportunity cost for students represents the value of reduced productivity or time lost because the student is away from his or her workplace while attending classes. This is a difficult figure to obtain but is extremely important. In this analysis, the lost opportunity cost was determined by calculating the average revenue that each sales employee contributes, dividing by the number of productive days and multiplying by the number of days away from the job at a training course.

The student cost comparison in Table 7-9 is shown by way of illustration since it represents the largest single cost element in the analysis.

The cost comparison between the two options—15 days of lecture/laboratory training and 8 days of Lecture/Laboratory plus 0.75 days of CBT and 0.5 days of EPSS—is shown in Table 7-10.

Table 7-10. The Comparison of Costs Clearly Highlights the Time and Money that Can Be Saved by Moving Some Courses from Lecture/Laboratory to CBT and EPSS

Cost Element	Lecture/Lab. Lecture/lab 15 days	Lecture/Laboratory + CBT + EPSS		
		Lecture/lab 8 days	CBT 0.75 days	EPSS 0.5 days
Student costs	$13,912,308	$7,435,897	$629,615	$419,744
Instructor costs	$138,846	$81,051	$11,628	$11,628
Instructional Development costs [a]	$121,074	$62,298	$83,551	$70,088
Facilities costs	$25,000	$13,000	$0	$0
Maintenance costs	$24,871	$14,785	$22,298	$17,743
Total Training costs	$14,222,099	$7,609,031	$747,092	$519,203
Total by option	$14,222,099		$8,875,326	
Annual cost per student	$47,407	$25,363	$2,490	$1,731
Total annual cost per student	$47,707		$29,584	

[a] Assumes that development costs are amortized over a 4-year period since the life of the courses is estimated at four years

The cost savings are substantial mainly because of the lost opportunity cost. Since it generally agreed that salespeople sell more products and services if they spend more, productive time in front of the client, the move to a combination of lecture/laboratory, CBT and EPSS appears to be a very satisfactory solution.

ROI Calculation

As shown above the course training time was reduced by 38 percent, which means that more time could be spent in front of the customer. It also means that fewer sales and sales support personnel needed to be hired to meet the company's goals and objectives. The total cost savings are equal to the training time saved per employee plus the salaries and overhead expenses for the employees that did not need to be hired.

As shown in Table 7-11, the savings are calculated by taking the number of weeks that new hires and existing employees would spend in training and determining the number of total number of person-weeks that will be saved by moving to the new training program. For example, the time saved for 100 new hires would be 300 multiplied by 38 percent or 186 weeks, which can be converted to a headcount reduction of 4 by dividing by the 47 weeks that an individual works each year.

Table 7-11. By Reducing the Number of New Hires per Year, Substantial Savings are Generated [a]

	Year				
	1	2	3	4	Total
New Hire Training					
New hires per year	100	110	125	138	473
Total training weeks	300	330	375	414	1419
Reduced weeks (-38%)	186	205	233	256	880
Headcount reduction	4	4	5	5	19
Recurring training					
Employee base	300	400	510	635	1,845
Total training weeks	900	1,200	1,530	1,905	5,535
Reduced weeks (-38%)	558	744	949	1181	3432
Headcount reduction	12	16	20	25	73
Total headcount reduction	16	20	25	31	92
Average employee cost ($80,000)	$1266	$1615	$2010	$2447	$7339

[a] Figures are in units except where otherwise shown

Total savings are determined by multiplying the total headcount reduction by the average annual salary of the employees.

The program costs in Table 7-12 include additional computer hardware, instructional development, recurrency development, maintenance, updates and implementation. Negative numbers are shown in parentheses.

Table 7-12. The Net Cash Flow is Positive in the Third Year [a]

Cash flow	Year				Total
	1	2	3	4	
Cash Inflow					
Reduced training time					
Headcount reduction	$1266	$1,615	$2,010	$2,447	$7,338
Training cost reduction	$462	$578	$723	$896	$2,659
Utilization factor	25%	50%	100%	100%	
Projected cash inflow	$432	$1,097	$2,733	$3,343	$7,604
Cash outflow					
Hardware	$500	$300	$300	$300	$1,400
Instructional development	$864				$864
Recurrency development			$300	$300	$600
Maintenance		$55	$55	$55	$165
Updates			$100	$100	$200
Implementation	$50	$100	$50		$200
Cash outflow	$1,414	$455	$805	$755	$3,249
Net cash flow	($982)	($340)	$1587	$2588	$4175
Cumulative cash flow	($982)	($340)	$1587	$4175	$8350

[a] Figures are in thousands

It would have been possible to quantify the cost savings and net cash flow that resulted from the change from paper-based to CD-ROM–based product documentation. However, the additional benefits were not needed to justify the initial program, which was directed at the training situation. As the project moves forward, each of the additions to the EPSS can be justified on a stand-alone basis as necessary. The additions could include decision-, proposal- and presentation-preparation modules as well as a competitive analysis section.

Much of the expenses of implementing the CBT and EPSS program can be considered capital expenses and depreciated over the life of the program, which is 4 years in this case. Money has been included in the fourth year (under recurrency development) for the major modifications to the original material that will be needed in the fifth year. The effect of depreciating the costs which are in parentheses is shown in Table 7-13. The numbers in parentheses are the total amounts to be depreciated. The first-year costs are reduced from $1,414,000 to $391,000 from the perspective of a balance sheet.

Table 7-13. Depreciation Reduces the Impact of the Hardware and Courseware Expenditures [a]

Depreciated Costs in Detail				
Capital expenses depreciated (Hardware, courseware)				
Year 1	($1364)	$341	$341	$341	$341
Year 2	($300)		$75	$75	$75
Year 3	($600)			$150	$150
Year 4	($600)				$150
Expenses not depreciated (Maintenance, updates, implementation)				
Annual expense		$50	$155	$205	$155
Total cost (depreciated)		$391	$571	$771	$871

[a] Figures are in thousands

The profit and loss for the first year is determined by subtracting the projected cost of $391,000 from the projected cash inflow of $432,000 as shown in Table 7-14. The cumulative ROI of 10 percent in the first year is calculated by dividing the cumulative profit and loss (P&L) impact of $41,000 by the projected cost of $391,000.

Table 7-14. Cumulative ROI for the Combined Training Program [a]

Return on investment	Year				
	1	2	3	4	Total
Projected cash inflow	$432	$1097	$2733	$3343	$7605
Projected cost (depreciated)	$391	$571	$771	$871	$2604
Annual P&L impact	$41	$526	$1962	$2472	$5001
Cumulative P&L impact	$41	$567	$2529	$5001	
Cumulative ROI (%) (P&L cost)	10%	92%	254%	284%	

[a] Figures are in thousands

The ROI is substantial, in part because of the fact that the analysis is for well-paid individuals. The analysis does not include the change from a paper-based to CD-ROM-based product documentation system. The addition of the documentation element to the EPSS would have increased the ROI for the overall EPSS. Other EPSS elements such as expert system and help system modules will be added in the future. It may be more difficult to measure the cash inflow for these additions, but it is clear that the overall system can be justified because of the impressive payback that occurs from the learning and documentation modules. In practice, it would have been better to prepare an overall justification for the entire EPSS, however, the complete set of information needed was not available to the authors.

THE HOLISTIC APPROACH

According to *The National Society for Performance and Instruction* the application of performance technology to "splinters" or groups does not allow for integration into an overall, cohesive framework that will deliver both organization and client payoffs (Kaufman 1986). A change in any one part of the organization has implications for all other parts, so changes should be designed to integrate and be mutually facilitating.

Multimedia capabilities can be implemented so that people will be comfortable with and know how to use technology and be able to tap its potential. The holistic approach to implementing applications can realize the power and potential of people on the job. It results in a move away from the traditional approaches based on independent training, documentation, and productivity software systems which seldom result in the promised improvements.

To link organizational effectiveness, organizational results and client consequences, the unit of analysis must include the whole organization. In the parlance of the human performance technologist, the whole organization is a candidate for analysis and hence the application of performance technologies based on multimedia capabilities. As such, the whole organization provides a holistic frame of reference which encompasses individual skills, the whole individual, the group, the organization, and the client.

By changing the focus to more holistic concerns, management can begin to ask how each part of the organizational contributes to the overall organization and client good. By linking organizational efforts, organizational results, and organizational payoffs in and for clients, any organization will be able to do the following:

- Determine gaps between current and desired results, both internal and external

- Determine where in the organization the needs exist

- Rank the needs

- Select the gaps with the highest priority to close

- Prepare objectives for closing the priority needs

- Identify causes and origins of the needs

- Identify the best methods and means to close the gaps

- Determine the effectiveness and efficiency of the methods and the means selected to meet the needs

The focus is on improving the competency of the organization on a results oriented basis rather than on improving achievement in one task area or decreasing documentation costs or delivering more effective business presentations. The holistic approach allows the organization to realize the benefits of multimedia capabilities in a systematized and prioritized way so that the technology infrastructure needed to support multimedia can be justified on a ROI basis.

The implementation of multimedia capabilities in business will continue to rise at dramatic rates over the next decade. Until multimedia reaches the pervade stage of its evolution, the documentation of ROI will be important to the continued growth of multimedia in all applications.

REFERENCES

Adams, Gregory L. Why Interactive? *Multimedia & Videodisc Monitor*: March 1992:20–25.

Burke, James. 1991. Keynote speech at the Multimedia Conference and Exhibition, American Museum of Natural History, October 7, 1991, New York, New York.

Fletcher, J. D. 1990. Effectiveness and Cost of Interactive Videodisc Instruction in Defense Training and Education. Institute for Defense Analysis.

Gery, Gloria J. 1990. Performance Support Systems: Concepts and Development Issues. Paper read at Computer-Based Training Conference and Exposition, 1-4 April 1990, Chicago, Illinois.

Head, Glenn E. 1985. *Training Cost Analysis*. Denver, Colorado: Marlin Press.

Ives, Bill, and Forman, David. 1991. Calculating Competitive Advantage. *CBT Directions* June 1991:10–18.

Kaufman, Roger. 1986. *Introduction to Performance Technology*. Washington, D.C.: The National Society for Performance and Instruction.

Peters, Tom. 1991. *Thriving on Chaos*. New York, NY: Harper Perennial.

Raybould, Barry. 1990. Building an Electronic Performance Support System. Paper read at Computer-Based Training Conference and Exposition, 1-4 April 1990, Chicago, Illinois.

Raybould, Barry. 1990. A New Approach to Using Computers to Improve Productivity in the Workplace. *Special Reports: Performance Support System Technologies*. Ariel PSS Corporation.

Trachtenberg, Peter. 1990. Training in the 1990's. Read at the Multimedia, Training and Information Conference, 11 October 1990, in San Francisco, California.

Weddle, Peter D. 1990. Human Capital: Reality or Rhetoric? *Human Capital Journal*, November 1990:45–47.

Ziegler, Richard. 1990. Integrated Performance Support Systems. *Human Capital Journal*, November 1990:40–42.

8

Computer-Generated Microworlds

SIMULATION AND VIRTUAL REALITY

Both graphics-based device simulation and virtual reality stem from the same phenomenon—the desire to create an interactive, real-time microworld that appears to be so "real" that it is highly conducive to the learning, information transfer or entertainment activity for which it was intended. The difference between the two is related to application, the type of user interface, and the manner in which the simulation represents the real world activity or system. There is not an easily defined demarcation point between simulation and virtual reality (VR). In fact, the VR community is debating the definition of the terminology.

The essence of the multimedia quest is to find pragmatic, utilitarian, and/or entertaining uses for real-world media data types in a fully digital, computer domain. The computer-generated microworlds of graphics-based device simulation and VR are firmly based on fully digital computer-based domains. Both simulation and VR attempt to create self-contained, software-based microworlds that behave according to their own laws of physics and behavior, most of which emulate real-world phenomenon.

These computer-generated microworlds are complex, dynamic, real-time environments that appear unpredictable. Such active/reactive/interactive environments come "alive" when a human interacts with or within them. Because the intent is to create the perception of "reality'" in the mind of the "beholder" (user or receiver), simulation and virtual reality seem to be a natural environment for the deployment of real-world media—audio, images, and/or full-motion video.

Both of these microworld capabilities take advantage of our ability to temporarily suspend "disbelief" while we are engaged in their environs. Most of us have experienced uncomfortable feelings when we see an actor hanging onto the ledge of a building in a movie. Logically we know that the actor is not in peril, but emotionally we are caught up in the drama because we believe that the scene is real.

Device simulation may be either two-dimensional (2D) or three-dimensional (3D), but the microworld is observed from a fixed point or plane of view. Virtual reality is always 3D and usually the viewer is surrounded by the microworld.

Both simulation and virtual reality will be used in business environments for training and education programs that requires "hands-on" experience. The goals of training and education are to change observable behavior and to increase awareness as shown in Figure 8-1. Instruction with a skill/knowledge focus can be handled by teaching in traditional lecture/laboratory environments or by providing simulators for the student to use. Learning that comes through practice cannot be taught using CBT.

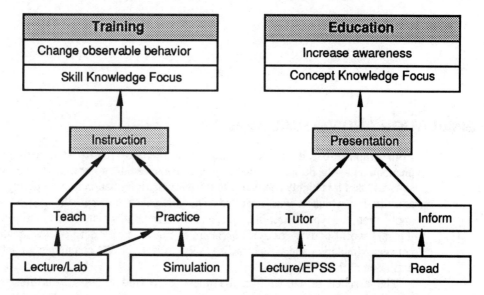

Figure 8-1. Simulation is valuable in both training and education applications. Source: Authenticity Incorporated.

Graphics-based device simulation provides a major opportunity for organizations to reduce the hardware dependency that results from the use of real equipment for training. Billions of dollars worth of captive equipment need not be consigned for training equipment operators or maintenance personnel.

In this chapter, we examine the application of off-the-shelf personal computers for graphics-based equipment simulation applications and explore a set of VR applications.

The solutions described for simulation are not limited to equipment simulations but can be used for learning complex processes and procedures and for sales demonstrations.

GRAPHICS-BASED SIMULATION

"To simulate" is defined in Webster's Dictionary as "to look or act like." In the multimedia environment, a simulation is a structured event with relationships between elements in a causative model that represents a slice of a real-world event or situation.

The combat and technical training requirements of World War II led to the birth of technology-based equipment simulation. The U.S. government was the first agency to fund the development and deployment of equipment training systems that were called "simulators." Simulators ("simulator/trainers") are especially valuable in military training because the complexity, cost, or danger of certain tasks makes it impossible to conduct comprehensive mission rehearsals.

Studies have shown that people reason or solve problems based on cases, examples, and experience, rather than by learning rules or procedures. Flight simulators are considered by cognitive learning scientists to be the best educational software ever written because pilots learn by experience in a very realistic microworld. However, flight simulators cost millions of dollars each. The same is true for nuclear and fossil fuel power generating plant simulators.

Because such complex systems cost hundreds of millions of dollars and operation of the actual system could be life threatening, full-fidelity, full-scale mockups have been created for training. Such systems incorporate both real-world and synthesized systems. For example, a flight simulator includes a full cockpit with all of the controls and instrumentation found in a real aircraft and elaborate computer-generated visual displays of real-world airports and flying situations. These hybrid simulators are so expensive that the only organizations that can afford them are the airline and power utility industries and the military.

Equipment manufacturers have been forced to use production units to provide hands-on technical training and to practise fault isolation. Equipment malfunctions and failures are "stimulated" through "jury-rigged apparatus" on a real device. In some instances the real devices are damaged or quickly worn out by this form of usage.

Graphics-Based Device Simulators

Graphics-based device simulators represent the real system using computer-generated graphics and a computer-mediated model of its affects and effects. The actual equipment is not required for this type of simulator since the microworld is completely generated by the computer.

In model-driven simulators the system responds to user actions according to a model of the device behavior. While users do not experience the kinesthetic sensations involved in touching and manipulating controls, model-driven graphical simulations offer a high degree of real-world visual fidelity. This is important because the dominant human perceptual sense is visual.

Government-sponsored research has proven that model-driven graphical simulations are extremely effective for teaching humans to

• Perform complicated procedures

• Comprehend complex processes

• Recognize and diagnose failures

• Respond appropriately in emergency situations

In fact, the virtual system created on a graphics-based device simulator can offer a number of advantages over stimulated real equipment or full-scale mock-up simulators including the following

• Easy exploration and observation of cause/effect relationships via a model

• Portrayal of internal effects that cannot be seen on the real device

• Experimentation/exploration without risk of hardware damage

• Passage of time can be adjusted (i.e., slowed down or speeded up)

• Simulation complexity can be tailored to individual needs (novice–expert)

The foregoing model-driven advantages notwithstanding, the primary business motivation for using a graphical simulation is the financial opportunity to dramatically reduce simulation delivery cost by using off-the-shelf computers. In addition, the development cost must be reasonable before businesses will find it an attractive alternative.

In the past, the use of graphics-based device simulators has been confined to situations where the expenditure of hundreds of thousands of dollars could be justified for development. In addition, expensive proprietary image-generation computer platforms from companies such as Evans & Sutherland or high-end reduced instruction set computer (RISC)-based UNIX workstations from Silicon Graphics were needed for high-fidelity graphics-based simulators.

Fortunately, a technological breakthrough known as Equipment Simulation with Intelligent Models (E-SIM) will make it feasible to implement desktop device simulators in 1993. Object-oriented technology forms the foundation and structure of E-SIM applications.

Although object-oriented technology has come into the limelight only recently, virtually all of the basic concepts of object-oriented programming were introduced during the late 1960s in Simula (acronym for "simulation language"), a seldom used programming language created specifically to support computer simulations of real-world processes.

It took more than two decades of research and development (R&D) to develop a commercially feasible technology because the evolution of E-SIM is directly linked to advances in

- Artificial intelligence (AI)

- Object-oriented technology

- Model-based intelligence

- Graphical user interfaces (GUIs)

An E-SIM application uses an expert system-like, object rule-base to interconnect all of the objects to their respective behaviors. The rules are combined with graphical representations of each visible object to form a device model of a simulated system, defined at a high behavior level. Extremely complicated system simulations can be composed of a number of relatively simple graphical objects, similar to the way that real systems are composed of physical objects. Developers don't need to deal with the huge number of possible combinations of device states. Instead they can focus on the ways that each individual part is affected by others. Figure 8-2 shows a simplified representation of the creation of an E-SIM object-based device model.

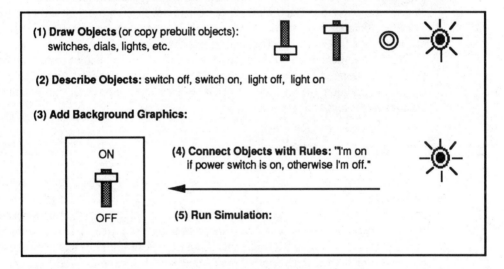

Figure 8-2. Creation of an E-SIM object-based device model. Source: Authenticity Incorporated.

Just as an automobile has an engine to make it move, an E-SIM application has a simulation engine that takes care of monitoring and managing the simulation as the user operates it. An active, object-based device model is composed of functional objects (graphical representations of object states plus their relevant behaviors), and effect propagation (caused by the multiplicity of ways that state variables affect one another, with or without a time dimension).

Hewlett-Packard Company is currently evaluating the cost and learning effectiveness of E-SIM for replacing the hands-on equipment used to train technical service personnel.

The current applications only use graphics and text but other media will be added in future. For example, audio will be used to simulate equipment alarms.

Hewlett-Packard is using E-SIM applications developed by Authenticity, Incorporated of St. Helena, California. The device simulations were created using Authenticity InSight, an E-SIM authoring system that will be released in 1993. Authenticity InSight represents a significant breakthrough because it reduces the development to delivery ratio to approximately 100 to 1, i.e., 100 hours of development time to prepare a simulation application that is 1 hour in length. In the past, the development cost of a modest, hand-coded model equipment simulation could amount to a million dollars. A simulation of medium complexity might typically involve three or more highly skilled computer programmers, working for a year or more in association with one or more subject-matter experts, in order to create a high-fidelity structural model. The development to delivery ratio was as high as 10,000 to 1.

The 10-fold decrease in the cost of development will prompt many high-technology companies to implement device simulators for training technical personnel. The potential savings are enormous since millions of dollars worth of equipment are being used in learning laboratories around the world. A significant percentage of this captive equipment can be replaced by E-SIM applications on personal computers.

The 10-fold decrease in development time will allow companies to stay in step with product development cycles that dictate that new products be introduced every 9 to 12 months. In addition, the authors expect that E-SIM applications will significantly reduce both instructor and student costs.

GRAPHICS-BASED VIRTUAL REALITY

Virtual reality is a conundrum as a term. How can something be both virtual, which is defined by Webster's Dictionary as "being so in effect, but not in actual fact or name," and reality, which is defined as "the quality or fact of being real"? Virtual reality enables users to participate directly in real-time, computer-generated, 3-D environments that convey information through sight, sound, and touch in a highly realistic manner. The human brain is "tricked" into believing that it is in the microworld created by the computer.

Virtual reality extends multimedia to a different level. The "VR experience" can include audio, images, and full-motion video but it does so in a manner that goes beyond what we currently expect of multimedia applications in business. Virtual reality enables the user to learn by doing since the computer-generated microworld is a replica of the real world, but without the threat of damage and injury to equipment and human operator. As discussed in the examples below, VR allows the user to exploit multimedia capabilities in the environment where the user needs to be immersed in the microworld to hear, see, and touch in order to achieve a new level of understanding.

Within the VR spectrum are high-end systems in which the participant is immersed in the computer-generated microworld through a VR suit with a stereoscopic display, audio system, and gloves. At the midpoint in the spectrum, the individual steers through a 3D world that is displayed on a computer screen using a control device such as a space ball or "flying mouse." At the other end, the viewer stands outside a video-projected VR world and communicates with characters or entities inside it.

Virtual reality is and will remain a research area for several years to come. The evolution of products and tools that are underway for other multimedia applications will reduce the limitations that exist for VR. However, there are many other areas that need to be addressed such as the special appliances that need to be worn.

Military and pilot training applications, surgical training, and other "life threatening" applications all are useful environments where the simulation must be realistic enough to ensure that the individual is well prepared to address the real-world situations. Tactile feedback can be very important to the user of the system. A pilot needs to experience the result of many actions through tactile feedback. A surgeon-in-training needs to have tactile feedback appropriate to the tissue or muscles that are being cut by the virtual scalpel.

Radiation therapy treatment planning allows the radiotherapist to examine multiple beam placements on a 3D model of the patient's body. Three-dimensional dose grids are calculated and registered on the patient anatomy model. The objective is to target multiple beams to a single location while minimizing the dosage on healthy regions of the body (Hughes and Latta 1991).

Boeing has demonstrated a virtual aircraft in a virtual space. The operator can fly around the V-22 Osprey aircraft which was parked on the ground, enter the cockpit, and operate the flight controls on a limited basis. In spite of the fact that Boeing has a complete database on the V-22, it was easier to create a model in Swivel 3D on a Macintosh from a plastic model purchased at a hobby store. This demonstrates one of the current limitations of VR technology.

Applications based on remote control of a distant device or system can be extremely realistic to the point that the user could not detect any difference between reality and virtual reality. The Woods Hole Oceanographic Institution used a personal computer connected via satellite links to demonstrate the exploration of a sunken vessel using an undersea robot to schoolchildren. The children's experienced a realistic undersea exploration that only lacked the smell of the sea and the pitch and roll of a ship. The operators were actually in control of an undersea robot named Jason.

The combination of computer-aided design (CAD) files combined with virtual reality systems can allow the buyer of kitchen applications and cupboards to construct a kitchen and rearrange elements using a data glove until the design completely suits their needs. The buyer of a building can walk through the design prepared by the architects using a virtual reality suit before a single brick is laid.

National Aeronautics and Space Administration (NASA) is using World Tool Kit from Sense8 Corp. for telerobotic planning and operation. The paths that robotic mechanisms trace during missions are subject to numerous constraints. NASA engineers need to be able to visualize the trajectory of the robots and change it on an interactive basis An advanced VR communications environment is provided using a head-mounted display. DVI generated photorealistic images are used to create realistic terrain, sea, sky, and space imagery.

With Virtus Corporation's WalkThrough, users can design a three-dimensional model and move through it interactively. Instead of traditional CAD elements such as polygons and vectors, WalkThrough provides familiar objects for modeling–such as doors, rooms, and furniture–whose shapes and colors can be edited by the user. To place a door, you select the door tool and position it in the program's two-dimensional Plan View window.

As WalkThrough assembles the 2D plan, a 3D perspective of the design space updates automatically in the WalkView window, so after placing a door, a user can immediately walk through it into an adjoining room simply by moving the mouse. Completed WalkThrough models can be exported to CAD programs for construction specifics.

Nippon Electric Company (NEC) is developing a virtual network computer-aided design system in which models of car designs can be manipulated in a networked environment.

The VR system is based on the existing design tools, with newly developed software that enables the definition of smooth surface models. Models displayed on the screen can be changed at will using data gloves to manipulate the model and tools for cutting and shaping. Components can be added from a parts library and designers can collaborate in real time over the network.

Current technology is challenged by the requirements of many VR applications. Hardware and software suppliers need to provide better user interfaces that allow easier input/output, higher resolution displays, open architectures to allow for easy interworking, and computer and storage systems that accommodate high-volume and high-speed data requirements.

REFERENCE

Hughes, Christine, and Latta, John N. 1991. Special Report. SIGGRAPH, Las Vegas, July 1991. *Media Letter* p 21–25.

9

Technology Infrastructure

INTRODUCTION

At this time it is still appropriate to refer to multimedia-capable personal computers, multimedia-capable servers, and multimedia-capable networks. After 1995, the term "multimedia-capable" will be redundant because the technology infrastructure will have encompassed all of the capabilities and functionality necessary for multimedia to become part of the normal work environment. The technologies and activities that are important to the successful implementation of multimedia applications are shown in Figure 9-1. Each of the areas will be explored in turn starting with computing platforms and ending with timelines for the pacing items in the evolution of multimedia.

The information in this chapter is specific to the platforms needed to implement multimedia in a business environment. Since personal computers from IBM and Apple Computer dominate the desktops of information knowledge workers, the focus is on their current and future products. The computing platforms needed by the professional creator/sender that are being developed by workstation suppliers such as NeXT, Silicon Graphics, Sun Microsystems, and others, are not directed at the application developer. Such platforms will be much more powerful and capable than those needed for playback by the receiver or for the non-professional creator/sender, i.e., the information knowledge worker.

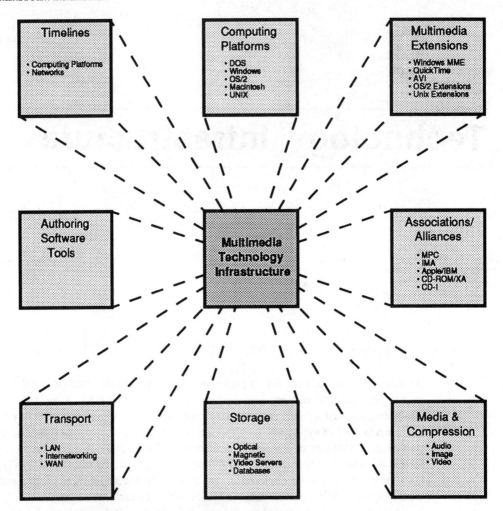

Figure 9-1. The technology infrastructure is moving ahead rapidly because of efforts by the information technology and telecommunications industries.

The authors recognize that market forces are blurring distinctions between high-end personal computers and low-end workstations. RISC technology will ensure that the performance needed for multimedia computing and communicating is available from the personal computer and the workstation vendors.

The time horizons for computing and telecommunications are significantly different. Innovation changes the computing world on an annual basis. In the telecommunications environment change has tended to occur over 5- to 10-year horizons.

The efforts of International Consultative Committee on Telephone and Telegraph (CCITT) to develop standards for BISDN. based on Asynchronous Transfer Mode (ATM) switching and Synchronous Optical Network (SONET) transmission technologies is generating a discontinuity in the networking world. For the first time there will be a common base for networking whether public or private, voice, data or image, or local or wide area.

Although the specifications are not yet complete, ATM technology is available now in intelligent hubs and T3 or SONET multiplexers. ATM is extremely attractive because it is capable of delivering dedicated Ethernet or token ring bandwidth to the desktop now and up to 600 Mbit/s in the future. Further, ATM offers network delay or latency characteristics that make it feasible to transport text, image, graphics, animation, audio, and full-motion video on the same network. Finally, all of the telecommunications vendors including the central office switching vendors are implementing products so that networking will be based on a common transport technology starting in 1995. Ubiquitous availability of BISDN will take more than a decade but the use of common technology by all players will decrease the time horizon.

COMPUTING PLATFORMS

The transition of the personal computer to a personal communicator will likely include a shift in the design philosophy of the computer industry. Existing personal computers have abundant CPU capacity but lack the I/O capability demanded by multimedia applications. The CPU in a personal computer is used for I/O activities in addition computing activities. Since the CPU is scheduled on a "fairness" basis rather than on "urgency," this can prove to be a performance bottleneck (Fox 1991). All of the major suppliers of personal computers and workstations are addressing the need for improved I/O capability.

Implementing multimedia in a personal computer is a tremendous technological challenge that will be transparent to the user. Full-motion video presents the most demanding requirements, followed by audio and still images . Full-motion video of television quality requires 720 kilobytes per frame at 30 fps. One second of video consumes 22.1 Mbytes of storage and requires network bandwidth of 176.8 Mbit/s.

The current de facto standard for distributing multimedia applications and content is the CD-ROM. With a capacity of 650 Megabytes and a transfer rate of 150 kbytes/s, the CD-ROM is capable of holding a total of 30 seconds of uncompressed video and it would take 5 seconds to display a single frame.

The challenge of multimedia applications demands compression ratios up to 160 to 1, transfer rates greater than 150 kbyte/s, and broadband networks with bandwidths greater than 1.5 Mbit/s and latencies appropriate to the continuous stream of data demanded by audio and video.

Existing LANs are optimized for "bursty" data, rather than streaming characteristic of audiovisual data. The contention schemes used in personal computers and networks cause all of the traffic to slow down when the system is busy which is inappropriate for audio, video, animation, and other real-time data.

The ideal solution will allow LANs to handle audiovisual data in addition to traditional data traffic using existing wiring and network software with multimedia-capable personal computers or workstations. Broadband WANs that provide bandwidth-on-demand will satisfy the need to interconnect LANs and individual personal computers or workstations.

There is no single computing platform that meets the needs of all the different types of users and multimedia applications classes. Multimedia platforms are being developed to meet the requirements of the application developer, the business user, and the consumer. Individual platforms are configured according to their intended use. The performance, complexity, and cost are highest for application development platforms and lowest for consumer products.

The current crop of operating systems is closely tied to the underlying hardware

• Microsoft's disk operating system (MS-DOS or DOS), Windows and OS/2to the Intel x86 family

• Macintosh to the Motorola 68000 family currently and to the PowerPC family of computers in the future, which is being jointly developed by Apple, IBM, and Motorola

• AIX to IBM's Power architecture

The cross-platform environments that are being developed—Windows NT, Pink, Solaris, and Open Desktop—will be able to run on both Intel x86 and RISC-based semiconductor chips. All systems promise interoperability and source code portability on the platforms on which they run.

It is clear that by controlling the lion's share of the desktops, IBM's PC (and clones) and Apple's Macintosh will be the platforms of choice for multimedia playback in the business environment. Developers and users in business will upgrade existing Macintosh, PC AT, or PS/2 personal computers. Older less powerful systems will be replaced. Admittedly, inroads will be made by UNIX workstations. It is clear that there is a major push for market share by Sun Microsystems, Silicon Graphics, and others.

Although multimedia application developers have been using platforms from Apple and IBM, the trend is toward high-powered, multitasking workstations with built-in networking capability from Sun Microsystems, Silicon Graphics, Digital Equipment Corporation (Digital), Hewlett-Packard, and others.

By 1995, all new workstations and personal computers will be multimedia capable and many existing units will have been upgraded to handle multimedia applications. The distinction between workstation and personal computer will have blurred as the personal computer becomes more powerful and the workstation becomes less costly. Intel and other silicon suppliers plan to include most of the functionality needed to handle audio, images, and video in the processing chips themselves so the number of discrete components will be reduced. Figure 9-2 depicts all of the functions that will be included in the personal computer or workstation of the future.

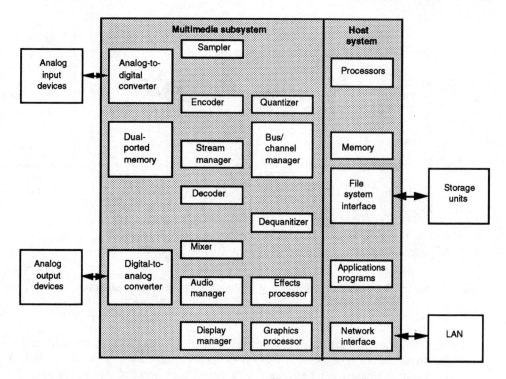

Figure 9-2. Future multimedia workstations may have all of the logical components as standard features. Figure reprinted with permission, from Computer 24(10):18, October 1991. © IEEE .

In business, the act of consuming, manipulating, producing, and communicating information is a group activity and must be done within the standard work environment of the group. Multimedia will not change this process (in fact it will greatly enhance the process), so we should expect that the battle for the desktop will continue to be Apple versus Microsoft and Intel X86-based PC vendors. The battle will continue even though Apple and IBM have chosen to jointly develop powerful new open system software platforms for the 1990s.

The installed base of IBM personal computers or clones that meet or exceed the revised MPC level 1 specification (i.e., 386SX or better) and the installed base of Macintoshes exceeds all other multimedia computer types as shown in Figure 9-3. The number of IBM clones includes those operating under DOS and Windows.

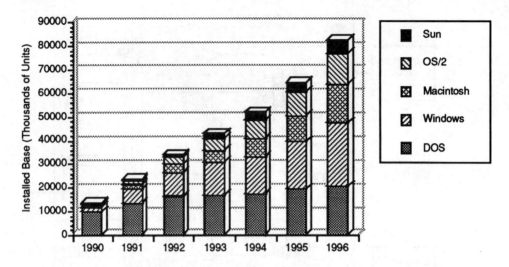

Figure 9-3. IBM's PC and clones represent the dominant potential audience for multimedia applications. Source: Scott Harmon, The Peregrine Group.

The computer industry is focusing on the technology infrastructure needed to develop broad market acceptance of multimedia applications. Desktop hardware and software is moving forward at a rapid pace because of the efforts of Apple Computer, IBM, and Microsoft. At this point in time, it appears that Microsoft Windows is the desktop operating system of choice.

However, the infrastructure must include multimedia networks and servers which are the domain of host computer suppliers such as Digital, IBM, and others as well as start-up companies such as Starlight Networks, Inc.. Office- and operations-centric applications can only be successful if the enterprise becomes multimedia-capable. Multimedia-capable desktop platforms will not satisfy the overall requirement by themselves.

The evolution of desktop operating systems is not being driven by "killer applications" but by the needs of all applications as they become bigger and more sophisticated with a need for more interoperability. To satisfy the requirements of multimedia applications, Apple Computer, IBM, and Microsoft have added extensions to their respective operating systems as described below under Multimedia Extensions.

DOS

DOS is not likely to make microcomputers an advanced platform for building and downsizing mission-critical networked applications or for long-term multimedia applications. Management information systems (MIS) organizations need a more robust foundation for integrating PCs into the enterprise and implementing an array of new technologies–GUIs, LANs, e-mail, client/server architectures, distributed relational databases, groupware, object-oriented programming, and multimedia.

However, DOS is far from dead. DOS is being used and will continue to be used for multimedia applications. The MS-DOS 5 upgrade released in June 1991 was greeted enthusiastically by the DOS community. A number of application development tools is available. In the short term, most of the applications will be implemented on DOS/Windows platforms. In the long term, DOS will become less attractive to the development community. The multimedia extensions to Windows that make it easier to develop and use multimedia applications will not be available to DOS developers and users.

Operations-centric applications will require networked server and more sophisticated operating environments. Such applications must be easy for the information knowledge worker to use which is somewhat dependent on the multimedia extensions. As multimedia evolves in this direction, DOS will become less and less attractive.

In the latter part of the 1980s, Microsoft reached some conclusions that dictated the future directions of DOS and Windows

• The Macintosh GUI provides an operating environment that is particularly valuable to multimedia and the future of personal computers. Microsoft decided to develop the Windows graphic operating environment on top of DOS. In fact, the entire microcomputer industry has moved to GUIs.

• DOS (which is really just a simple loader/control program) restricts applications to single-task functionality. Since the computing needs of the 1990s would outstrip the capabilities of DOS, Microsoft began development of the OS/2 operating system in 1987 to sustain the alliance with IBM.

IBM and Microsoft agreed that OS/2 would have a different graphic environment (Presentation Manager or PM) than DOS (Windows). Thus software developers were forced to develop applications for two operating system/graphic environments.

The fact that Windows was evolving more quickly than OS/2 was evident to software developers. With enhancements to DOS and the sophisticated system features built into Windows, DOS/Windows evolved into a "real operating system." At the end of 1989, IBM and Microsoft positioned Windows and OS/2 as complementary operating systems and reinforced their commitment to OS/2. However, by the spring of 1990, it was clear IBM and Microsoft were moving down different paths. IBM took over development responsibility for OS/2 while Microsoft focused on DOS and Windows.

In addition, Microsoft decided to start work on a future operating system known as New Technology or NT. IBM decided that OS/2 would be capable of running both DOS and Windows applications. In the long term DOS users will migrate to either NT or OS/2 to get access to richer and more robust operating environments for multimedia and other applications. The networked and distributed computing environment will benefit from the capabilities that both companies are building into their respective operating systems.

Windows

More than 14 million copies of Windows 3.0 were shipped since its introduction in 1990 and 3 million copies of Windows 3.1 shipped in the first 6 weeks after the product was released. By 1995, Windows will likely be the number one operating system. In the multimedia community, Windows is clearly the dominant operating environment. Microsoft began shipping Microsoft Windows with Multimedia Extensions (MME) 1.0 to original equipment vendors in August 1991. Windows 3.0 with MME 1.0 was the first standard for combining text, graphics, animation, and audio.

Windows 3.1 which began shipping in April 1992 incorporates much of the functionality of MME. By so doing, Microsoft is ensuring that individuals that buy operating systems in future will not face the daunting task of adding MME to Windows 3.0. Microsoft is creating a sizable potential market for multimedia applications in the future. Applications developers will know that potential users have the software-base for running multimedia applications. Users who upgrade their PCs to meet the MPC standard will have complete systems that are multimedia-capable. Refer to Multimedia Extensions, below, for more information.

Direct support for external devices such as CD-audio and videodisc players and joysticks is only available under MME. However, all of application programming interfaces (APIs), data formats, and application calls are the same, so applications developed under Windows 3.0 with MME are compatible with Windows 3.1. In addition, the Windows 3.0 MME can run on Windows 3.1.

Device drivers for the musical instrument digital interface (MIDI) sequencer and mapper as well as the wave audio is included in Windows 3.1. (Refer to the Media section below for more information about MIDI.) Thus developers of traditional business and productivity applications can add voice annotation to their products.

Microsoft intends to support two operating systems in the long term: a mainstream, midrange offering—Windows on DOS, and a high-end, advanced offering—Windows NT. Both operating systems will share a single-user interface and run the same applications base. Microsoft will continue to upgrade character-mode DOS for low-end hardware.

Support for 32-bit applications and preemptive multitasking will appear first in the high-end NT operating system and over time in the mainstream offerings. The Win32 API is designed so that an existing 16-bit application can be converted 32-bit, and continue to be used.

The Win32 API announced in March 1992 enables developers to create a single 32-bit application that will run on either Windows 3.1 or on Windows NT. The Win32 API is a binary-compatible subset of the Win32 API that will be supported by the Windows NT operating system. Win32 technology was made available to qualified Microsoft C and C++ developers in July 1992.

Windows NT is expected to ship in 1993. In April 1992, independent software vendors (ISVs) demonstrated more than 50 applications for the Microsoft Windows NT operating system, only 5 months after receiving the first version of the NT operating system. The demonstrations included a range of future products including PC productivity, server, and workstation applications software, and development tools from leading developers for the MS-DOS, Windows, OS/2, UNIX, and Macintosh platforms.

By mid-1993, the first 32-bit version of Windows on DOS will ship. This release will require a new version of DOS. Microsoft notes a new release of Windows will be made available every 12 to 15 months.

Windows 3.1 features several key improvements: better performance; greater application integration with Dynamic Data Exchange (DDE), Object Linking and Embedding (OLE), and drag-and-drop features; better handling of Unrecoverable Application Errors (UAEs), TrueType fonts an improved file manager; and a host of cosmetic changes. Developers can take advantage of more 300 new API functions, most of which support Version 1.0 of the OLE protocol.

OLE is supported by utilities such as Recorder, PaintBrush, Cardfile, and Write, and by a number of application software packages. OLE provides a means of inserting information from one document in another document similar to familiar cutting and pasting operations. However, the information in the destination document is updated automatically when the source document is updated.

The NT operating system will fully support current DOS, 16-bit Windows applications, and future applications written to the 32-bit Win32 API. The first release will have limited support for 16-bit OS/2 character-based applications such as Microsoft's SQL Server and Communications Manager. More complete support of PM-based OS/2 applications will be included in a future NT release.

The NT operating system is based on an object-oriented architecture which supports distributed computing and symmetric multiprocessing (in addition to multitasking capabilities). The native graphic operating environment for NT will be Windows. Windows 32 and NT will appear to be identical to the user and to application software.

NT will be ported to Digital's RISC-based Alpha computers and MIPS RISC computers.

OS/2

IBM is committed to supporting OS/2 with a 32-bit release (Version 2.0), and is jointly developing a new object-oriented operating system (Pink) with Apple Computer.

Two jointly owned companies were formed as part of the IBM/Apple agreement: Taligent (from talent and intelligence) and Kaleida (from kaleidoscope). Taligent is developing a new object-oriented environment, and Kaleida will be responsible for developing multimedia products.

Although IBM and Apple are designing a completely new object-oriented environment, development work at Taligent did not start from scratch. Apple brought over 3 years of development and more than a million lines of code from its Object-Based Systems division to the new company. IBM contributed technology resulting from its Patriot Partners joint venture with Metaphor Computer Systems, Inc. IBM and Metaphor started work in September 1990 to design an object-oriented operating system and to develop visual, object-oriented programming tools.

Object-oriented technologies from Taligent will appear in both OS/2 and AIX (Leghart 1991). For example, the object-oriented Workplace shell is going into OS/2 now, and Object Rexx will be coming in the near future. Microsoft's OLE technology will initially be supported in OS/2 2.0 via Windows applications. IBM will provide support for OLE in PM applications in a future product release.

The evolutionary path for IBM's operating system remains unchanged: migration from DOS to OS/2. IBM is moving in the direction it committed to in 1987. The development of object-oriented operating systems and multimedia capabilities (with Apple, Taligent, and Kaleida) has not changed their commitment to OS/2.

IBM notes that OS/2 Version 2.0 can run multiple DOS and Windows applications side-by-side as well as applications developed specifically for 32-bit microprocessors.

OS/2's virtual memory paging architecture provides more conventional memory to DOS applications (over 640 kbytes). For Windows applications, OS/2 offers better protection—UAEs no longer crash the entire system, only the DOS virtual machine they are running in.

The OS/2 2.0 version of PM began shipping in September 1992. Multimedia PM/2 includes multimedia extensions that take advantage of the 32-bit environment, including preemptive multitasking, available under OS/2.

OS/2 2.0 features a new user interface, called the Workplace Model, which is based on Common User Access (CUA) 91 specifications. It is more like the Macintosh interface than Windows which complies to the older CUA standard.

Windows Under OS/2

Under OS/2 2.0, Windows runs in a DOS virtual machine as an extended DOS environment. Windows acts like a DOS Protected Mode Interface (DPMI) client. The Windows kernel runs in native mode and uses DPMI to access portions of its virtual copy of the hardware.

DDE is supported between PM and Windows applications. Under OS/2 2.0, users can launch Windows programs directly from the PM workplace shell, or launch the Windows program manager and run their applications from that interface.

If OS/2 2.0 can run character-mode DOS applications faster than DOS, and Windows-based applications faster than Windows, then OS/2 2.0 could pose a serious competitive challenge to Microsoft's Windows strategy.

Early performance tests indicate that DOS applications run faster, and certain Windows functions run faster under OS/2, but others run slower. IBM claims an overall 33 percent performance improvement for 32-bit applications compared to their 16-bit applications.

32-Bit Applications

IBM says over 300 vendors are moving their 16-bit applications to 32-bit, of which 30 vendors have committed to providing 32-bit PM applications. Some of the major PM applications for OS/2 2.0 will include: Lotus' 1-2-3/G spreadsheet; DeScribe's DeScribe 3.0 word processor; the CorelDraw graphics package, from Corel Systems Corp., Ottawa,

Ontario; and the ObjectVision graphical application development tool, from Borland International, Inc., Scotts Valley, California.

One of the most important 32-bit OS/2 applications will emerge from IBM's alliance with Lotus. Under an agreement signed in June 1991, key elements of Lotus's Notes technology will be included in 32-bit OS/2 offerings, such as: IBM's OfficeVision/2, Notes, and cc:Mail.

IBM is offering its own programming environment and C compiler Watcom, Waterloo, Ontario, Canada will be supplying Fortran and Borland is providing its Turbo C++ compiler for OS/2 2.0.

IBM's Ultimedia Systems

IBM announced a broad array of multimedia products under the Ultimedia banner. The products offered range from fully configured systems to board level products and from content to application tools.

The following capability is available in every Ultimedia model:

• Minimum CPU: IBM 386 SLC 20 MHz processor or more powerful follow-ons with 4 Mbytes of memory and a small computer system interface (SCSI) controller

• High-performance CD-ROM XA drive with an average access time of 380 ms or less, transfer rate of 150 kbit/s and the CD-ROM XA interleaving capability (selected models may be offered without the CD-ROM XA drive)

• 160-Mbyte hard disk

• 2.88-Mbyte, 3.5-inch floppy disk drive

• Extended graphics architecture (XGA) graphics

• CD-quality audio subsystem with 8- or 16-bit capture and playback, up to 44,100 samples per second, MIDI synthesized playback

• Multimedia front panel

• Microphone

• OS/2 2.0 with support for DOS and Windows applications

The ActionMedia II display adapter and capture option is a joint development of IBM and Intel. The Model 8513 Touch Select add-on touch screens snap on to PS/2 monitors, either 12- or 16-inch units, and hook directly into the computer's mouse port for easy installation.

Updated M-Audio Capture and Playback Adapter and Video Capture Adapter/A include new APIs and audio device drivers for Microsoft Windows 3.0 and Multimedia Extensions.

The PS/2 TV is a fully integrated external audio/video tuner which allows the PS/2 to receive and display NTSC signals.

While the Ultimedia platform has everything necessary for multimedia personal computer (MPC) certification (with the exception of MIDI-in), IBM does not guarantee that MPC-approved software will run on Ultimedia systems. In addition, IBM does not endorse the MPC specification and believes that the MPC specification defines a system that cannot support serious multimedia computing. In spite of this, Microsoft's Windows 3.1 and NT operating systems combined with PCs that meet the MPC specification are the dominant force on the multimedia desktop.

UNIX

UNIX is an established operating environment for open systems computing. Many leading hardware manufacturers and more than 200 software vendors are moving or have moved from MS-DOS and proprietary environments to UNIX-based open systems. The move is global, including a growing list of European vendors, but penetration for desktop personal computer applications is trivial and it is not growing.

UNIX has served as the de facto operating system standard for heterogeneous computing and has established ready linkages to variations such as Xenix, Ultrix and Berkeley. UNIX connectivity is growing from a solid base, supporting open systems interconnection (OSI) Layers 1 through 4, Institute of Electrical and Electronics Engineers (IEEE) evolving Portable Operating System Interface for UNIX (Posix), and the Cambridge, Massachusetts-based X/Open establishment which, working with UNIX V.4, was seeking to unite UNIX variants into a single environment.

In addition, UNIX made gains in linking up with RISC-based parallel processing. UNIX has become virtually the obligatory operating system for an entire new generation of RISC workstations which breathed new life into sales of workstations and software support.

UNIX has grown to be identified with open systems. UNIX proponents operate on the premise that the ability to use the same UNIX system on every machine makes it an open system. The object of open systems is not to reduce computing to a single operating environment, but to expand and facilitate computing in diverse environments.

UNIX lacks the application portability and system interoperability inherent in the definition of an open system. Depending on the application, a great deal of specialized programming may be required to port applications between a UNIX and a non-UNIX operating environment. Distribution of processing is similarly encumbered.

Macintosh

Motorola 68000 Line

Apple claims that all Macintosh computers are multimedia-capable today. However, most Macintosh computers will need to be upgraded to meet the requirements of multimedia applications. The upgrades may take the form of a CD-ROM drive, more memory, and/or a video board, depending on the application. If video at 15 fps in a small window is not acceptable, a video board will be needed.

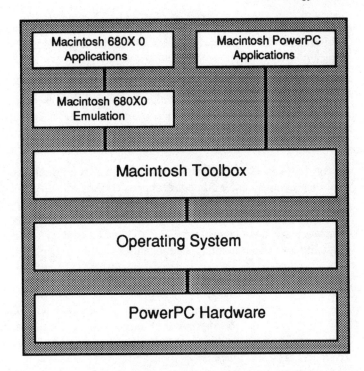

Figure 9-4. Macintosh system software is being enhanced for the PowerPC architecture with an expanded Toolbox. © Apple Computer, Inc. used with permission.

All of the Macintoshes released since 1991 have built-in support for sound and graphics. The Macintosh LC and IIsi include 8-bit video and digital audio as standard features as do the Quadra models.

Apple expects that the needs of many of their customers will continue to be met by the 680X0 complex instruction set computer (CISC) architecture and the capabilities of System 7 (Apple Computer 1991). They anticipate introducing desktop, portable and low-cost systems well after the release of the RISC-based systems in 1994–1995. Work environments and networks will support 680X0 and RISC models using the toolbox shown in Figure 9-4. Users will be able to move disks, files, data, and applications easily and seamlessly between the two environments.

System 7 will be enhanced with the following improvements to the basic operating system, Toolbox layers, and the desktop environment.

• Enhanced navigation—future versions of the Finder will extend the Find facility to include access by content in addition to file name.

• Improved help—System 7 Balloon help will be enhanced to include context-sensitive help in addition to shortcuts and power user tips.

- Speech integration—text-to-speech and speech-recognition capabilities will augment the visual interface. These technologies will enable remote access to desktop resources using the telephone.

- Multimedia enhancements—QuickTime provides an architecture for time-based media including audio, video, and animation. Application tools such as word processors, spreadsheets, and databases can incorporate audio and video clips, animation, or images. New compression schemes, add-on hardware such as digitizer boards, and other media peripherals can be added without modification to application programs.

- Imaging—Apple believes that a breakthrough in color publishing is just around the corner. Costs for color printers, scanners, copiers, and displays is dropping rapidly. Digital photography will become an important extension to the desktop. Apple plans to deliver additional type, type-layout, and printing capabilities. The new line layout manager and enhancements to TrueType font technology will provide typographic-quality text layout to all applications tools.

Apple's Open Collaboration Environment

Apple Computer, Inc. plans to enhance System 7.0 with the Open Collaboration Environment (OCE), to support user interaction and collaboration through personal computers. The OCE will include uniform directory, security, and transport services for developers to create collaborative applications.

Apple intends to provide a complete set of programmatic interfaces, foundation services, user-level capabilities, and servers. The key characteristics of the collaboration environment are:

- A full suite of tools and programmatic interfaces in the areas of messaging, directory, privacy, security public-key based digital signatures, and e-mail, which extend and complement the Inter Application Communication (IAC) capability of System 7.0.

- An open-system architecture providing the ability to integrate existing and emerging alternative message transports, directory services, e-mail, and emerging industry standards such as X.400.

- Interfaces include the Open Messaging Interface (OMI) for mail and messaging services, which will enhance portability of mail-enabled applications across different computer platforms.

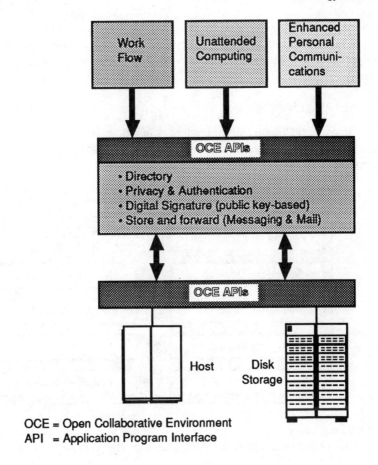

Figure 9-5. The OCE will make it possible to build applications that collaborate on different types of tasks. © Apple Computer, Inc. used with permission.

Macintosh users will have the capability to interact with others anywhere, anytime, and regardless of their location—home, office, classroom, or on the move. The system will include a consistent, intuitive, and integrated facility for directory look-up and common collaborative functions such as addressing and mailing letters and documents from any application.

OCE defines APIs that application developers can use to write a common set of network services. In addition, the vendors that provide back-end components such as database servers can use APIs to the same set of services as shown in Figure 9-5.

Users can anticipate innovative, new communication–rich applications that support business activities such as information, activity, and communication management, workflow, and special service agents. For instance, everyday work activities such as the preparation, approval, and processing of work orders, expense reports, and other business documents will be automated by using applications that build on the OCE. Furthermore, Apple's new system facilities will enable network-based service agents such as news clippings and stock market monitors to deliver customized information to Macintosh users.

PowerPC Line

The PowerPC family of computers is based on the PowerPC architecture, which is being jointly developed by Apple, IBM, and Motorola, will give Apple two product families as shown in Figure 9-6.

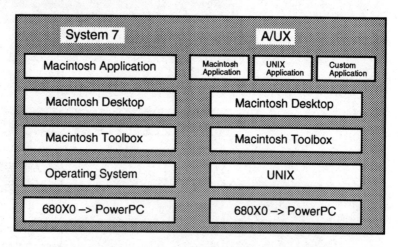

Figure 9-6. Apple will have two product families, defined by System 7 and A/UX system software architectures. © Apple Computer, Inc. used with permission.

This new architecture is based on IBM's Performance Optimized Enhanced RISC (POWER) architecture. Current POWER models deliver up to 56 million instructions per second (MIPS) and 23 million floating point operations per second (MFLOPS). It is expected that the design and production expertise of the partners will enable them to exceed these performance specifications. Products will be available in the 1994–1995 time frame.

The PowerPC will be supported by the PowerOpen software reference standard, which integrates Apple's A/UX®, IBM's AIX, and the OSF/1 UNIX kernel. A/UX is the foundation for Apple's open-systems line of Macintosh workstations. A/UX provides the same GUI and runs the same applications as System 7, but it is based on a UNIX foundation.

The power of the RISC and the expanded Toolbox will enable people to interact with the PowerPC in the following ways

• With 50 to 100 MIPS available, speaker-independent speech recognition with a large vocabulary will be possible without add-on hardware.

• Language technologies such as foreign-language translation, syntax, and semantic analysis will provide on-line writing support. When combined with speech recognition, these technologies will lead to support for dictation.

• Three-dimensional graphics and simulation applications with real-time compression/decompression and real-time three-dimensional data manipulation will be available to mainstream computer users.

• Standard application tools such as word processors and databases will include real-time acquisition and editing of sound, 24-bit graphics, and digital video.

• Telephony, videoconferencing, and other workgroup applications will be facilitated.

The computers will incorporate multimedia functions so that word processing programs will be able to include graphics and digital video in documents and support videoconferencing.

Apple will continue to introduce new Macintosh personal computers based on Motorola, Inc. 68000 processor family after the PowerPC versions appear—and the latter will be upward-compatible with the former. These commitments appear in a new *Blueprint for the Decade* (Apple Computer, 1991), which also says that System 7 will be enhanced to support applications written for Microsoft Windows and MS-DOS and be capable of reading Windows disks.

Apple expects demand for multimedia players for the home to grow rapidly, suggesting they will broaden access to a wider audience, "and we anticipate that their high-quality graphics, sound, video, and animation will cause the entertainment and education segments of the technology market to grow rapidly, especially as prices drop" (Blueprint for the Decade 1991).

Although Sony Corp. was believed to be Apple's chosen partner on the consumer market, the Blueprint notes that Apple has enlisted the support of several other consumer electronics firms besides Sony. Apple also promises to offer color laser printers and three-dimensional workstations.

In a foreword, chairman John Sculley says, "As the computer industry increasingly requires complex interdependencies for the development of new industry standards, Apple will no longer go the distance alone." Apple intends to work more closely with major companies in an effort to develop leading edge products through partnerships and licensing arrangements.

MULTIMEDIA EXTENSIONS

QuickTime

QuickTime is a significant and fundamental extension to the Macintosh operating system that provides capabilities for combining video, sound, graphics, and text by simply cutting and pasting. QuickTime consists of four major components: system software, file formats, Apple compressors, and human interface standards. The system software includes Movie Toolbox, image compression manager, and component manager. In future, Apple has committed to deliver the additional functionality listed under "future attractions" in Figure 9-7.

A new file format called "Movie" specifies dynamic data such as audio, video, and animation. The Movie Toolbox makes it easy for developers to incorporate support for movies in their applications.

The PICT file format (an object-oriented graphic file format) is extended to support image compression, so that users can open a compressed file from within any existing application.

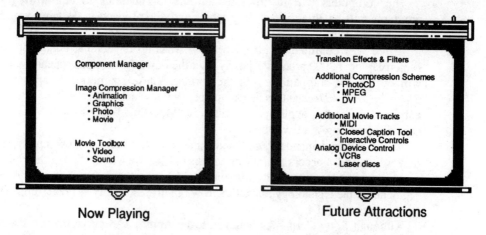

Now Playing   Future Attractions

Figure 9-7. QuickTime makes it easy to use dynamic media and planned improvements will extend its usefulness in multimedia applications.

Three compressor/decompressors are included for still images, animation and video. Photo compression is implemented in accordance with the JPEG standard as part of the system software. Animation compression is based on run-length encoding principles to compress computer-generated sequences from 1 to 32 bits in color depth. This compression scheme handles animation at acceptable speeds on all Macintoshes. Video compression, based on an Apple proprietary scheme, allows digitized sequences to playback from hard disk or CD-ROM in real time in a 160 by 120 pixel window at 15 fps.

The human interface guidelines ensure ease of use and consistency across applications when dealing with dynamic data.

In January 1992, Apple announced that it will begin development of tools to allow users of other computers to integrate dynamic data such as sound, video, and "Movie" into applications on other computer platforms.

The Apple announcement was made a year after Microsoft released beta versions of its Multimedia Development Kit (MDK) to independent software developers (ISDs), including those developing on the Macintosh. The MDK, officially released in August of 1990, includes a Movie converter disk for moving QuickTime Movies to Microsoft Windows multimedia applications. Apple ISDs can leverage the investment they make in Apple QuickTime-compatible products by porting them to the Microsoft Windows MPC platform.

The QuickTime Movie Exchange Toolkit for developers will support a wide range of platforms including MS-DOS, Cray, Silicon Graphics, Sun, Digital, and IBM computers. The kit will contain utilities to allow a developer on another platform to convert the multimedia application program to QuickTime. The completed conversion can then be distributed over a network or on a floppy disk.

Corel Systems Corp. file format translators are included as a part of a Macintosh utility in the QuickTime Starter Kit. The Corel translators allow for the conversion of the MS-DOS and Windows format presentation, graphics, and animation files to the Apple QuickTime Movie file.

Microsoft supports the full-motion video program by implementing QuickTime as an add-in to Microsoft Excel and Microsoft Word. By using QuickTime as an add-in to Excel, a user could place a series of charts in QuickTime and play them back in a movie format to show changes in data over a specified time period.

In Microsoft Word, users who install QuickTime will have an "insert/movie" command on their menu. Any movie developed in QuickTime format can be posted into Word and played back.

QuickTime movies in Word could be used to train new customer service employees by placing short movie scenarios in on-line customer service manual. Travel agencies could include short movies of various vacation locales into an electronic travel guide for viewing by vacation planners.

Apple's version of UNIX, A/UX 3.0 integrates QuickTime into the Macintosh running the UNIX operating system. A/UX 3.0 is one of the first UNIX-based systems in the computer industry to integrate dynamic data "movies" into documents.

The first generation of QuickTime is capable of video playback at 10 to 15 fps depending on the speed of the Macintosh. Adding the QuickTime extension to the system folder enables any color Macintosh (an LC or better) to play back prerecorded movies. Third-party video boards, developed specifically for QuickTime, handle compression and the video display to provide full screen movies at 30 fps.

New Video Corp.'s board lets Macintoshes compress and play QuickTime movies with full-screen at 30 fps on displays as large as 16 inches, along with stereo sound. The EyeQ Delivery board is a NuBus card that uses Intel Corp.'s i750B video processor and DVI compression technology. This is the same capability used by IBM in the ActionMedia product. Using DVI, New Video's board compresses video and sound in ratios of up to 160 to 1. Thus a CD-ROM can hold an hour of full-screen, full-motion video with 16-bit stereo sound.

A QuickTime Developer Toolkit is available from Storm Technology. The kit includes Storm's NuBus accelerator card, documentation, and a QuickTime JPEG image compressor called Quickpress that runs on the card.

Premiere 2.0 from Adobe Systems, Inc. can be used by information presenters or professional-level video editors to edit QuickTime movies. Premiere 2.0 features include CD-quality audio, Society of Motion Picture and Technology Engineers (SMPTE) time code support, chromakeying, luminance keying, and many other video editing and control capabilities. Premiere 2.0 can be used with the Digital Film card from SuperMac Technology. The Digital Film card supports real-time recording of National Television Systems Committee (NTSC) and phase alternating line (PAL) video with a resolution of 640 by 480 pixels at 30 fps and simultaneous digitization of CD-quality audio.

The products mentioned above transform QuickTime movie capability from the realm of jerky video in small windows to full-screen, full-motion video.

Microsoft's Multimedia Extensions to Windows

Microsoft's MME1.0 added support for a wide range of multimedia devices and data types including audio, animation, motion video, and images to the core functionality of Windows, and enabled multimedia applications to run on Multimedia PCs. MME provides consistent access to a variety of external devices through the Media Control Interface (MCI), file formats, Dynamic Link Libraries (DLLs), and limited compression technologies shown in Figure 9-8. Key features include the following

• MCI provides a standard, extensible mechanism for supporting a range of time-based media and devices including videodisc and videotape, audio, animation, and digital motion video.

MCI gives applications a standard way to access and play videodisc players, MIDI sequencers, audio digitizers and scanners. The MIDI is described in detail later in this chapter under the Media section. CD-ROM is a standard because it is included in the basic MPC specification. Microsoft's Multimedia Movie (MMM), which evolved from the animation-player technology licensed from Macromedia, provides a consistent file format that incorporates animation, sound, and some scripting in the form of MCI commands.

• New end-user accessories including Sound Recorder, Music Box, and Media Playerimmediately enable users to experience, create, and control multimedia elements. HyperGuide provides a graphically based, on-line help facility for Windows with Multimedia with more than 20,000 links and 3000 topics. New Control Panel applets ease the process of installing new multimedia devices and accessories.

• Audio services provide a device-independent interface that developers can use to bring high-fidelity sound to PC applications. Joystick and Timer services provide support for joysticks and high-resolution event timing. A total of 144 new APIs provide support for multimedia functionality using Windows with Multimedia.

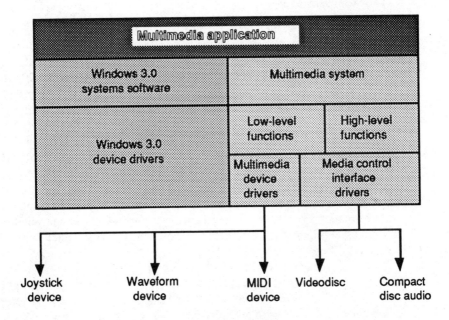

Figure 9-8. MME provides the device and interface drivers needed for a variety of external analog and digital devices.

The audio cards used in MPC computers allows MIDI to be played back directly through the computer. Thus it is practical to use the more efficient MIDI format as an alternative to digitized music in multimedia applications.

Compression capability is limited to 4-and 8-bit still images or 16 and 256 colors.

Object Linking and Embedding

OLE for Windows, defined in 1991 by Microsoft, provides a standard mechanism for media integration. Developers of existing OLE-compatible Windows applications are able to embed multimedia objects such as sound into their applications without writing any new code. OLE allows developers to integrate video simply by copying from a source and pasting it into the new application. Applications that supported OLE in mid-1991 included Microsoft Excel 3.0 and Lotus 1-2-3.

Microsoft began providing a software development kit for OLE on the Macintosh in early 1992. OLE technology provides a powerful set of capabilities for integrating information created by different applications. The OLE specification enables developers to access these capabilities by making extensions to existing graphics applications that run under System 7.0 on the Macintosh computer.

Video for Windows

In order to make digital-motion video available to Windows, Microsoft developed a least-common-denominator compression method optimized for software-only decompression that works on Multimedia PCs that was released in November 1992. Video for Windows (formerly known as Audio-Video Interleaving or AVI) is a set of tools for playback, creating, editing, and integrating digital video in Windows 3.1, Modular Windows, or Windows NT. The Windows Sound System, a complementary product, enables the delivery of sound and video for multimedia applications.

One of the compression approaches used is the Video for Windows format which combines lossless run-length encoded intraframes with Delta Frame compression. This is a simple predictive method that is not compute-intensive. Video for Windows increases or decreases the number of frames per second to meet the required data transfer rate. Both frame rate and resolution scale seamlessly from low- to high-end computing platforms. Color resolution from 16 to 32,000 colors in supported. Video for Windows will also include other algorithms that make it competitive with QuickTime from Apple Computer.

Video for Windows was designed to decompress images quickly from any digital storage device. However, the standard was tuned for the data transfer rate of a CD-ROM which is 1.2 Mbit/s. Video for Windows can be used to create a 160- by 120-pixel image in 256 colors on-screen with a display rate of 15 fps. The system allows you to make a larger image at a slower frame rate or to use a higher compression ratio with some loss of picture quality.

The video components of Video for Windows are Digital Video Media Control Interface (DV-MCI), AVI file format, and the Media Player. The DV-MCI is a device driver that developers can incorporate into their products.

Microsoft co-developed the Digital Video command set for the DV-MCI with Intel and partnered with Media Vision on the development of the technology for the Microsoft video codec.

Video for Windows is an interim solution pending the completion of the MPEG standard. In addition, Microsoft licensed fractal compression technology in February 1992 from Iterated Systems; for use in its multimedia products. Future compression schemes for images and video may be based on fractal compression, which has great potential. For more information, see fractal technology in the Media section below.

MotiVE from Media Vision

With Microsoft's Video for Windows, digital videos can be captured and played back only on personal computers under Windows 3.1. MotiVE was developed by Media Vision to allow movies prepared in the Windows environment to be played back under Macintosh or DOS operating systems. MotiVE provides system independence for digital video clips that are compatible with Video for Windows.

MotiVE is bundled free with Media Vision's Video capture card, the Pro Movie Spectrum. This runtime version can play back Windows for Video files that were captured using the Pro Movie Spectrum card on virtually any machine.

ASSOCIATIONS AND ALLIANCES

Platform Independence

Multimedia will not live up to its potential as an integral part of computing until uniform standards are available across the industry. Platform independence is a desirable condition for the growth of multimedia. Today, no authoring software tool is able to ensure that applications and titles can be played back on any platform, regardless of the platform used for development. As shown in Table 9-1, there are several incompatible operating systems and different GUIs.

Even though the market for applications and titles is restricted to the installed base of any given platform, the leading players have been willing to make major investments.

A great deal of money has been invested in titles: IBM invested $400,000 in Ulysses and $1.2 million in Columbus; Philips AIM funded the development of more than 50 titles at $300,000 to $400,000 each; and Commodore has paid for 30 to 40 titles at $200,000 to $300,000 each.

Table 9-1. The Lack of Standard Platform Interfaces Makes it Difficult for Developers to Choose

Hardware	Operating System	Graphical User Interface
Apple Macintosh	Macintosh System 7	Proprietary
Apple PowerPC	Pink	Proprietary
IBM PC-AT	MS/DOS	Windows 3.1
IBM PS/2	OS/2	Presentation Manager
IBM RS/6000	UNIX: OSFI/AIX	Motif/AIX Windows/NeXTStep
HP9000	UNIX: OSFI/HP UX	Motif
Sun SPARC Station	UNIX: System V.4	OpenLook
Commodore Amiga	Amiga	Proprietary
Philips CD-I	OS/9 (CD-RTOS)	Proprietary
DECStation 5000	UNIX: OSFI/AIX	Motif/DECWindows

In the battle that will ensue between computer makers and consumer electronics companies, it is interesting to note that both will use the same platforms for the development of titles.

Architectures, standards, and enabling software designed to remove communication restrictions between incompatible hardware, operating systems, and databases are rapidly becoming available. The open systems model—enterprise-wide shared, desktop access to corporate databases in a transparent, multivendor computing environment—is an unfolding reality. It also represents a significant reversal in the design and marketing strategies of the major technology vendors.

"Platform-independent" computing is common misconception of open systems. Open systems is trying to make computing "technology-transparent." Open systems, by definition, must be able to accept technological diversity. The Open Software Foundation's DCE, for example, was designed to work transparently from the desktop with a variety of networks and operating systems supported by open systems standards. It is unreasonable to expect that a single operating system could provide the same solutions.

Multimedia PC

Microsoft spearheaded a major effort to obtain the support of hardware and software developers for a de facto multimedia standard. The original standard involved three levels of technological sophistication, each of which added incremental media support.

- Level 1 (sound) business system was a 10 MHz 286, with video graphics array (VGA) display, bundled CD-ROM drive, 2 Mbytes of random access memory (RAM), MIDI (three-voice synthesizer, 8-bit audio in and out), joystick port, a 30-Mbyte hard disk, and a floppy. Over 5 million PCs exist that could have been upgraded to the level 1 configuration for under $1000, including a CD-ROM drive. Level 1 was intended to support Microsoft Windows 3.0 with multimedia extensions.

- Level 2 (image) system was based a 386 as a minimum, with a built-in Digital Signal Processing (DSP) chip, as well as support for still images.

- Level 3 (video) system was to have included fully integrated full-motion video.

Following criticism from IBM and a number of other organizations, the MPC Marketing Council raised the minimum standard for an IBM-compatible PC.

The current minimum MPC standard (i.e., Level 1) is an IBM or compatible PC with a 386SX central processing unit, 2 Mbytes of RAM, a 30-Mbyte hard disk, a video graphics display (VGA), a CD-ROM drive, an audio board, and Microsoft Windows 3.0 with the addition of the Multimedia Extensions 1.0. The CD-ROM drive must have a data transfer rate of at least 150 kbyte/s, a maximum seek time of 1 second, and it cannot utilize more than 40 percent of the computer's central processing unit (CPU) power. The sound card must meet the minimum of 8-bit samples at 11 kHz for the input sampling rate and 8-bit samples at 22 kHz for the output sampling rate.

Microsoft and the Multimedia PC Marketing Council, a subdivision of the Software Publishers Association, introduced the MPC trademark in 1991. The term "multimedia personal computer" (MPC) is administered by the MPC Marketing Council. To qualify as an official MPC system, a computer must run Microsoft Windows with the Microsoft

MMEs—on a platform meeting the new Level 1 specification. All multimedia products bearing this designation will comply with the MPC specifications. The original Level 1 definition has been superseded and the Level 2 and Level 3 definitions shown above have been indefinitely suspended.

The Multimedia PC Marketing Council consists of the companies listed below that support the new MPC standard, which includes Multimedia Extensions to Windows 3.0:

CompuAdd Corp.	Creative Labs, Inc.
Fujitsu	Media Vision
Microsoft Corp.	NCR
NEC Technologies	ING. C. Olivetti
Philips Consumer Electronics Co.	Tandy Corp.
Zenith Data Systems	

MME 1.0 is shipped with MPC labeled computers and upgrade kits from a variety of manufacturers. MME brings new media such as stereo sound, synthesized music, CD-audio playback, and animation to the Windows environment and adds 144 new functions to the 600 functions in Windows 3.0 API itself.

Microsoft's previously announced specification for OLE, an extension to DDE allows compliant applications, such as Lotus Notes, Micrografx Charisma, and Excel 3.0, to embed audio waveforms directly in the applications data file by simply pasting from the clipboard.

A file format called Resource Interchange File Format (RIFF) is standardized with MME. RIFF was codeveloped by IBM and Microsoft. It can be used for both playback and recording of multimedia content and is designed to serve as a data exchange medium between platforms. An equivalent format on Motorola platforms called Resource Interchange File (RIFX), is the same as RIFF except for the integer byte ordering.

The Level 1 MPC specification calls for VGA; which implies 4-bit color depth (16 colors) at a resolution of 640 by 480 pixels. Photorealistic images require a minimum of 8-bit color depth (256 colors) to be acceptable. As a result, applications based on photorealistic imagery will look poor with 4-bit color depth. However, most of the current VGA adapters are super VGA boards which support 256 colors at 640 by 480 pixels (i.e., VGA resolution).

The number of data development tools is growing. Image preparation tools and scanners, sound sampling hardware and MIDI sequencing software packages are available but require refinement. High-level authoring tools such as Toolbook, IconAuthor, Authorware, and Guide have been modified to support MME. These tools will be preferred by the corporate business developer because they are relatively easy to learn to use and new data types can be incorporated easily.

Interactive Multimedia Association

The Interactive Multimedia Association (IMA) is a nonprofit organization that has formally constituted a 26-member steering committee. The steering committee established four technical working groups charged with creation of platform-independent software specifications for a variety of multimedia services. The working groups will cover architecture, digital audio, digital video, and data exchange.

A special interest group (SIG) has been established to focus on platform-specific product specifications and the steering committee invited the MPC Marketing Council to form a similar SIG, under IMA oversight, to support and evolve MPC-related compatibility specifications.

The SIG structure creates an appropriate separation between the results of the technical working groups which can be implemented on any platform and specific groups of products.

The IMA Compatibility Steering Committee members are listed below.

3M Corporation	Arthur Andersen & Company
Apple Computer	Chinatown Group
Compaq Computer	Digital Equipment Corporation
Department of Defense	Eastman Kodak
IBM Corporation	Interactive Multimedia Association
Intel Corp.	Jostens Learning Corporation
Lotus Development Corp.	Meridian Data
Microsoft Corp.	National Bureau of Standards and Technology
NCR	NEC Technologies
New Media Graphics	Philips Consumer Electronics
Phoenix Technologies	Pioneer Communications
Sony Corporation	Video Associates Labs
VideoLogic, Inc.	Visage, Inc.

IMA will develop specifications for programs that will run on a number of standard, IMA-defined "classes," or hardware/software combinations. One class might be Apple's Macintosh computer; another might be IBM-compatible PCs that run Microsoft Windows 3.0 and are equipped with CD-ROM drives. Eventually, IMA would like to merge as many of the standards as possible so that applications can run on many different computers.

IBM/Intel Alliance

In 1988 IBM and Intel decided to collaborate on the development of ActionMedia™ II products based on Intel's Digital Video Interactive or DVI®. ActionMedia II integrates full-motion video, high resolution still images, and stereo audio in an all digital environment on the PC.

ActionMedia II add-in delivery and capture boards and system software run under the OS/2, Windows, DOS-based LinkWay™ Live! and Macintosh operating systems. Since identical DVI content can be used in all of these environments, developers can amortize their expenses across the widest possible market.

IBM feels that DVI a strategic technology—one that has the long term commitment of IBM behind it. Intel and IBM will continue to develop future implementations that will support new video compression standards. Eventually the technology will migrate to the motherboard of the PS/2 computer that is part of the Ultimedia system.

Apple/IBM Alliance

Apple Computer, Inc. and IBM are working to create powerful new open system software platforms for the 1990s. The companies will develop and market new technologies which both Apple and IBM intend to integrate into existing and future products, as well as offer for use on other vendors' computers.

The agreement covers four areas:

• Joint venture for object-oriented software

• Apple Macintosh computer integration into IBM's Enterprise Systems

• IBM POWER RISC architecture

• Common multimedia platforms for the industry

Joint Venture for Object-Oriented Software

Apple and IBM intend to create a new open system software platform that will be based on object-oriented technology. The new platform will offer major new user and system functionality, while greatly simplifying the process of application programming. It will span a wide range of computing platforms from laptop computers to large servers and is expected to run on major industry hardware platforms, including Intel's x86, Motorola's 680X0, and IBM's RISC System/6000 POWER architecture. Apple and IBM intend to use object-oriented technology in future product offerings, as well as in current operating systems, assuring that applications written for current operating systems, including AIX, OS/2, and Macintosh, will run in these new environments.

In order to implement this plan, Apple and IBM have formed a new system software company, Taligent, which is jointly owned and independently managed. Taligent's operating system will be able to run applications written for IBM's OS/2 and AIX as well as Apple's System 7. The software will be offered for sale for both IBM and Apple computers and marketed widely for use on other vendors' systems.

Apple Macintosh Computer Integration into IBM's Enterprise Systems

IBM and Apple plan to work together to further integrate Macintosh into the client/server enterprise environment in two ways. First, Apple and IBM will develop, market, and support networking and communications products that extend the ability of the Apple

Macintosh computer to operate in the IBM enterprise environment. Second, IBM and Apple will develop and market an enhanced AIX (IBM's industry standard UNIX operating system) which combines the best of IBM's open systems with Macintosh and its thousands of user-oriented productivity applications. The enhanced AIX will span the range from desktop workstations to servers, and will offer Macintosh and OSF/Motif user interfaces.

IBM POWER RISC Architecture

Apple intends to adopt future single-chip implementations of IBM's RS/6000 POWER architecture—called POWER PC—in future Apple Macintosh personal computers. Both companies will use POWER PC microprocessors in workstations and file servers. Motorola, Inc. and IBM will use their expertise to design and manufacture a new family of world-class POWER PC chips. Motorola will serve as a source to IBM, Apple and other open systems vendors. Motorola intends to market the POWER PC microprocessors in configurations that will target a broad spectrum of systems.

Common Multimedia Platforms for the Industry

IBM and Apple plan to work together to create and license platform-independent software environments that will stimulate widespread industry development of this new technology. New multimedia technology resulting from this effort also will be made available for use on other vendors' products.

A second joint venture called Kaleida is being created to promote standards for multimedia. Both Apple and IBM will license multimedia technology they've developed independently to Kaleida. Kaleida will make the technology available to other vendors.

CD-ROM XA

CD-ROM XA, or Extended Architecture, was developed jointly by Sony, Philips and Microsoft in 1989 and is used in IBM's Ultimedia systems. Software developers can take advantage of two key features: a compression scheme known as ADPCM and the ability to interleave audio with text and graphics.

Both CD-I and DVI use ADPCM to compress audio. Audio can be compressed by a factor of 4 to 1 using ADPCM on CD-ROM XA. In addition, CD-ROM XA provides multiple audio tracks so that an application could support fully synchronized sound with different sound or music clips.

CD-ROM XA drives interleave audio with graphics and text. CD-ROM players that don't support interleaving must treat audio and text and graphics information as separate files. In such cases, two searches are needed to find the information and the CPU of the multimedia computer is responsible for synchronizing audio with text and graphics. CD-ROM XA drives are capable of transferring a continuous stream of information. This enables faster access times and continuous playback of multimedia information. Both the CPU and the system memory of the multimedia computer are free to perform other tasks.

CD-I™ Consortium

The consumer-oriented Compact Disc Interactive (CD-I) is being promoted by Philips, Sony, and Matsushita. The three companies formed the Japan CD-I Consortium in December 1990 to promote the dissemination of CD-I players, titles, and peripheral hardware and software products. The Green Book describes a complete system consisting of the disc format, player hardware, and system software. The specification defines a low-cost audio/video/computer product suitable for use in the consumer market or other markets where cost is a major issue.

The disc format is compatible with the CD-ROM High Sierra scheme and goes beyond to specify the structure of the contents of files and the characteristics of associated hardware and software. Philips and Sony have licensed the specifications to many companies to encourage the development of CD-I hardware and software.

The fundamental CD-I hardware package could be placed inside a box the size of a VCR. The CPU is a Motorola 68000-family processor that runs a unique operating system called Compact Disc–Real-Time Operating System (CD-RTOS). CD-RTOS has the real-time, multitasking features that are needed to handle video and audio.

CD-I Audio

CD-I audio has four different modes, which can be used as appropriate on the same disc. The highest level is CD-DA audio based on Pulse Code Modulation (PCM), which uses the entire CD data stream. There are three modes based on ADPCM that do not use all of the data stream so that video and graphics can be combined with audio. The audio modes are shown in Table 9-2.

Table 9-2. CD-I Audio Modes Source: MULTIMEDIA & VIDEODISC MONITOR

	CD-DA	"A"	"B"	"C"
Sampling rate	44.1	37.8	37.8	18.9
Mode	PCM	ADPCM	ADPCM	ADPCM
Bits/sample	16	8	4	4
Mono or stereo	stereo	mono and stereo	mono and stereo	mono and stereo

CD-I Video

CD-I provides a range of video or graphics modes as shown in Table 9-3. The CD-I video hardware provides two separate image planes in memory, each of which can store a complete image. The planes can be combined in a keying or overlay fashion. There is also a separate image plane for the cursor image and a background plane for displaying an incoming real-time image along with information from the other planes.

Analog sources such as slides, flat art, or an RS-170E video source is converted to the universal digital format RGB888 (Isbouts 1991). The digital image is then converted to any of the CD-I formats in Table 9-4. Color Lookup Table (CLUT) 8, 7, and 4 provides varying levels of compression. In the YUV image format, Y is the luminance component and the U and V plane represents the color values for a frame of video.

Although CD-I is capable of handling small-screen or low-frame-rate video, full-motion video is constrained by the CD data rate and the lack of hardware capable of decompressing images that are highly compressed.

Table 9-3. CD-I graphics modes. Source: MULTIMEDIA & VIDEODISC MONITOR

Type	RGB888	RGB555	DYUV	CLUT8
Description	Not a CD-I format	5 bits each for RGB	Delta YUV	8 bit color lookup table
Resolution	Normal	Normal	Normal	Normal
Colors	16,777,216	32,766	16,777,216	16,777,216
Plane	NA	Both	A or B	B only
Bits/pixel	24	16	16/2 pixels	8
Use	Source	Detailed images	Photographic images	"Graphics"

Type	CLUT7	CLUT4	RLE7	RLE3
Description	7 bit color lookup table	7 bit color lookup table	run-length var CLUT7	run-length var CLUT4
Resolution	Normal	Double	Normal	Double
Colors	128/16,777,216	128/16,777,216	128/16,777,216	128/16,777,216
Plane	A or B	A or B	A or B	A or B
Bits/pixel	7	8/2 pixels	7	8/2 pixels
Use	"Graphics"	"Graphics"	"Cartoon animation"	"Cartoon animation"

Abbreviations: NA, not applicable; RLE, run-length encoding.

Competitive pressures are forcing the proponents of CD-I to add options that respond to the need for full-motion video. The initial release in October 1991 supported JPEG images but not full-motion video. Full-motion video will be available in 1993 using a video codec add-on that complies with the MPEG standard.

CD-Recordable Consortium

The success of CD-ROM makes it highly desirable to have a technology that makes it easy and inexpensive for authors and developers to write on CD-ROM discs. The CD-Recordable (CD-R) Consortium was established in 1990 to promote CD-R applications in the professional marketplace and to stimulate the use and broad acceptance of this technology. The foundation for the Consortium is the "Frankfurt Group" standard file format, which is based on the Philips/Sony "Orange Book," specifying the physical standard for "write-once" CD media.

Founding members of the Frankfurt Consortium include Philips, Meridian Data, Taiyo Yuden, Ricoh, Sony, Teac, Sun Microsystems, Elektroson, Kodak, Jet Propulsion Labs, and Optimage.

CD-R discs written according to the rules of the "Yellow Book" or the "Green Book" are in fact fully compatible with CD-ROM, CD-ROM XA, and CD-I discs. The Frankfurt standard and the CD-R technology also ensure backward compatibility. This means a CD-R drive that adheres to the Consortium's standard will be able to write and read a conventional CD-ROM, CD-ROM/XA, and CD-I.

STORAGE MECHANISMS

CD-ROM

CD-ROM has a capacity of more than 600 Mbytes and a manufacturing cost of less than a dollar and has been in use since 1985. CD-ROMs are currently the most effective way to distribute multimedia applications and content. CD-ROMs are related to compact disc digital-audio (CD-DA). Both support direct access to individual sectors of data that can store 2336 bytes in CD-DA format or 2048 bytes in CD-ROM format, with the remainder reserved for error correction.

The transfer rate of the CD-ROM is 1.2 Mbit/s and data can be accessed in less than 1 second. A CD-ROM drive that cannot support a continuous data rate of 1.2 Mbit/s will impair the quality of audio and video. Thus a 600 Megabyte CD-ROM is capable of storing just over 1 hour of audio and video.

The International Organization for Standardization (ISO) 9660 specifies the volume and file characteristics allowing access through nearly any CD-ROM drive and personal computer operating system. The efforts of Rock Ridge Group have extended ISO 9660 to include UNIX systems and servers.

Philips Information Systems Co., Sony Corporation of America, and other companies created a specification called the Orange Book which defines the physical format of a write-once medium readable by existing CD-ROM drives. The joint effort also specifies basic drive characteristics.

As noted above the Frankfurt Group is attempting to create a format that is general enough to allow hard disk emulation on any operating system platform. The proposal released at the Microsoft Corp. CD-ROM Conference in March 1991 is intended to be used with the International Standards Organization's ISO 9660 standard.

ISO 9660, which originated from the 1986 High Sierra Working Paper, specifies a volume and file structure for CD-ROM media, i.e., a generic file system. Although this file system can accommodate all the requirements of MS-DOS files, it does not accommodate those of UNIX and other operating systems that have long file names, file name case sensitivity, and symbolic links.

The Rock Ridge Group was formed in 1990 to address the shortcomings of ISO 9660. Two preliminary CD-ROM specifications were submitted to the National Institute of Standards and Technology (NIST) covering the System Use Sharing Protocol (SUSP) and the Rock Ridge Interchange Protocol (RRIP). These specifications extend and are completely compliant with ISO 9660.

The SUSP allows multiple file-system extensions to coexist on one CD-ROM disk as allowed for, but undefined by, ISO 9660. The RRIP, which is built on top of SUSP, supports the POSIX files and directories. Rock Ridge Group members include Digital, Hewlett-Packard, Philips, Sun Microsystems, Meridian Data, Highland Software, Mentor Graphics, The Santa Cruz Operation, Silicon Graphics, and Young Minds.

O-ROM

IBM and Mitsubishi Kasei Corp. have cooperated since the middle 1980s on the development of rewritable optical disk drives and 3.5-inch optical disk products. The development of proposed standards by the ISO/IEC and ANSI committees characterizes the physical and logical requirements of 3.5-inch rewritable, ROM (read-only), and partial ROM optical disks (O-ROM). Each type of 3.5-inch optical disk is designed for use in 3.5-inch rewritable disk drives.

O-ROMs are identical in appearance to the 3.5-inch rewritable optical disks. Unlike CD-ROM which was adapted from consumer electronic audio technology, the 3.5-inch O-ROM optical disk cartridges have been developed specifically for interchange of computer data (Rogers 1991). The characteristics of O-ROM and CD-ROM are contrasted in Table 9-4.

Users of 3.5-inch optical drives have the capability of performing either rewritable or read-only operations. Both operations can be performed on the same disk by using ISO proposed 3.5-inch Partial-ROM media.

O-ROM disks will store up to 122.8 Mbytes of prerecorded data and the 3.5-inch rewritable disk up to 128 Mbytes of user-recorded data. A total of 128 Mbytes of combined ROM data and rewritable user space is provided by a 3.5-inch Partial-ROM. The ROM and rewritable areas can be sized in accordance with application needs. Depending on the manufacturer, the rewritable 3.5-inch optical drives have access times ranging from 35 to 83 ms and transfer rates of 3 to 6 Mbit/s (compared to approximately 350 ms and 1.2 Mbit/s for CD-ROM).

The capacities of the next generation of 3.5-inch optical media will be increased to more than 256 Mbytes by reducing the track pitch and adopting zoned recording format (ZCAV). Further increases will be realized using optical technologies to reduce the spot size of the laser beam.

Table 9-4. Comparison of O-ROM and CD-ROM Specifications. Source: Verbatim Corp.

	O-ROM	CD-ROM
Drive form factor	3.5 inch (90 mm)	5.25 inch (130 mm)
Disk diameter	86 mm	120 mm
Cartridge size	90 by 94 by 6 mm	None
Capacity	122 Mbytes	600 Mbytes
Data transfer rate[a]	3-6 Mbit/s	1.2 Mbit/s
Average access time[a]	35-83 ms	350 ms
Average seek time[a]	26.7-66 ms	300 ms
Rotational latency[a]	8.3-16.7 ms	56-150 ms
Rotational speed[a]	1800-3600 RPM	200-535 RPM
Rotational mode	CAV	CLV
Modulation method	PPM	PWM

Abbreviations: PPM, pit position modulation; PWM, pit width modulation.

[a] Hardware dependent performance specifications.

Erasable Optical Drives

Unlike other optical disc technologies, erasable optical drives are read/write devices just like magnetic disks. The drives are based on magneto-optical technology which uses a laser beam to read and write information on a plastic disk. The optical head can be much farther away from the recording surface that a magnetic head can be for floppy disk or hard drives. As a result, optical discs are not subject to the wear and tear of magnetic disks and are ideal for long term archival storage applications.

Each 5.25-inch cartridge can hold up to one gigabyte of information but the cartridge must be flipped over to access the information stored on the other side. The drives are capable of writing data at transfer rates of 1.5 to 2.0 Mbyte/s and reading data at rates from 476 kbyte/s to 1.04 Mbyte/s based on ISO standard media for drives with rotational speeds of 1800 to 3600 RPM.

Erasable optical drives begin to be cost effective when compared to hard disk drives at approximately 650 Mbytes and becomes much more effective as the storage needs increase into the gigabyte range.

Videodisc

Storage and retrieval of large quantities of audio, image, and video information in analog format was made possible in the late 1970s with the availability of the videodisc. A videodisc player is required to play back the videodisc on a personal computer or a standard television monitor. Storage capacity is up to an hour of high-quality, full-motion video plus two audio tracks that can be played separately or together. Each side holds up to

54,000 images or 30 minutes of motion video if the images are played in sequence at 30 fps and run concurrently with stereo sound. There are two distinct formats, CLV and CAV:

• Constant linear velocity (CLV) videodiscs provide up to one hour of extended play per side and are good for linear viewing.

• Constant angular velocity (CAV) videodiscs provide thirty minutes of extended play per side but allow random frame access, fast and/or slow motion playback, scanning (displaying occasional frames as it traverse the disc), and search by specific frame. These features are critical for true interactive videodisc applications.

The video disc output goes directly to the monitor of the personal computer or workstation. Additional boards are needed so the computer can overlay text or graphics on the video output or digitize the analog video signal.

Preparation of video discs is a relatively expensive process, costing several thousands of dollars for mastering and reproduction and $100,000 or more for a complete project.

Videodiscs are likely to be replaced by digital storage media, either optical or magnetic devices since the analog environment is alien to personal computers and digital networks.

Floppy Disk

The floppy disk has moved steadily up in capacity from 400 kbytes to more than 20 Mbytes but the storage potential of the technology pales against the massive storage requirements of multimedia computing. Very-high density (VHD) floppy disk drives provide more than 20 Mbytes. The average seek times are of the order of 50 milliseconds (ms). The VHD units are read/write compatible with 720/800 kbyte and 1.44-Mbyte floppy disk drives. If the VHD floppy becomes the standard floppy drive in the personal computer environment, it will be useful for "sneaker net" distribution of multimedia files.

The industry is expected to develop floppy disks with capacities greater than 50 Mbytes in the future.

Low-capacity floppy disks are being used to deliver CBT material by companies such as Northern Telecom. Northern needed to provide courseware that was compatible with both Macintosh and IBM personal computers that would be used to teach customers how to maintain the latest generation of central office switching equipment, the DMS SuperNode. The floppy was chosen for distribution because it is common to the wide variety of personal computer platforms used by Northern's major customers.

It is likely that floppy disks will continue to be used for some applications because there are few storage media that are common to the several different platforms.

Fixed Magnetic Disks

Hard drives continue to evolve to higher areal densities, lower access times, higher transfer rates, and lower costs per megabyte. Drives spin at more than 5400 rpm to improve access and transfer rates, and use multiple zone recording techniques increase the amount of data that can be stored to 150 Mbytes per square inch. Suppliers of 3.5-inch drives provide more than 1 gigabyte at a cost of $1.00 per Mbyte or $1000 per gigabyte. Capacities of 2 gigabytes per drive will be available in the near future.

Disk drive sizes include 2.5-, 3.5-, 5.25-, 8-inch, and up to 14-inch models. With seek times of less than 20 ms and transfer rates of 40 or 50 Mbyte/s, hard disks have highly desirable characteristics for use in the multimedia environment.

The arrival of redundant array of inexpensive disks (RAID) technology makes it possible for vendors to provide file servers that offer very fast access times and transfer rate and provide highly reliable mass storage of data.

A network file server—a tower of storage power—was on display and in use at DECWORLD '92. The tower can store more than 58 gigabytes and is comprised of individual 1-gigabyte drives in an array with RAID technology and 384 Mbytes of RAM.

Removable Magnetic Disks

Portability was the driving force behind the creation of the 44-Mbyte SyQuest SQ555 cartridge. It became the industry standard that desktop publishers used to transport information to service bureaus in the Macintosh community. The 44-Mbyte Bernoulli box that is championed by Iomega was used by PC users. Both technologies are now used in drives for either type of computer.

SyQuest and Iomega have been able to pack more information onto each tracks and more tracks on a disk to increase the capacity of the cartridges to 88 and 90 Mbytes, respectively. Both manufacturers provide 32-kbyte cache memories to improve the effective access time.

Access times are approximately 20 ms for either mechanism. The SyQuest drives have average read/write throughputs of 800 kbyte/s and the Bernoulli drives have slightly more at 940 kbyte/s. Although the performance of the cartridge drives is less than that of fixed drives, it is more than adequate for multimedia computing applications assuming that the storage capacity is sufficient.

Cartridges are available at computer stores and mail order houses for approximately $75 for 44 Mbytes and $140 for 88 or 90 Mbytes.

A number of firms use cartridges for distributing the large files associated with CBT courses to field offices. Cartridges are also useful as archival or backup devices for the information on fixed hard disk drives. Although the cost per bit is more than magnetic tape, the cartridges offer random access which is important for many applications, including multimedia computing. Anyone that has used floppy disks to back up hard disk files will appreciate the capacity and performance of the cartridge drives.

Network Servers

Given the large file sizes that are required for real-time media such as audio, video, and animation, it is unlikely that the desktop storage will be viable for long-term storage. It is likely that network servers will be deployed at the group or departmental level, the establishment and enterprise levels, and in the public network. Several companies are creating the technologies that will enable existing file server platforms and networks to satisfy the needs of networked interactive video applications.

Multimedia applications based on full-motion digital video will not enjoy widespread success until networks are capable of providing easy access to full-motion video. Multiple users need simultaneous access to digital video databases from the desktop so that multimedia applications can be fully integrated into their work environment.

Computer networks and existing servers are not a good solution since they are optimized for small-packet, asynchronous data communications. Real-time media, such as full-motion video, audio, and animation demand isochronous (time-sensitive) network services with acceptable levels of network latency or transmission delay. Real-time media are highly sensitive to variations in latency, while small variations are of no consequence to data traffic.

A number of companies are developing the enabling technologies for storage of digital video files on servers and retrieval over networks. The solutions will first enable small groups to share digital video and evolve to provide enterprise-wide access.

The enabling technologies must address the following

- Servers: Simultaneous, real-time data management

- Networks: Sufficient and reliable bandwidth

- Desktops: Protocols and session management

- Compression: Real-time compression and decompression

When these technologies are combined with i386, i486, and RISC-based platforms to create multimedia servers, users will be able to simultaneously access video information using Ethernet, token ring, or fiber distributed data interface (FDDI) LANs. The number of simultaneous users will depend on the bandwidth of the LAN or the capabilities of the intelligent hub.

For example, Fluent, Inc. notes that each full-motion video session will consume 2 Mbit/s on average, so that an Ethernet LAN can only support three to six concurrent users and FDDI networks 25 to 30. Third-generation wiring hubs such as 3Com Corporation's LinkBuilder 3GH provide dedicated access to the 10 Mbit/s bandwidth of Ethernet or to 100 Mbit/s FDDI and support large groups of personal computers.

Starlight Networks, Inc. has developed the StarWorks video networking solution to enable enterprise networks to accommodate digitized, full-motion video, and multimedia applications. An i486 EISA computer running StarWorks software functions as a server for up to 20 simultaneous users on DOS, Windows, and Macintosh computers. StarWorks consists of video application server software and video network interface software for desktop computers as shown in Figure 9-9. All of the current digital video systems are compatible with StarWorks including DVI, QuickTime, Video for Windows, and Fluency as well as systems compatible with MPEG and JPEG.

StarWorks is independent of the networking operating system and only manages the video streams. Data streams are managed by the existing data network protocols. By using arrays of Winchester disk drives and a Streaming RAID™ algorithm (patent pending), the architecture provides "no compromise" access for many simultaneous users. For example, simultaneous access to the same video file can be provided to 20 users with 20 different starting times.

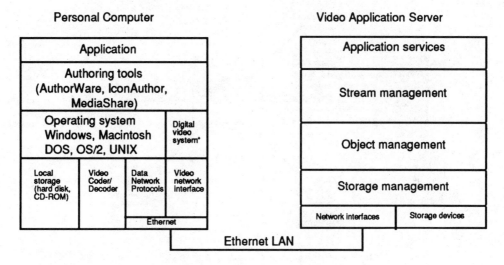

* Digital video system: DVI, QuickTime, AVI, Fluency, etc.

Figure 9-9. StarWorks provides a client/server solution for networked video applications. Source: Starlight Networks, Inc.

Personal computers or network hubs can be connected directly to the Starlight MediaServer or via high-performance switched hubs or superhubs (refer to IEEE 802.X LANs under the Transport section below). The switched hubs support multiple Ethernet segments and are capable of providing MediaServer access to hundreds of users.

Figure 9-10 notes that up to 20 users can have simultaneous access to video files. The actual number of simultaneous users depends on the bandwidth requirements of a given video format and the number of Ethernet connections to the MediaServer.

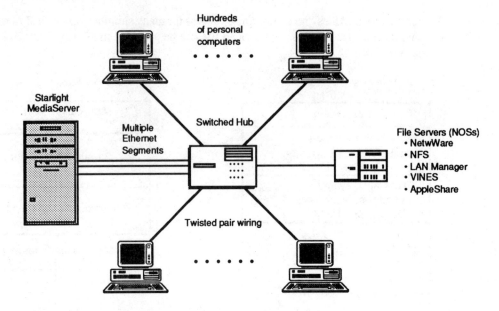

Figure 9-10. Superhubs can be used to provide access to the MediaServer for large number of users. Source: Starlight Networks, Inc.

Fluent intends to provide products that support networked video. The Fluency™ line of products provide the ability to retrieve and transmit video objects on networks and the ability to adjust video frame rates in response to network loads. By using a programmable video signal processor, Fluent can support DVI video streams as well as Px64, JPEG, and MPEG standards. This positions Fluent to address video presentation and production applications as well as videoconferencing.

Initially Fluent's client/server products were designed to integrate full-motion video into applications designed to work with Microsoft Windows. Fluency includes two add-on boards for AT-compatible personal computers and FluentLink server software. In future, OS/2 and UNIX versions of the products will be made available.

FluentLink enables digital video files to be stored on a server and transmitted on Ethernet or FDDI networks. The product, which works with Novell, Inc.'s NetWare 386 Version 3.11, was made available at the end of 1991.

The software enables users to integrate live video into an application or create their own video files. Video is recorded using a camera or videocassette recorder and stored in a file created within Windows applications. Compression rates and resolution are controlled using menus. The maximum resolution of 320 by 120 pixels is below the standard VHS quality of 640 by 480 pixels.

Fluent's architecture supports multiple full-motion video feeds to a personal computer. Scalable video is supported so that the resolution, picture quality, and bit rate can be matched to the requirements of specific applications. The ability to adjust video quality in response to network loads overcomes many of the barriers to using existing networks to transport digital video.

Although CD-ROM has played and will continue to play a useful role for transporting multimedia applications and information, either in a networked or "sneaker net" environment, it is not adequate for business operations-centric applications. Such applications demand storage capacities in the gigabyte and terabyte range and a database management system that has been extended to include the new types of information that are used in multimedia applications.

Digital Equipment Corporation realized that they are a very late entrant into the desktop computing wars and that their traditional strength is multivendor environments, distributed computing, and networking–an ideal combination to enable database solutions of the scale and performance demanded by networked multimedia applications.

On March 10, 1992, Digital and Fluent, Inc. announced a strategic agreement to develop and market a family of products for integrating full-motion video and audio into network computing solutions. They are developing a new family of hardware and software products based on Fluent's Fluency products. The new Digital products include system software and programming interfaces that allow images and full-motion video to be integrated into desktop applications. Networking software will support image, video, and audio playback over networks. In addition, Digital will provide add-in boardsets for real-time capture, compression (using JPEG now and MPEG when available) and overlay of still images and full-motion video segments with synchronized audio. The combination provides a good solution to multimedia networking requirements.

The network file server on display and in use at DECWORLD '92 can store more than 58 gigabytes and is comprised of individual 1 gigabyte drives in an array with RAID technology and 384 Megabytes of RAM. The tower can be equipped with one or more Intel 486 processors operating at 66 MHz and multiple Ethernet or FDDI interfaces. Data are striped across multiple disks so that access time is reduced and input/output capability is improved. The availability of two gigabyte drives will increase the overall capacity to roughly 120 gigabytes in the near future.

The tower is capable of storing 100 full-length feature movies in digitized form. When equipped with two Intel 486 processors and two or more FDDI links, the tower has sufficient input/output capacity for simultaneous playback of all 100 movies. This is an excellent device for business operations-centric applications serving large numbers of users that need simultaneous access to audio and video files.

IBM is developing a video server capable of storing hours of compressed video with the input/output capability for sending video streams to users over a network (Boudette 1991). The video server is expected to consist of two separate machines: one to control massive storage systems holding more than 1 terabyte of data, and a second, high-performance front-end system to handle the compute-intensive task of routing the video to the client.

Multimedia Database Management Systems

A comprehensive set of tools is needed to integrate the information available in a variety of digital media. Without such tools, multimedia applications will result in "islands of information" that were created with different application development platforms, with no effective capabilities to integrate them.

Current database management systems are fully capable of supporting traditional business applications. However, the features must be extended to handle the new types of information (audio, video, and image) that are used in multimedia applications. In addition to support for large data objects which may span several physical blocks, the database system may need to support dynamically changing blocks. The following extensions will need to be supported:

- The storage manager needs to be able to manage dynamic data types. Audio and video information must be compressed to appropriate levels before it is stored on disk.

- Users need to be able to retrieve and/or modify part of a document, image, audio, or video file because the files may be large.

- At the logical level, the database system must provide the capability to define the logical schema containing multimedia objects in a uniform manner. Operations that are provided in standard record-oriented database systems such as join, union, etc. may be needed for multimedia.

- Objects must be shown in the media that is appropriate. For example, text will be shown by a browser, pictorial data as a graphics interchange format (GIF) file, image as a picture, and records as a table.

- The database system must provide a level of performance that is acceptable for the application, even with the large files associated with audio, images, and video.

TRANSPORT

The telephone industry has successfully implemented a single, seamless, worldwide network which is almost completely hidden from the user. We are able to pick up a phone and dial anywhere in the world without concerning ourselves about who built the switching or transmission equipment or the telephone sets. Our only concern is whether we share a common language with the party at the other end of the line. Circuit switching technology is well suited to handle voice and low speed data.

The data network is comprised of millions of separate and often incompatible computer networks because there has never been central planning function such as we have had with the operating telephone companies in North America or the Postal Telephone and Telegraph companies (PTTs) in Europe and other parts of the world. Both circuit and packet switching technologies are used in current data networks.

The standards for public network transmission services such as T1 (1.544 Mbit/s), T3 (45 Mbit/s), and SONET (155 and 622 Mbit/s) are specified by the CCITT. In June of

1989, the study group agreed on a recommendation which set two broadband user-interface rates: 155 and 622 Mbit/s for BISDN services. In 1990, a platform of international agreements in CCITT enabled manufacturers to begin development of BISDN switching systems. BISDN will use ATM for the transfer of information and SONET transmission facilities.

ATM is capable of delivering all types of traffic including text, graphics, image, animation, audio, and video at rates of 155 and 600 Mbit/s to the desktop. ATM is a switching and multiplexing scheme which supports both continuous and variable-rate (bursty) traffic by organizing the payload on fiber transmission facilities.

Although multimedia applications do not dominate network traffic as yet, they could speed up the evolution of broadband networking if they continue to proliferate as rapidly as expected. Multimedia applications, particularly because of dynamic media communication requirements, will promote the establishment of a common network infrastructure, based on ATM. The same core technology will be used in the LAN, internetworking, and WAN environments. Users will have access to a network that is as transparent, seamless, and adaptive as the voice network.

These applications also hold the possibility that a common network infrastructure based on ATM will develop, providing the same core technology to communicate across a building, across town, or across the country.

Although the definition of ATM began with CCITT, the standard is being defined through a collaborative effort on the part of the computer and the telecommunications industries on a worldwide basis. In the 1990s, we will begin to develop a new network that will handle all media types, provide broadband services, and give us a new opportunity to improve the compatibility of the computer networking environment. It is ironic that a technology intended for WAN use will be deployed first in the LAN environment. Intelligent hubs and bridge and router functions based on ATM technology have already begun to appear. Refer to the LAN and WAN sections below for more detail.

In the 1970s and 1980s, data networks grew out of applications developed in a terminal/host computer environment and were justified as part of the overall application development cost. This often spawned the creation of multiple independent data networks based on 9.6 or 56 kbit/s leased lines. There was little opportunity to consolidate even though the networks often served the same locations.

In 1984, the general availability of 1.544 Mbit/s T1 circuits and premise-based multiplexing equipment put unprecedented access and control in the hands of the user community. For the first time, bandwidth could be managed to suit the quality of service, cost objectives, and applications requirements of individual business environments. Voice and data shared the same transmission facilities on corporate backbone networks in many Fortune 1000 companies.

Another phenomenon occurred in 1984 as the personal computer moved from the hobby to the business environment. Almost immediately there was a need to connect to other personal computer users. As a result, personal computer networks grew from the individual to the workgroup, from the workgroup to the department or establishment, from the establishment to the organization, and finally from organization to organization.

The internetworking requirement that resulted from this growth was satisfied by bridges and routers.

Over the next decade, businesses will be able to choose digital facilities at bandwidths from Nx64 kbit/s to 155 Mbit/s, as dedicated lines or switched services in circuit switched or fast packet switched mode. Frame relay and Switched Multi-Megabit Data Service (SMDS) represent a major push by the Regional Bell Operating Companies (RBOCs) and the IECs into the data networking market. Both frame relay and SMDS are stepping stones on the path to BISDN. BISDN will provide services for all digital media at bandwidths that range from 155 Mbit/s to 2.4 gigabit/s.

The elements that will be available for deployment in the broadband network of the 1990s are shown in Table 9-5.

Table 9-5. Multimedia Networks Are Being Implemented Using Broadband Network Elements in Addition to Current Networking Technologies

FDDI	100 Mbit/s fiber LAN–Products are available now Driven by the computer industry for premise/campus applications Developed for data initially, but evolving to multimedia
SONET	Synchronous Optical Network–Products are available now LEC solution for fiber networks Hierarchy based on multiples of 51 Mbit/s–155 and 600 Mbit/s, 1.2 and 2.4 gigabit/s
IEEE 802.6	Metropolitan Area Network (MAN)–trials in 1991 Driven by LEC desire to serve the LAN interconnect market Data initially with evolution to multimedia BISDN compatible
SMDS	Switched Multi-Megabit Data Service–trials in 1991 and 1992 Defined by Bell Communications Research (Bellcore) Operate initially at 1.5 and 45 Mbit/s with evolution to higher speeds Service "envelope" for voice, data and video applications on the MAN Will evolve to be compatible with BISDN
BISDN	Standard available in 1992 Carrier solution for multimedia services (audio, text, graphics, animation, image, and video) ATM 53-byte cells with interfaces defined at 155 and 600 Mbit/s

Abbreviations: MAN, metropolitan area network

Local exchange carriers (LECs), including the RBOCs, have not been successful in selling data services in the past, partly because they did not have strong data service offerings. In addition, they were hampered by regulatory constraints on pricing and operations. Historically, the LECs have been a strong channel to the small business and residential markets.

However, the RBOCs are particularly intent on developing new lines of business. Since divestiture, they have done an admirable job of reducing costs, but little has been done to generate new revenue. As a result, the RBOCs are determined to provide new, revenue-generating services for the multimedia communications market.

The Communications Utility

As noted above, voice and data networks were developed as separate entities using different switching and distribution schemes. In most offices, separate wiring systems are used to deliver telephone and computer communications services. Until codecs that operated at 56/64 or 112/128 kbit/s became available, videoconferencing services required a third network. Communications switching vendors have had limited success in efforts to add data networking to their portfolios and LAN vendors have not been able to successfully add voice to data networks.

While it is clear that ATM-based products combined with broadband transmission facilities will offer a homogenous network capable of transporting all media types including video, it will take several years to evolve to this new network. An alternative that is available now may satisfy the needs of networked multimedia applications. Enabling technology developed by First Pacific Networks of Sunnyvale, California is capable of delivering voice, video, and data to the desktop simultaneously on a single wiring scheme.

Wideband distribution systems based on fiber/coax, thin Ethernet coax, or shielded twisted pair (STP) wiring can be used. The bandwidth of the distribution system is subdivided into individual radio frequency channels and into blocks of bandwidth for receiving and transmitting information. Bandwidth can be allocated for telephone, data communications, and analog and digital video services.

First Pacific Networks' Personal Xchange system treats communications as a utility and allows voice, data and video networks to coexist on a single wiring system. As shown in Figure 9-11, the intelligence is located at each end-user device, similar to the way that LANs are implemented, instead of in a central system, such as a private branch exchange (PBX) or host computer. Intelligent interface units support telephones, personal computers, shared network devices (such as file servers, printers, gateways, and bridges), NTSC, or other video devices.

The *Personal Xchange* supports all major voice, data and video standards including ISDN primary rate, Ethernet, PC Network, Transmission Control Protocol/Internet Protocol (TCP/IP), NTSC and High Definition Television (HDTV).

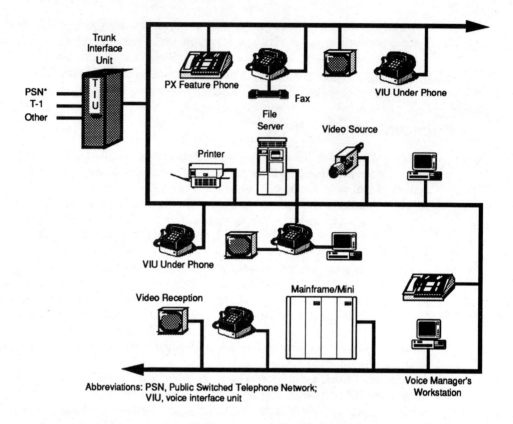

Figure 9-11. The intelligent distribution system channels and distributes several forms of information. Source: © First Pacific Networks., Inc.

Local Area Networks

The personal computer engendered an entirely new way to build large networks. Previously networks were constructed by building a backbone first. Service was extended from the backbone to the establishment over the network tails and then to the individual desktop.

Although personal computers were stand-alone devices in the beginning, the nature of the applications soon created a need for interconnection of the individuals in a workgroup. This was followed by the need to connect workgroups in an establishment and finally by the need to interconnect establishments. For the first time in history, networks were created outward from the user to the backbone rather than from the backbone to the user.

LANs have become a universal mechanism for large numbers of users to share relatively high bandwidths on a contention basis. Network resources such as file servers and print servers can be shared by all parties on the LAN and all parties connected to the LAN through bridges and routers. LAN operating systems provide services on a "democratic" basis to all users experience the same level of performance over a full range of operating conditions. This type of operation is well suited to the bursty type of traffic that is generated by desktop applications based on the use of text, graphics, and image files. However, it is not appropriate for time-dependent media such as audio, video, and animation. The LAN industry is taking a number of steps that enable the worldwide installed base of LANs to cope with dynamic media.

The LAN industry is moving to intelligent switched hubs that will allow Ethernet, token ring, and FDDI bandwidth to be dedicated to individual users. In some cases, ATM technology is being used to switch individual LAN segments so that the full bandwidth of the LAN is available to each individual connected to the hub.

IEEE 802.X

Data networking pioneers conceived Ethernet as a 10 Mbit/s data highway based on "fat" cable to carry terminal traffic and occasional file transfers. In the beginning Ethernet was used for connecting terminals to host computers but became the preferred solution for interconnecting personal computers and minicomputers. Token ring was introduced by IBM to satisfy the needs of their computer users.

The "fat cable" LANs gave way to network hubs which used twisted pair wiring in a physical star configuration to create logical LANs. The growing popularity of minicomputer and personal computer LAN applications created a need for bridges and routers which were used to segment LANs on a local and long distance basis.

Multimedia trials have already demonstrated the need for high bandwidth LANs. A 16 Mbit/s token ring network will support four or five users of interactive digital video, with questionable video quality. The streaming nature of audio and video is at odds with the contention schemes used in LAN operating software.

As yet, multimedia has not had a major impact on existing LANs or WANs. Multimedia applications have been implemented in a stand alone-mode, which is the first wave of market penetration. Information is often transported on CD-ROM, disk cartridges, or video discs using "sneaker net." However, the impact of business operations-centric applications will be significant since they will be networked applications. Existing 802.X shared media LANs will simply be unable to support multimedia traffic even when combined with the streaming technology offered by Fluent, Inc. and Starlight Networks, Inc..

As bandwidth requirements increase, the number of users on 802.X LANs will decrease to the point of becoming desktop LANs that serve a single user. This trend has prompted the development of hubbing concentrators which allow the LAN to be segmented so that each user has access to the full bandwidth of Ethernet or token ring on a dedicated basis. These so-called superhubs or switched hubs preserve the investment made in wiring, network interface cards and network software—only the hub in the wiring closet needs to be changed.

3Com provides a third-generation enterprise hub which can provide either shared or dedicated access to Ethernet bandwidth. In effect, users that need bandwidth for multimedia applications can have a private LAN. The third-generation hub or superhub will be a cost-effective method of delivering 10 Mbit/s to the desktop over the next 3 to 5 years.

A number of companies including Alantec, Inc., Hughes LAN Systems, SynOptics, and Ungermann-Bass have entered or plan to enter the superhub market with products that deliver 10 Mbit/s or more to the desktop on a dedicated basis. By dedicating (rather than sharing) the full bandwidth of Ethernet to each desktop and by implementing the video streaming capabilities offered by Starlight Networks, Inc., the enterprise can be "multimedia ready." ATM technology will be used by all of the hub vendors, initially to provide dedicated bandwidth at 10, 16, or 100 Mbit/s depending on the type of LAN and eventually at 155 Mbit/s or 600 Mbit/s to match the user network interface rates of BISDN. ATM-based LANs will let the user preserve investments in wiring, network interface cards, and networking software.

FDDI

Fiber Distributed Data Interface (FDDI) is an established LAN access methodology which follows American National Standards Institute (ANSI) Standard X3T9.5. FDDI is an outgrowth of token ring and emerged as a higher-speed alternative to Ethernet and token ring LANs.

FDDI runs at 100 Mbit/s and is implemented using a counter-rotating ring topology. Up to 500 nodes can be attached to each ring with a maximum distance between each node of 2 kilometers (km), with a total network coverage of 100 km. Workstations can be attached to one ring or to both. The cost of connecting workstations to FDDI has constrained the market to organizations that want to network high-performance workstations and compute servers.

Several federal agencies, including the Department of Transport (DOT) and Sandia National Labs, have elected to install FDDI networks. DOT's Ethernet LANs did not have the capacity to support the engineering documentation and design workload. Fiber will be run to the desktop to support 15,000 personal computers and workstations.

A number of companies are working to develop a standard that would enable FDDI to operate on STP and unshielded twisted pair (UTP) wiring which would reduce the network interface cost for workstations and take advantage of the installed base of twisted pair wiring.

FDDI enjoys greater success as a backbone technology and will continue to be used in the manner in the future. It is a good approach for interconnecting network devices such as intelligent hubs, including the new superhubs, concentrators, bridges, and routers.

Although FDDI offers 100 Mbit/s, it was not designed to support time-dependent continuous media and is not a suitable transport mechanism for digital audio and video traffic. Dynamic media cannot tolerate delay and there is no synchronization mechanism on FDDI or any other LAN. FDDI II will offer a circuit switched or isochronous, data service on top of FDDI's packet-switched data service. It is being defined as an upward compatible, fiber-based LAN that incorporates the current data capabilities and adds the ability to handle voice and compressed video traffic. FDDI II aims to support multimedia applications by providing multiple 6 Mbit/s channels that are dynamically allocated to support voice and video.

FDDI II networks will likely be used as backbone networks initially to interconnect hubs and evolve to accommodate BISDN applications such as image and full-motion video transmission.

Products and applications based on FDDI II will lag 2 years behind FDDI, due to the nature of the standards activity and the services required by customers.

FDDI is being squeezed by the migration of Ethernet and token ring to superhub technology which dedicates 10 or 16 Mbit/s, respectively, to individual users and by the implementation of ATM-based devices that will be able to deliver broadband services directly to the desktop. It is unlikely that the costs of FDDI network interface cards will drop to the level of Ethernet or token ring connections.

ATM enjoys the support of both the computer and telecommunications communities and is fully capable of handling all media types including dynamic media. Dozens of vendors from the intelligent hub, interconnect, multiplexer, and computer industries have joined the telecommunications equipment manufacturers in the race to enter ATM marketplace. This may mean that ATM will quickly eclipse FDDI as a the technology of choice for networking multimedia at the desktop.

Interconnect

Bridges and Routers

Standard corporate networks were implemented as layered structures consisting of a backbone and workgroup LANs. The fastest technology was used for the backbone and the slower technologies were used to connect workgroups. Workgroups were connected through bridges to departmental segments which were linked to the corporate backbone via routers.

The capacity of the backbone is limited by the solution that is chosen—10 Mbit/s for Ethernet, 16 Mbit/s for token ring, and 100 Mbit/s for FDDI. All LAN segments contend for the bandwidth on the backbone network. Network latency or delay increases every time a data packet is transferred through the bridges or routers that are used to connect workgroup segments to the backbone.

Organizations created complex data networks with multiple hops between LANs to handle the bursty data traffic generated by productivity and business software. The contention schemes used in LANs share resources equally between users. When the network is busy, everything and everybody slows down. This arrangement is not satisfactory for transporting digital audio and video.

Kalpana, Inc. is using ATM technology to implement a product with low latency that switches individual Ethernet segments. The switch handles data packets on a traditional Ethernet network using the parallel architecture used by PBXs to serve the voice world.

The EtherSwitch links workstations and servers using the star topology common to PBXs and processes multiple data communication sessions at the same time, as shown in Figure 9-12.

Kalpana's EtherSwitch and other similar products eliminate the delay inherent in the store-and-forward process employed by a traditional bridge or router. In addition, the switch provides parallel data transfer between connection ports. EtherSwitch processes multiple packets simultaneously, yielding an aggregate data transfer that can be many times higher than 10 Mbit/s.

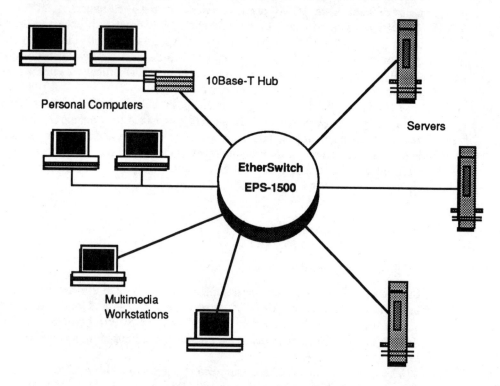

Figure 9-12. Kalpana's EtherSwitch servers as a backbone network and bridge/router to provide switched access to multiple LANs and servers. Source: Kalpana, Inc.

Multiplexers

As is the case for the major vendors of intelligent hubs, the T1 multiplexer vendors are aimed squarely at ATM technology for future products. Several vendors have developed T3 products based on a SONET switching matrix, which allows them to move to 155 Mbit/s or higher when SONET facilities are available. The current interfaces for the SONET-based products are T1 and T3, since both are available on a widespread basis.

The multiplexer market enjoyed incredible growth in the 1980s as major corporations were able to use multiplexers on private T1 networks. Voice transmission costs were the critical factor that made it feasible to justify the cost of establishing a private T1 network. Multiplexers used ADPCM to double the number of voice calls that a T1 link could carry. Analog voice is normally converted to a 64 kbit/s digital signal using an international standard known as PCM. Businesses were able to convert from analog networks to digital networks, carry both voice and data traffic, and save money. Typical payback periods for a T1 multiplexer investment were 12 to 18 months.

As the bandwidth requirements of corporations increased because of data center consolidation, increased use of LANs and implementation of high-bandwidth applications for imaging, concurrent engineering, and CAD/CAM, T3 multiplexers started to emerge. With 28 times the bandwidth, the tariff for a T3 link is roughly the same as five to eight T1 links. Thus T3 services provide economies of scale to companies that need large amounts of bandwidth between individual sites.

However, voice is no longer the dominant factor and in many cases businesses choose to use the virtual private network services offered by the major carriers rather than continuing to operate private networks. The focus of the multiplexer companies has shifted to multimedia and other high-bandwidth applications. As a result multiplexer products are incorporating router functionality and will incorporate intelligent hub technologies so they can serve the desktop.

SONET multiplexers will continue to be attractive to businesses that want to operate private data networks and have sufficient aggregate traffic between company sites to justify the cost of dedicated lines. The addition of frame relay and/or SMDS interfaces to a multiplexer allows private network operators to lease sufficient dedicated line capacity to satisfy the average load and to use switched network services to accommodate the peak load.

Hub vendors intend to use ATM technology to satisfy the bandwidth requirements of the desktop and to add WAN switching and routing capabilities. As shown in Figure 9-13, multiplexer vendors will use ATM technology to handle WAN switching and routing and add LAN hubbing capabilities. By the middle of this decade, it will be difficult to distinguish between the products offered by the different vendor communities. Both will be offering an integrated enterprise switch.

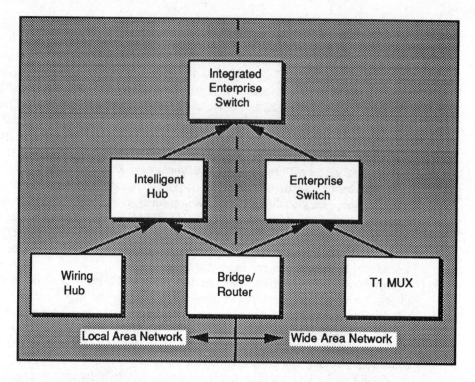

Figure 9-13. Although the starting points are different, the LAN hub and multiplexer vendors are headed on a collision course because ATM technology can serve both environments.

Wide Area Network

The WAN is served by the LECs and the IECs who provide an array of services that is being augmented by the addition of frame relay and SMDS in the near term and BISDN in the long term. Figure 9-14 covers the array of services that will be available from LECs or IECs in the 1990s.

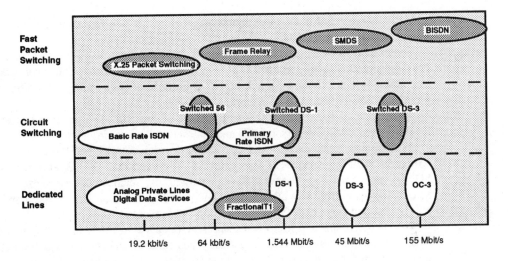

Figure 9-14. The gaps in traditional service offerings are being filled with the addition of new circuit switched and fast packet switched services.

Point-to-Point Services

Leased lines are available at speeds from 9.6 kbit/s up to 45 Mbit/s on a widespread basis and on a limited basis at 155 Mbit/s on SONET transmission facilities. The backbone networks of IECs such as AT&T, MCI and Sprint are all digital and the RBOCs can provide digital facilities to most business locations. Large corporations will likely continue to use leased lines to interconnect major facilities because they are more economical for heavy usage. Smaller facilities will use switched 56 kbit/s services and ISDN basic rate to connect to the corporate backbone network.

Many large businesses are moving to the virtual private network services offered by the major carriers for their voice networks. The telephone companies are well equipped to provide reliable, cost-effective voice services to all business organizations. In the near term, businesses will continue to implement, maintain, and manage their own data networks. However, as more switched services are made available, all of the carriers will attempt to convince businesses to use switched facilities rather than leased lines.

Switched Services

In the voice world, circuit switching technology has been applied on a worldwide basis, in both public and private networks. In the data world, X.25 packet switching technology has been applied for computer networking. Neither technology will play a major role in public or private multimedia networking, simply because they do not have the bandwidth and/or latency characteristics needed in this environment.

Cell relay or ATM is the most significant technology that has resulted from CCITT's efforts to standardize BISDN.

Frame relay, SMDS, and cell relay take advantage of the reliability and extremely low error rates of modern digital lines to provide fast packet switching. Cell relay is designed to support data rates that are much higher than those of frame relay (56 kbit/s to 1.544 Mbit/s) or SMDS (1.544 to 45 Mbit/s).

Although cell relay was developed as part of the BISDN standards process, it is beginning to find application in LAN and internetworking environments.

In addition to switched services such as frame relay, SMDS, and BISDN, the carriers will offer switched services at fractional T1, T1, fractional T3, T3, and eventually at SONET rates. Switched services make data networking much simpler since each LAN can be one hop away from any other LAN. Data networks based on leased lines can become so complex that they are difficult to understand and manage.

Switched 56 kbit/s and ISDN basic rate services are available on a widespread basis at this time. The telecommunications industry has ensured that the two are compatible so that a communications session can begin at location A on switched 56 kbit/s services and terminate at location B on ISDN basic rate services.

Switched data services must be available on a ubiquitous basis if business is to adopt them the same way that has been done for voice services. This brings up an interesting issue as several different types of switched services are being promoted by various factions. Fortunately all of them are based on the fast packet switching concept shown in Figure 9-15.

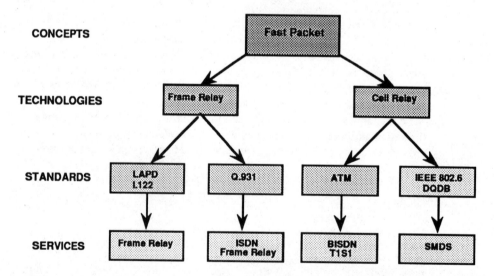

Figure 9-15. Fast packet switching is a concept that is being defined through standards efforts for several different types of services.

Both frame relay and SMDS can run over ATM networks assuming that the adaption layers are modified to support both. Both frame relay and SMDS are gaining momentum in the market so ATM will be forced to accommodate them.

Frame Relay

Frame relay is not a high-speed network. The specification defines the connection between a LAN internetworking device such as a router, and a switch at the local end of the wide area link. Frame relay defines an efficient scheme for moving packets between LANs and WANs at 1.544 Mbit/s or lower.

Frame relay possesses some characteristics of both packet switching and circuit switching. Like X.25 packet switching, frame relay networks use bandwidth only when there is traffic to send. However, like circuit switching, frame relay is transparent to most data communication protocols in use today.

Since users can easily upgrade existing equipment to frame relay, costs should be lower. Private networks can be upgraded to provide high-performance packet switching services. When price is a major issue and users need to stay with private networks, frame relay will be an attractive alternative.

Frame relay represents the best short-term upgrade path to X.25 packet switching users and is expected to capture a significant portion of the market until SMDS and BISDN services are available.

Frame relay is often positioned as a competitive offering to SMDS. Although the two technologies are different, both are based on the fast packet switching concept and both are used to interconnect LANs.

SMDS

SMDS is a connectionless, public, packet-switched data service that provides LAN-like performance and features over a metropolitan or wide area. SMDS, which is based on the IEEE 802.6 MAN standard, uses fast-packet, cell-switching technology which is believed to be the most efficient and economical way to handle data traffic (Kessler 1991).

SMDS was defined by Bellcore to

• Provide a high-speed data service within a metropolitan area

• Provide high throughput and low delay

• Allow easy integration of the service within existing systems and provide the capability to evolve gracefully with the network

• Define and implement security features, such as closed user groups

• Provide a connectionless, high-speed packet service

As currently specified, SMDS will provide the MAN service using the Distributed Queue Dual Bus (DQDB) as the underlying transport network. Bellcore released the first in a series of Technical Advisories (TAs) defining the requirements for SMDS was released in October 1989. These documents include specifications for the user interface, service structures, network components, billing elements, and network management. SMDS Technical References (TRs) appeared in 1991, and SMDS demonstrations, trials, industry groups, and related standards have also started to appear. SMDS is a very important initial step to offering BISDN services.

During this same time period, the IEEE 802 committee was developing its MAN standard. The DQDB standard was adopted as IEEE 802.6 in late 1990. DQDB describes a physical layer and Medium Access Control (MAC) sublayer to support packet and isochronous (time-sensitive) data transport over a metropolitan area. DQDB describes a transport network, not a MAN service.

SMDS operates over an underlying DQDB subnetwork. DQDB is a cell-relay network that switches and transmits 53-octet cells, which have the same format as those defined in BISDN standards. In addition, SMDS data frames use a format that is similar to DQDB data frames. Thus, DQDB provides a compatible format to carry SMDS data and interoperate with ATM.

Network access is via a dedicated link, typically from a customer's network directly into the public MAN. Initially SMDS will be available at speeds of 1.544 Mbit/s and 44.736 Mbit/s. In the future, SMDS will dovetail with SONET and operate at 155 Mbit/s. The high bandwidth, scalability, and packet switching orientation of SMDS will make national and international internetworking possible. Users who feel comfortable that the common carriers can operate, maintain, and manage such networks, will find SMDS an attractive alternative.

Figure 9-16 shows a typical SMDS network. User Site A is a collection of end systems connected via a LAN. The LAN itself is attached to the SMDS network via a bridge or router. The Subscriber Network Interface (SNI) describes the access point to the SMDS service and is the point where the public network ends and the customer premises' network begins. The SMDS Interface Protocol (SIP) contains three protocol layers that describe the network services and how the user accesses those services. The SIP defines the frame structure, addressing, error control, and data transport at the SNI. SMDS is directed at companies that

- Have multiple, geographically dispersed, business locations, each with its own LAN and/or host computer system

- Need to exchange information among locations or with other businesses

- Expect growth in data traffic and require a high-speed backbone with greater capacity than is currently available or affordable

- Want a public network service rather than a private network approach

Organizations in these markets are likely to be heavy users of document imaging processing systems, multimedia capabilities, videoconferencing and collaborative computing applications as well as CAD/CAM, concurrent engineering, and other high-bandwidth applications.

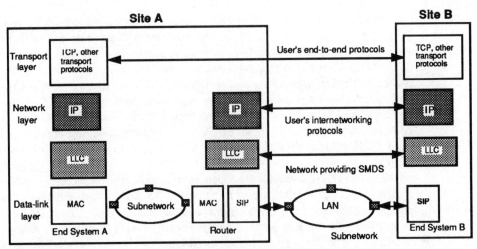

Figure 9-16. SMDS networks make every LAN one-hop away from every other LAN to reduce the complexity of data networking. Copyright 1991 by Network World, Inc., Framingham, MA 01701—Reprinted from Network World.

SMDS tariffs remain an open issue. Both flat-rate and usage-sensitive schemes have been proposed by the RBOCs. Initially flat rate services will be offered since billing systems are not yet available to handle usage-sensitive schemes. The most likely result will be to create a fee schedule that combines both flat-rate and usage-sensitive rates.

BISDN

The deployment of BISDN, that is, an integrated services digital network operating at bandwidths of 1.5 Mbit/s and above, will meet the needs of multimedia applications for virtually unrestricted capacity and allow the cost savings that result from shared resources. Just as the shared switch made it feasible to offer universal service in the voice network, BISDN will provide a universal platform for high-speed voice, data, and video services in the future.

The CCITT classifies the services on BISDN as "interactive" and "distribution" (Stallings 1991). *Interactive services* are those in which a two-way exchange of information takes place between users or between a user and service provider. *Distribution services* are those in which information transfer is one way—from service provider to user.

Interactive services are further classified as conversational, messaging, and retrieval. Distribution services are classified as with or without user presentation control. Distribution services without user control are also referred to as *broadcast services*.

BISDN is derived from the combination of two important new technologies: ATM and SONET. ATM is a switching and multiplexing scheme that supports both continuous and variable bit rate (bursty) services by organizing the payload on SONET transmission facilities. ATM is a form of packet switching that uses fixed-size packets (53 bytes) or cells and common channel signaling. SONET is a fiber optic transmission system based on a 51.84 Mbit/s building block that will be used to transport SMDS and BISDN services.

ATM and SONET provide for video, high-speed LAN interconnect, and loop carrier systems on an all digital network starting at 45 Mbit/s with existing networks and equipment, evolving to 155 Mbit/s, 600 Mbit/s, and 2.4 gigabit/s as SONET equipment is installed. SONET can perform add/drop multiplexing of channels. A key feature of SONET is its ability to create higher speed interfaces by simply interleaving the streams of lower speed SONET channels. SONET speeds will range from 51.84 Mbit/s to more than 13 gigabit/s.

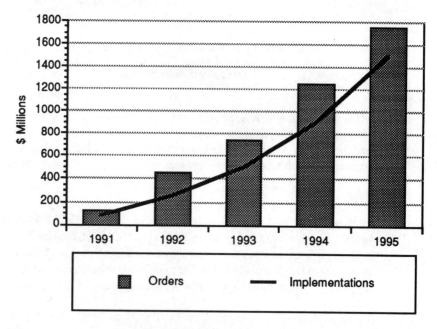

Figure 9-17. The pace of deployment will be driven by demand and is expected to increase in the last half of the decade. © 1992 ryan hankin kent, inc.

In 1990, a platform of international agreements in CCITT enabled the development of critical technology elements for BISDN (Walters 1991). At present, manufacturers worldwide are developing products that conform to the CCITT agreements. Most vendors have demonstrated BISDN switches, and several intend to provide commercial products in the 1993–1994 time frame.

Although a general BISDN framework and principles have been established, comprehensive BISDN specifications will not be completed until the end of the 1989–1992 study period.

BISDN deployment will likely occur in several phases. First, SONET transmission equipment will be placed into networks, which is a process that began in 1989. Many vendors provide the products needed to create a SONET backbone. The pace of deployment shown in Figure 9-17 will dictate the availability of widespread broadband services.

The rollout of SMDS in 1992-1993 represents an important step toward BISDN by providing switched, high-speed data communications services. Small ATM switching systems capable of handling approximately 100 subscribers appeared in 1992. Even though signaling and congestion control are not yet determined, the deployment of these small switches was an important step.

Assuming that the standards for signaling and congestion control are finished in 1993-1994, it is reasonable to expect ATM switches capable of handling up to 1000 terminations by 1994. Beyond 1995, wider deployment will depend on the technological advancements needed to enable manufacturers to build the large BISDN switching system needed for nationwide deployment of BISDN.

ATM

ATM is an emerging international standard for transport and routing in a multivendor environment that is independent of services (voice, data, image, video); independent of rate (T1, T3, FDDI, SONET); and independent of media (fiber, coax, twisted pair, microwave radio).

ATM provides simple fixed-length packets or cells, composed of destination address, priority, and service type to self route the packets through the network.

Three transmission services are defined: full duplex at 155 Mbit/s, asymmetrical with 155 Mbit/s from the subscriber to the network and 600 Mbit/s in the reverse direction, and full duplex at 600 Mbit/s. However, BISDN is not restricted to the channel rates noted above. The user and network provider can negotiate the channel capacity appropriate to the application.

The 1990 BISDN draft recommendations describe the functions to be performed at each layer of the ATM protocol reference model. Refer to Figure 9-18.

Two layers of the BISDN protocol architecture relate to ATM: an ATM layer common to all the services that provide packet transfer capabilities; and an ATM Adaption Layer (AAL), which is service dependent (Stallings 1991).

Services carried within ATM cells must be adapted to ATM (Walters 1991). The AAL performs this function. The AAL can be used end-to-end by BISDN network users or can be terminated within the network depending upon the service being offered.

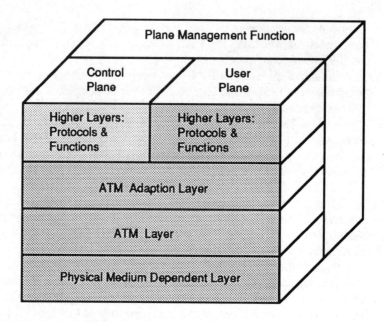

Figure 9-18. Protocol model for ATM. Source: CCITT.

For example, the AAL will be carried transparently through ATM switches for ATM connections between user stations. For connectionless service or signaling message transfers, the AAL will be terminated in the network. In either case, AAL elements are not processed by ATM switches. These deliver the entire ATM payload intact. Although several types of AALs can be identified, only two will be mentioned here. One will carry packet information and the other will carry circuit types of information.

	Class A	Class B	Class C	Class D
Timing relation between source and destination	Required	Required	Not required	Not required
Bit rate	Constant	Variable	Variable	Variable
Connection mode	Connection-oriented	Connection-oriented	Connection-oriented	Connectionless

Figure 9-19. ATM adaption layer service classes are based on the timing relationship between source and destination. © March 18, 1991 by Network World Inc., Framingham, MA—Reprinted from Network World.

As shown in Figure 9-19, BISDN supports four classes of services:

- Connection-oriented for voice (fixed rate) and videoconferencing services (variable rate), where timing is important; and

- Connection-oriented or connectionless for data transfer, where timing is not so important and bit rates vary.

The classification is based on the nature of the timing relationship between source and destination, whether applications require a constant bit rate, and whether transfers are connection-oriented or connectionless.

In ATM, transmission capacity is assigned to a connection based on subscriber requirements and on available capacity. Two types of connection concepts are used: virtual channel and virtual path.

A virtual channel, which is much like an X.25 circuit, provides a logical packet connection between two users. A virtual path defines a route from source to destination through the network. Multiple virtual channels may be bundled together to use the same virtual path.

Each 53-byte cell consists of a 5-byte header and a 48-byte information field. Fixed-length cells make processing more predictable in the switches and support the exact provision of certain bit rates.

Initial ATM standards, consisting of thirteen recommendations, were approved at the CCITT Study Group XVIII meeting held on November 26, 1990. More work needs to be completed on signaling, congestion management, and on ATM Adaption Layers.

SONET

SONET, an acronym for Synchronous Optical Network, was originally conceived by Bellcore as a standard optical interface to help local telephone companies and long-distance carriers interconnect the various types of fiber-optic transmission systems used in backbone or interoffice networks. Equipment that adheres to the SONET standard ensures that different vendors' equipment can be connected anywhere along a fiber span and communicate intelligently.

The telephone companies have major incentives for upgrading the network to SONET because of potential savings in maintenance and capital equipment. Much of the equipment that is used to connect the local exchange carrier facilities to the inter-exchange carriers point of presence is eliminated.

The SONET transmission standard was developed by ANSI and the T1 committee of the Exchange Carriers Association. The initial definition of SONET supported only the North American hierarchy of digital services (1.5 and 45 Mbit/s), but was modified by the CCITT to incorporate the European hierarchy of 2, 8, 34, and 140 Mbit/s.

The Synchronous Digital Hierarchy (SDH) in Europe specified a transmission rate of 155.52 Mbit/s. SONET was modified to be compatible with SDH and became the North American standard based on a building block which is one-third of 155.52 Mbit/s or 51.84 Mbit/s. This rate allows for commonality of interfaces at 155.52 Mbit/s and above.

It also allows SONET to be backward compatible with the existing 45 Mbit/s DS-3 network.

The basic SONET signal, which operates at 51.84 Mbit/s is called the Synchronous Transport Signal 1 (STS-1). It is made up of digital frames, each 125 microseconds long. Each STS-1 signal is divided into two portions, one for transport overhead and the other for the payload that is to be transported.

The portion of the frame containing the data is called the Synchronous Payload Envelope (SPE). The SPE can be used to transport DS-3 signals, digital video, or a number of lower speed telephone services.

SONET speeds are based on an optical carrier channel of 51.84 Mbit/s (OC-1) and increase in multiples of that speed to 13.271 gigabit/s as shown below.

- OC-3   Channel of 155.52 Mbit/s

- OC-12   Channel of 622.08 Mbit/s

- OC-48   Channel of 2.4 gigabit/s

- OC-96   Channel of 4.9 gigabit/s

- OC-192   Channel of 9.95 gigabit/s

- OC-256   Channel of 13.271 gigabit/s

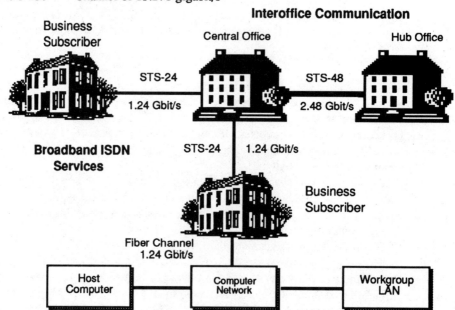

Figure 9-20. SONET deployment will allow telephone companies to provide broadband services to business subscribers. Copyright Lightwave 1991.

SONET will be deployed to serve business customer as depicted in Figure 9-20. Although it would be desirable to serve residential customers with fiber-to-the-home, it is likely that fiber will be run to curb and the existing copper wiring will continue to used.

BellCore's Asymmetric Digital Subscriber Line (ADSL) will allow telephone companies to use existing copper wiring to deliver 1.544 Mbit/s service to the home. AT&T has developed a technology called carrierless, amplitude/phase modulation or CAP which can deliver to 3 Mbit/s over two twisted pairs. Undoubtedly, improvements in digital signal processing technology will allow both groups to deliver even higher bandwidths using the installed copper plant.

New recommendations drafted in 1990 cover basic compatibility between different fiber optic systems and define the parameters for setting up a local fiber communications network and enabling it to interconnect with similar networks via optical links. The recommendation were ratified at the end of 1991.

SONET comprises three layers: the section layer, the line layer, and the path layer.

The section layer transports a Synchronous Transport Signal frame over the optical fiber. The line layer uses the section layer to transport STS synchronous payload envelopes over the optical fiber. The path layer deals with the transport of network services such as DS-1 and DS-3.

Although much work remains, SONET now provides local exchange carriers with a new set of tools for designing lower cost, more flexible and more manageable network access. To benefit fully from the potential of SONET, the remaining SONET standards issues and network transition issues (such as an enhanced operations support environment) need to be resolved.

MEDIA

The challenge of multimedia computing is to transform the media that existed in the analog world—images, audio, and video—into compressed digital files that can be stored, retrieved, manipulated, and transmitted in the computer and data networking environments. The focus of this section is on the dynamic media—audio and video—and on image media.

Compression technology is a key enabling technology for multimedia. Real-world audio, image, and video files are too large to store and manipulate in the personal computer environment, and too large to transmit in the current networking environment.

Compression and bandwidth are inextricably linked by the need to store and transmit audio, full-motion video and image files. Effective compression techniques based on international standards will ensure that information content can be moved from platform to platform.

As noted in Table 9-6, standards do not exist for compressing all of the media types.

Table 9-6. Compression Is a Key Enabling Technology for Multimedia Computing and Networking

Media Type	Lossy or Lossless	Standards	Compression Ratios
Audio	Lossy is acceptable	Standards set by the audio CD industry	4 to 1 achievable
Image	Lossy is acceptable	JPEG	25 to 1 with JPEG
	Lossless	JBIG	Varies with the application
Text	Lossless	None	3 to 1 is achievable
Video	Lossy	MPEG	160 to 1 is achievable

The MPEG, JPEG, and Joint Bi-Level Imaging Group (JBIG) compression standards are important to the implementation of multimedia applications. MPEG applies to full-motion video, JPEG to continuous-tone images, and JBIG to text or bilevel still images. Full-motion video is gated by the amount of information to be sent (up to 1 Mbyte per frame for color images) and the frame rate, which is 25 or 30 fps to give the appearance of realistic, smooth motion to the eye. Thus full-motion video requires 30 Mbytes/s or 240 Mbit/s which is a tall order for current storage, manipulation, and transmission technologies. All of the types of video communications represent represents a significant challenge to compression technology and to networks.

Acceptable compression levels for audio, still images, and video are dictated by the amount of content loss (i.e., "lossy compression") that can be tolerated. For text or data or medical imaging, compression must be lossless so that the integrity of the information is retained.

Lossy compression is acceptable for all other media up to a point. Image compression algorithms that eliminate redundant data as is done by JPEG, are called lossy. JPEG compressed images appear to be virtually indistinguishable from the original but the number of bits that go in is much greater than the number that go out.

The network requirement for multimedia can be estimated by determining how much bandwidth each media type will require. For static digital media, the content of a page can be measured in megabits. The peak communication rate is determined by the minimum acceptable delay times for transmission of a page. For example, a color photograph that is transmitted in 0.25 seconds requires a transmission rate equivalent to 22 Mbit/s. It is generally accepted that 0.25 seconds is an effective instantaneous response rate for browsing. Studies show that worker productivity improves with faster response times.

The transmission requirement for audio and video is determined by multiplying the amount of information per sample times the number of samples per second. As noted above, full-motion video could require 240 Mbit/s. A sampling rate of 44.1 kHz with 16 bits per sample provides high-quality sound and represents a bandwidth requirement of 1.368 Mbit/s.

Table 9-7 points out the need for more bandwidth to the desktop than can be delivered by current IEEE 802.X LANs, unless they are dedicated to one or two simultaneous users. Full-motion video, even when compressed using MPEG I, still requires a minimum of 1.2 Mbit/s. MPEG II will increase the minimum bandwidth to 4 Mbit/s. Note that the compressed transmission rate depends on the compression ratio.

Table 9-7. Network Requirements Depend on the Average and Peak Communication Rates for the Individuals in the Office as Well as the Number of Concurrent Users on the Network

Digital Media Type	Information Content (Megabits)	Network Requirement		
		Peak	Compression	Compressed
Full-motion video	240	240	MPEG II	4.0
Color photograph (4x5 in.)	5.4	21.6	JPEG	1.44
B&W photograph (4x5 in.)	1.8	7.2	JPEG	0.48
Audio (LP record quality)	0.68	0.68	ADPCM	0.17
Voice	0.064	0.064	ADPCM	0.016
Videoconferencing (QCIF)	0.560	0.560	H.261	0.128
Text page	0.020	0.08	Lossless	0.04
Graphics page	0.100	0.4	Lossless	0.2
Animation (20 fps)	3.0	3.0	JPEG	0.2

Abbreviations: B&W, black and white; QCIF, quarter common intermediate format

It appears that LAN networking solutions that offer dedicated bandwidth (i.e., either 10 or 16 Mbit/s) to an individual desktop will satisfy the initial needs of multimedia users. However, the bandwidth requirement will grow as applications become more sophisticated, multiples windows are open and operational simultaneously, and higher quality is demanded.

Audio

By 1995, voice functionality will be built into most workstations and personal computers. Voice will be used to enhance existing desktop applications and will be widely deployed across enterprise networks. Starting in 1991, Apple provided digital audio on the Macintosh LC and IIsi as a standard feature. Voice user interfaces represent the next wave of user friendliness on personal computers and workstations.

To be convinced of the value of audio in multimedia applications, one need only watch any video presentation with the sound turned off. Audio in the form of speech, music, and special effects adds a great deal of information to the communication and provides a powerful affective element.

When sound is digitized, it is sampled and quantized using PCM. According to sampling theory, samples should be taken at least twice for each cycle of the highest frequency component to be recovered. A sampling rate of 44.1 kHz is used since the human ear doesn't detect sounds at frequencies greater than 20 kHz. To provide a large dynamic range and a signal-to-noise ratio greater than 95 dB, each sample is 16 bits.

With this approach, 1 minute of audio requires more than 10 Mbytes of storage which is equivalent to 1.368 Mbit/s. Thus a single stereo source almost consumes an entire 1.5 Mbit/s communications channel and it exceeds the 1.2 Mbit/s transfer rate of a CD-ROM player.

There are a number of techniques to reduce the amount of storage that is needed, but all of them reduce the quality of reproduction

• Use mono instead of stereo

• Sample at rates less than 44.1 kHz

• Use fewer bits per sample

    With CD-I, there are three sound levels

• Level A—680 kbit/s which is comparable to an LP record

• Level B—340 kbit/s which is comparable to frequency modulated (FM) radio

• Level C—170.4 kbit/s which is comparable to amplitude modulated(AM) radio.

ADPCM provides even greater reductions in the storage and transfer rate requirements. ADPCM works by recording the difference between successive samples which usually requires fewer bits that the actual sample and by computing parameters which link a value scale to the rate of change of amplitude.

In a multimedia application, audio must play continuously and cannot be interrupted without the interruption being heard. Thus it is a real-time operation on a personal computer. Many of the current operating systems (such as MS-DOS) do not provide for real-time operations and must be bypassed. Although audio does not consume the raw bandwidth of video, it is more difficult to compress because there is no structure for the compression algorithms to use.

The CD-ROM XA standard from Philips and Sony uses ADPCM with 4 bits per sample to deliver adequate audio quality.

Musical Instrument Digital Interface

Computer music has existed as a formal application of computer science for at least 35 years (Baggi 1991). The field of musical composition is changing dramatically. Computers have allowed the composer greater flexibility and a richer source of sounds. The advances resulted from the marriage of computer and musical expertise. Computer music has come to mean the direct synthesis of sound by digital means and computer-assisted composition and analysis.

Modern hardware allows the sound to be heard immediately after it has been conceived. Sound synthesis and algorithmic composition tends to have merged. Most users are satisfied with the sounds created by modern synthesis machines, which are readily available and inexpensive.

MIDI was a significant factor in the advances that have been made. MIDI is a hardware specification for a serial port and a protocol for transmitted symbols that represent note, velocity, channel specification, controllers, and exclusive messages to control a device. At a higher level, MIDI is also standard for structuring files of musical data.

MIDI has defined the communication between musical devices such as synthesizers, expanders, keyboards, and MIDI instruments. The instruments may be wind controllers, saxophones, guitars, trumpets, drums, and even digitized voice in the case of pitch-to-MIDI converters.

A major trend in modern computer music is that of multimodiality. This is the combination of music and other expressive media. A typical example is the combination of video, such as graphic synthesis and sound.

Music encoding has been reduced in size by going from pulse code modulation to MIDI by at least four orders of magnitude.

Image

Two types of image processing are important in the multimedia computing environment. The first is document imaging in which paper or film documents are converted to bit-mapped images at typical resolutions of 200 or 300 dots per inch (dpi). The second is the photorealistic image or photographic image which is captured using a camera. As camera technology moves from analog to digital technology, the need to scan images and convert them to digital form will disappear. Kodak's Photo CD strategy was developed to satisfy the desktop color imaging requirements of electronic publishing, video production, presentation graphic, multimedia, and other applications. Photo CD preserves the resolution of the photographic image which is 3000 dpi.

Document Imaging

A document image processing system is a computer system that converts paper or film documents into digital (bit-mapped) images that can be viewed at a workstation, stored on random access media, transmitted across networks, and printed. As shown in Figure 9-21, once documents or photograph have been scanned and indexed for later retrieval, they are incorporated in the database and can be retrieved over LANs or WANs (Salamone 1991).

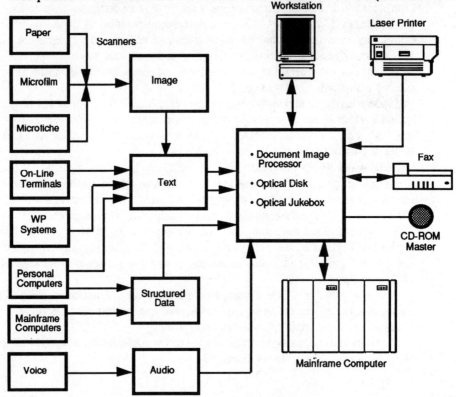

Figure 9-21. The image processing environment represents the integration of image and information processing technologies.

With the development of powerful workstations and personal computers, large capacity storage devices, and effective data compression techniques, images of source documents of all types can be captured, stored, and retrieved on-line in seconds. The uncompressed image of a typical page at 300 dots per inch (dpi) requires 1 Mbyte of storage. Lossless compression techniques reduce the storage requirement to between 85 and 135 kbytes and make it possible for Ethernet and token ring LANs to handle small-document imaging systems.

Image systems save money through improved productivity and reduced storage requirements for archiving documents. Image networks improve productivity by reducing the time spent filing, indexing, and retrieving documents. Cost savings vary from 30 to 50 percent with the type of business.

In 1990, the document imaging and computing industries joined forces. The relationship is symbiotic: imaging enhances the functionality of existing information systems while building on the same platforms and sharing the same components as other applications. Imaging moved into the mainstream with links to the corporate databases.

Although document image processing systems were designed to capture paper documents, documents originate from a variety of sources as shown in Figure 9-22.

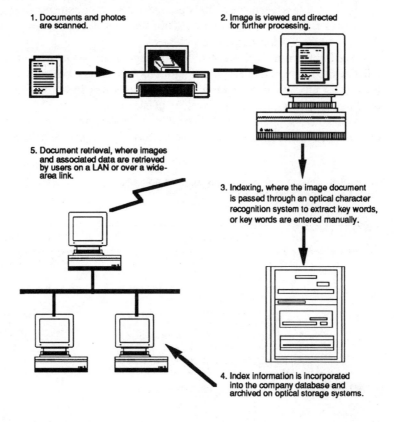

Figure 9-22. Document imaging is often described as a workflow process that captures documents and photographs. Copyright February 18, 1991 by Network World Inc., Framingham, MA - Reprinted from Network World.

Some documents are created electronically using a computer and others are created manually. Some documents have already been converted to microfiche or microfilm. A good deal of documentation comes from outside the office in the form of correspondence, forms, invoices, news clippings, published reports, and books. Voice documents created on voice messaging or through voice annotation systems represent another form of document.

Digitizing scanners are used to convert the documents into bit-mapped images that can be stored, retrieved, and used on the system. Scanning a document converts a page into a bit-mapped image by illuminating the document and converting the reflected light and dark areas into a string of bits called a *bitmap*. Most business documents are scanned at 200 to 300 dpi.

An 8 1/2 by 11-inch letter takes almost 500 kbytes of storage space if scanned at 200 dpi, or more than a megabyte at 300 dpi. The storage requirements double for a 50 percent increase in scanning density because 200 dpi requires 40,000 dots per square inch, and 300 dpi requires 90,000 dots per square inch.

Scanning color or black-and-white photos requires even more storage. More than 1 bit must be used to represent each dot. Eight bits represents a dot with one of 256 shades of gray, or 24 bits represents a dot with one of more than 16 million colors (i.e., 8 bits are used for the red, green, and blue intensity of each color).

Documents and photographs that are already in electronic form can be read directly into the system. The file sizes of images can be very large as shown in Table 9-8.

Table 9-8. Image File Sizes Vary According to Image Size, Resolution, and Number of Gray Levels or Color Depth

Scanned Image	File Size
Magnetic coded bank check	40–80 kbytes
CAT scan magnetic resonance image	1.5 Mbytes
Chest x-ray	8 Mbytes
Black and white photograph (4 in. x 5 in.)	1.8 Mbyte
Color photograph (4 in. x 5 in.)	5.4 Mbyte

Abbreviations: CAT, computer-aided tomography.

To reduce the storage requirement and the bandwidth that is required to transmit bit-mapped images, document imaging systems use compression algorithms, many of which are proprietary.

International imaging standards—JPEG and JBIG, which is still pending—offer improved compression and will have a positive impact on image networking.

JPEG is a general-purpose technique for desktop publishing, graphic arts, color images and facsimile, news-wire photo transmission, and medical imaging (Haber 1991).

JBIG will be used to compress bilevel images, such as black-and-white photographs or pages of text. This technique will be useful for fax machines as it will offer superior image compression when compared to CCITT Group III and Group IV fax standards.

The main difference between the two is that JPEG deals with continuous-tone images which are complex and dense. Such images can be subjected to lossy compression since pixels can be eliminated, to a point, without the loss being perceived. JBIG must be lossless since the loss of pixels in such simple images would easily be seen.

Once images are digitized, key words are assigned according to company policies and procedures. Some document imaging systems work with host computers to automate the identification process.

The general uses for document image processing systems can be summarized as follows

- Records management—Industry sources estimate that 50 to 60 percent of documents originate from outside sources. Imaging systems treat all documents, regardless of source, as images. Thus all related information can be collected together and managed electronically.

- Records preservation—Images stored on optical disks have an indefinite shelf life compared with paper and film.

- Archiving—The Association of Information and Image Management estimates that almost 3 billion pages of paper are produced every day by U.S. companies. Image processing systems provide a highly effective method for archiving paper documents.

- Forms management—Forms were developed as an efficient way to collect information for use in obtaining reimbursements, ordering goods and services, filing incident reports, applying for services, jobs, loans and, of course, filing income tax returns. A document image processing system archives and manages the forms. Paper flow can be improved by routing the forms electronically for review and approval.

Applications for installed document image processing systems are almost equally split between archiving and transaction processing. The transaction processing segment will grow faster now that imaging has become part of information processing solutions.

Imaging systems are used for a broad range of horizontal and vertical applications and markets and are listed below according to installed base

- Records archiving

- Customer service

- Financial services

- Insurance processing

- Legal document management

- Personnel records

- Loan processing

The factors that dictate imaging network and compression requirements are image quality and image size. Although the transmission requirements for video tend to be a dominant factor in multimedia networking, images present high-bandwidth, bursty traffic to the network. The sporadic nature of imaging traffic can best be served by high-bandwidth switched services.

Kodak's Photo CD

In 1991, Eastman Kodak outlined a business strategy for desktop color imaging and announced several new products to facilitate consistent, cost- effective use of color and photographs in desktop applications. Developed jointly by Kodak and Philips Electronics NV, the Photo CD system combines the convenience and excellent image quality of 35 mm photography with the benefits of digital technology and compact discs.

The Photo CD system allows high-resolution 35 mm film images to be converted to digital form, stored on compact discs, and used in a variety of applications. These range from desktop publishing, using a personal computer equipped with a CD-ROM XA drive, to casual viewing of the images using a conventional television set, and a dedicated Photo CD player or a CD-I player.

Up to 100 images from 35 mm negatives or slides can be transferred to a Photo CD disc by photo finishers using the Photo CD Imaging Workstation (PIW). The PIW consists of a high-resolution Kodak film scanner, a Sun Microsystems SPARCstation computer, Kodak image processing software, discwriter, and a thermal printer. Negatives or slides are loaded into the Kodak scanner which prescans each image. The operator checks each image on the SPARCstation monitor before it is scanned at high resolution and digitized. After each image has been checked for color density, it is compressed and written to compact disc.

New products and technologies include two software packages, Kodak's Photo CD development toolkit and Photo CD accessory that allow vendors, value added resellers (VARS) and end users to work with Photo CD images; a color interchange space specification called PhotoYCC that Kodak will provide to the industry as a method for representing color in digital form efficiently; the Kodak color management system that is a set of tools and utilities to provide consistent color across all devices and computer platforms; and the Kodak Diconix Color 4 printer, a color ink-jet printer designed to provide quality output for users of IBM-compatible and Macintosh computers.

Kodak's color strategy is based on its belief that demand for color and high-resolution photos in electronic publishing, video production, presentation graphic, multimedia, and other applications will be the basis for a market category to be called desktop color imaging, which the company estimates will reach $5 billion by 1995.

Kodak intends to lead this new market three ways—by providing the core technologies for ease of integrating color and photos into desktop applications; by working with third parties to create comprehensive desktop color imaging; and by offering a range of application software, systems, and peripherals required for desktop color imaging.

Supporting or endorsing Kodak technologies were a number of computer industry leaders including Adobe Systems, Inc., Aldus, Apple, Autodesk, Hewlett-Packard, IBM,

Macromedia, NeXT, Olivetti, Oracle, Software Publishing, Sun Microsystems, Truevision, and Videologic.

Philips intends to publish prerecorded Photo CD titles which will contain up to 800 digitized images at television resolution or 72 minutes of full CD audio, or any combination of the two. Prerecorded Photo CD discs will be easy to produce and will be ideal for extending the library for CD-I with low-cost titles, especially for art, sports, and nature collections.

Kodak says photofinishing services for Photo CD images will be available worldwide at 100,000 photofinishing retail outlets by the end of 1992. Kodak will allow images to be annotated with voice, graphics, and text at the beginning of 1993.

QuickTime™ Support for Photo CD

Apple Computer and Kodak announced in March 1992 that the two companies planned to include Photo CD in Apple's next release of QuickTime. Apple licensed Photo CD technology from Kodak and is making it directly accessible in QuickTime. QuickTime supports all industry standard image compression schemes in a seamless fashion.

Photo CD images can be accessed by a computer through a CD-ROM XA-compatible drive, or Kodak's Photo CD player or Philips' CD-I player.

Macintosh users can access "thumbnail" versions of images stored on Photo CD discs by clicking on a Photo CD icon. QuickTime translates the images from Photo CD to PICT format on the fly so they can be integrated directly into applications. This capability will allow users to create multimedia titles, presentations, or publications that combine video, animation, and photographic-quality still images.

Apple says the AppleCD SC Plus can read single-session Photo CD discs now, but plans to enhance the CD-ROM drive to better support Photo CD using a multisession Photo CD drive.

Image Compression

JPEG

The JPEG committee was formed in 1986 by the CCITT and ISO standards bodies to set worldwide standards for image compression. ANSI is the body that provides input to the committee on behalf of the United States. The standards work is technically complete. The committee draft was sent for balloting early in 1991, and it will be approved as International Standards Organization/International Electrotechnical Commission (ISO/IEC) Standard 10918 by 1992.

JPEG algorithms provide lossy compression at various levels up to 160:1. The assumption is that some data in the file can be safely eliminated (Haber 1991). JPEG proceeds on a pixel-by-pixel basis. It has multiple modes of operation but features a core mode known as the baseline system. This is common to all modes of operation and will be sufficient in its own right for some applications.

The baseline system is a sequential system based on an 8-by-8 Discrete Cosine Transform (DCT), which is the main component of JPEG (Haber 1991). During the transform encoding, the picture is sampled from left to right and from top to bottom in 8 by 8 pixel blocks (i.e., 64 pixels per block). Redundant data are removed using the DCT.

The second step, which is quantization, removes additional information in a manner that is optimized for the human visual system.

The final step, entropy coding, achieves additional compression with no further loss of image quality, by discarding data that are not visually significant. Entropy encoding in the baseline system is achieved by using variable-length encoding or Huffman encoding. Huffman encoding replaces frequently occurring data patterns or characters by shorter bit patterns to reduce the overall number of bits.

If more compression or greater pixel precision is needed, the extended system provides arithmetic encoding as an alternative to Huffman encoding. In addition, the extended system provides progressive operation using progressive encoding and hierarchical encoding.

With progressive encoding, each component of the image is encoded as multiple scans so that the image is built up from low to high resolution. In a database application, a user could search the database using a low resolution to find the right image. Once found, the image could be built up to high resolution.

Hierarchical encoding uses pyramidal encoding for applications in which a high resolution image must be accessed by a low-resolution device with insufficient buffer space to reconstruct the image at full resolution. For example, an image that is scanned and compressed for printing on a high resolution printer must also be displayed on the low-resolution monitor of a personal computer. pyramidal encoding

A lossless setting is included for applications such as magazine-quality prepress. It guarantees excellent fidelity with exact recovery of every source-image pixel value. Medical imaging applications must be able to ensure that there is no loss of image information, from both a medical diagnosis and litigious perspective.

The multimedia industry has adopted the draft as a standard. C-Cube Microsystems is shipping chips that comply with the current revision and U.S. European, and Japanese suppliers have declared their intentions to develop devices in accordance with the standard.

JBIG

JBIG is a lossless compression technique that is needed because bilevel and certain types of gray scale images cannot afford any distortion (Haber 1991). The final version of the JBIG standard will not be available until 1993 or 1994. A number of vendors (AT&T, Eastman Kodak, Hewlett-Packard, IBM, Mitsubishi, and NEC America) are interested in using the proposed standard, but there are no implementations available at this time.

Developed by JBIG, this standard is expected to have a major impact in the facsimile and imaging markets. JBIG was created by ISO and CCITT.

JBIG shares these parent organizations with the JPEG that currently has a proposed standard for continuous-tone image compression in international ballot. The committee was charged with the development of bilevel and limited bit-per-pixel image compression standards useful for broad application in both data processing and telecommunications. Although a single standard was desirable for image compression, it was not possible because of the difference between continuous tone and bilevel images. It is likely that JPEG and JBIG will be used together in applications that contain both images and text.

Currently, the compression standards developed for Group 3 (G3) and Group 4 (G4) facsimile are widely used for storage of images in the vast majority of image database and archival systems in addition to facsimile applications. These techniques were designed for compression of black/white text and line drawings, but perform poorly on images that have halftone or dithered content.

JBIG's goal is to develop a technique that is significantly more efficient than G3 and G4 on all types of bilevel images while also providing new capabilities suitable to a mixed delivery environment containing display terminals and printers. To do this, JBIG provides both a sequential mode for top down scan line compression and a progressive mode that can deliver images as low resolution icons that build definition until the desired resolution is reached. JBIG's compression ratios exceed G4's by 2 to 30 times on gray scale images rendered with halftone or dithering and by 1.1 to 1.5 times on scanned text and line drawings. These advantages hold true for both the sequential and progressive modes.

JBIG achieves its higher compression efficiency through the use of an adaptive arithmetic encoding techniques. Unlike the current techniques which use fixed coding tables, the JBIG coder "learns" the characteristics of the image and dynamically adjusts to efficiently encode it.

The sequential forms JBIG will be used as a high-performance compression scheme for traditional G3 and G4 facsimile. Other applications that require higher compression and greater flexibility will use it as well. An example is the minimization of the buffer memory between a page description language interpreter that generates a bitmap image and its physical printing engine.

Video

Current representations of images are based on a two-dimensional array or raster. Video is assumed to be a sequence of images. Full-motion video is gated by the amount of information to be sent (up to 1 Mbyte per frame for color images) and the frame rate which is 25 to 30 fps, to give the appearance of realistic, smooth motion. Thus full-motion video requires up to 30 Mbytes/s or 240 Mbit/s, which is a tall order for current storage, manipulation, and transmission technologies. Motion video playback is not possible on a personal computer without levels of compression in excess of 100:1.

The resolution achieved for National Television Systems Committee (NTSC) television is 360 by 240 pixels. The international standard for digital video is defined as 720 lines by Recommendation 601 of the International Radio Consultative Committee (CCIR). For NTSC, there are 480 pixels and for phase alternating line (PAL) , the European standard, there are 576 (Fox 1991).

The CCITT uses the Common Intermediate Format (CIF) for video telephony, which has a resolution of 360 by 288 pixels. Quarter CIF has a resolution of 180 by 144 pixels.

Images are also defined by pixel depth, which is the number of pixels used for each picture element. Monochrome uses a single bit and gray scale often uses 8 bits to provide 256 shades For color graphics, 4 or 8 bits may be adequate, and for color images, 8, 9, 16, or 24 bits are standard. With 32-bit color, 24 bits are used for color and the remaining 8 bits indicate the degree of transparency or mixing with other image planes.

Pixel depth relates to the choice of color space. Cameras and scanners separate the red, green and blue components (RGB) and quantize each component. For example, RGB 5:5:5 is used with CD-I and RGB 8:8:8 for 24-bit color. The human eye is not as sensitive to color (chrominance) as it is to intensity (luminance) which allowed for the development of other color spaces. PAL uses YUV which has also been adopted by CD-I and Intel's Digital Video Interactive (DVI). For color television, two planes represent each image. In the YUV image format, Y is the luminance component and the U and V plane represents the color values for a frame of video. Analog television uses 4.5 MHz for luminance (Y) and 1.5 MHz each for the two chrominance channels (U and V).

Table 9-9. The Video Information Rate of Television Sets and Computer Displays Indicates the Difference in Image Quality . Source: William B. Welty, Volpe, Welty & Company

Device	Screen Refresh Rate	Screen Display Format (pixels)	Total Video Information (Mbit/s)
NTSC television	30 per second	525 by 330	77.6
Zenith HDTV proposal	60 per second	800 by 600	216.0
Japanese HDTV proposal	60 per second	1024 by 768	353.6
VGA quality monitor	66 per second	640 by 480	220.8
Photo realistic quality computer monitor	66 per second	1025 by 768	565.6
Super VGA quality monitor	66 per second	800 by 600	230.4

Abbreviations: HDTV, high definition television

With CCIR Recommendation 601 for digital video, chrominance is subsampled to provide a 4:2:2 scheme that provides twice as many samples for luminance. The 9-bit compressed video format of DVI uses 4 to 1 subsampling in each dimension which results in 1 bit of chrominance for every 8 bits of luminance.

The three factors that determine image quality are motion, color (particularly color change), and resolution, in descending order of sensitivity (Welty 1991). Modern black-and-white VGA monitors have twice the resolution of a color television receiver, but this is not easily perceived since motion and color rank higher than resolution.

The difference in picture quality between a single frame from a color NTSC signal and a single image generated by the computer using 24-bit color is striking. This is because the NTSC television displays colors to a depth of 15 bits. Television sets are capable of displaying 33,000 colors while a 24-bit color VGA monitor can display 16,700,000 colors. Table 9-9 contrasts the video information rates for television and color computer monitors.

Smooth-motion video requires 25 to 30 fps. They are usually interlaced so that each frame is made of two fields containing alternating lines, and two fields are shown during each frame time. Noninterlaced displays such as those of computer monitors could be refreshed with a full image at 60 times per second.

Playback of compressed images at the standard video rate of 30 fps demands a system capable of decompressing images in 1/30 second or less which requires substantial processing power. For example, a board based on the 35 MHz version of C-Cube's CL550 chip is capable of attaining 30 fps.

Table 9-10. Video Quality Is Inextricably Linked to Compression Levels and Network Bandwidth

Type of Video	Bandwidth	Standards
Business videoconferencing	56 kbit/s–1.5 Mbit/s	H.261
Desktop videoconferencing	56 kbit/s–128 kbit/s	H.261, QCIF
Multimedia quality video	1.2–5 Mbit/s	MPEG
	4–9 Mbit/s	MPEG II
Full screen broadcast quality	16–24 Mbit/s	None
Digital video	120 Mbit/s	NTSC
Digital video	216 Mbit/s	CCIR-601
VCR+ quality	2 Mbit/s	None
Studio quality video	8–45 Mbit/s	None

Abbreviations: QCIF, quarter common intermediate format; VCR, video cassette recorder

Bandwidth requirements can be estimated using the total number of samples per second for the various schemes. For digital video that is quantized at 8 bits per sample, the bit rate is 216 Mbit/s with a sampling rate of 13.5 MHz for luminance. Contrast the 1.2 Mbit/s rate of a CD-ROM with the bit rates of the video schemes in shown in Table 9-10.

DVI

DVI technology was originally developed at the David Sarnoff Research Center in Princeton, New Jersey (Bunzel and Morris 1992). In October 1988, Intel acquired the DVI Technology Venture from General Electric and set up the Princeton Operation as part of Intel's Microcomponents Group.

Intel's DVI was the first compression technology developed to address the need for a personal computer-based, interactive, all-digital audio/video system capable of playing television-style video and audio. Fundamentally, DVI technology is a set of video processors and software that allows computer vendors to implement a multimedia platform capable of handling audio, images, and video.

DVI technology consists of a set of hardware elements, a C language software interface, compression and decompression algorithms, and disc file formats which allow powerful digital audio/video capabilities to be added to a number of different personal computer platforms. The video processors (Intel's i750 PB/DB pixel processor and display processor) are high-speed, special-purpose computer chips that are dedicated to the tasks of compressing, decompressing, and displaying video in a personal computer. As shown in Figure 9-23, the DVI chip set will be integrated into the microprocessor by the year 2000.

The current DVI technology (Fox 1991) uses a 25 MIPS pixel processor, 82750 PB, which can

- Decode a 640 by 480-pixel JPEG compressed image in less than a second;

- Compress or decompress images up to 768 by 480 pixel resolution using a proprietary format in a fraction of a second

- Compress 128 by 120-pixel resolution full-motion video at 30 fps with fair quality into a special representation called Real-Time Video (RTV) on hard disk

- Playback compressed on a 64-processor Intel computer into another special representation called Production Level Video (PLV) at 30 fps with good quality at 256 by 240-pixel resolution

Third-party developers provide higher level software support. For example, MediaScript is a high-level language interpreter which eliminates the need to program in C. Other tools support painting and rendering (e.g., Lumena™ from Time Arts, Inc.), animation building, and hypermedia (Authology: Multimedia from ATI).

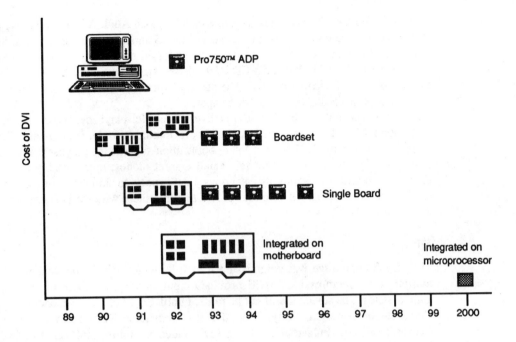

Figure 9-23. DVI product evolution from chip set through to integration on the microprocessor itself. Source: Intel Corporation.

Most multimedia platforms, including IBM's Audio Video Connection (AVC) and Multimedia PC or MPC provide the ability to show digital still images and to play digital audio on the PC. DVI adds compressed motion video, compressed audio, and compressed still images to the array of media choices (Bunzel and Morris 1992).

DVI allows all media–video, images, and audio–to be captured, stored, retrieved, manipulated, and transmitted in the same manner as text, graphics and animation files. Video files can be cropped to eliminate unwanted portions; alternate audio tracks can be added to the video; special effects such as zooms, wipes, and fades can be written in software; and graphics can be added to video.

Each frame in a full-motion video signal must be compressed on average to 5 kbytes or 40 kbits to match the transfer rate of CD-ROM (i.e., 40 kbits x 30 fps = 1.2 Mbit/s). Compression at 160:1 allows up to 72 minutes of full-motion, full-screen video (and high-quality audio and images) to be stored on a CD-ROM. Video transmission at 1.2 Mbit/s is practical on existing networks. This capability is key to the proliferation of multimedia applications in business and consumer markets.

Although DVI is proprietary, Intel has announced that future chips will support current DVI algorithms, JPEG, MPEG, Px64, future enhancements to DVI, and other advanced algorithms. This flexibility is possible because the chips are programmable.

A consortium of 70 Japanese companies called Digital Audio Video Interactive Society (DAVIS), have announced the establishment of the "Standard DVI® Player." The Standard DVI Player is a hardware/software specification based on Intel's ActionMedia Series II card, an 80286-based CPU, and a CD-ROM drive. The system software is NewWorld, a product of Digital Video Arts, Ltd. The standard was established to allow developers to create new products and be assured of compatibility.

DVI users need the ActionMedia II Delivery Board for playback, and the ActionMedia II Capture Module for digitizing, which are available only from Avtex Research (Campbell, California), IBM, and Intel. Application support for playback of DVI-based video has also been limited to a few small market niches, most notably in the video editing and multimedia authoring categories. Intel expects to ship the Audio Video Kernel (AVK) and Developer's Kit, a low-level API that interfaces with the DVI hardware in the third quarter of 1992.

MPEG

The MPEG committee was commissioned in 1989 to set worldwide standards for full-motion video compression. ANSI provides input to the committee on behalf of the United States. The standard will not be ratified until 1993 but has been endorsed by JVC Company of America, Sony, IBM, Philips Consumer Electronics Company, and Matsushita Electric Industrial Co. The MPEG–Video committee draft balloting took place in 1991.

There are three parts to the MPEG standards effort: MPEG–Video, MPEG–Audio, and MPEG–System. Although C-Cube demonstrated the first single-chip MPEG video system capable of decompressing digital video signals in real time at the CD-ROM Conference and Exposition in March 1991, it is important to note that the MPEG standard is far from complete. The video effort refers to work with video compression with television resolution—360 by 240 pixels—down to 1.2 Mbit/s. This rate is suitable for use with CD-ROM, T1 communication channels and limited numbers of users on Ethernet or token ring LANs.

All MPEG decoders should be able to operate with a "core" bit stream with the following upper bounds

• Resolution of 720 by 576 pixels

• Speed of 30 fps

• Bit rate of 1.86 Mbit/s

• Decoder buffer of 46 kbytes

Another MPEG project is investigating compression for digital video CCIR Recommendation 601 at bit rates up to 10 Mbit/s.

MPEG–Video specifies a layered bit stream that consists of a video sequence header and layers for sequence, a group of pictures, pictures, slices, macroblocks, and blockers (Le Gall 1991). The two lower layers include motion compensation and DCT data. The algorithm provides features that will be attractive for a range of applications

- Random access

- Fast forward and reverse searches

- Forward and reverse playback

- Audio/video synchronization

- Robustness against errors

- Delays limited to 150 ms

- Edibility

The MPEG–Video algorithms uses motion compensation on 16 by 16 blocks and DCT coding on 8 by 8 blocks, followed by quantization and entropy coding. Motion compensation uses both predictive and interpolative coding. Predicted (interpolated) frames are determined on the basis of the nearest reference or predicted frame on both sides. Motion information is statistically encoded.

The MPEG–Audio standard was fully specified in 1991. Although CD-ROM quality requires two audio channels of 706 kbit/s, the compressed bit rate will be two channels of 128 kbit/s or 64 kbit/s. Compression will be either 5.5 to 1 or 11 to 1. Input sampling rates of 32, 44.1, and 48 kHz with 16-bit samples will be supported; delays will be no more than 80 ms; and addressing will be possible to units of less than 1/30 second. The resultant sound quality will be close to the original.

In the future, the MPEG–System will provide a complete approach to encoding television-quality audio and video into a single stream at approximately 1.5 Mbit/s. However, there is growing concern about the limitations imposed by this bandwidth which has prompted greater interest in MPEG II, which would cover CD technologies with transfer rates of 2.5 to 5 Mbit/s.

JPEG

Although JPEG was intended for still images, it is a leading technology for playback of motion video. JPEG became a popular compression scheme, in part because of ratification by the CCITT and ISO standards bodies much sooner than MPEG. The acceptance by standards organizations and the relative ease of implementation are key to the widespread success of JPEG in both imaging and motion video applications.

H.261 or Px64

CCITT has been developing a series of recommendations for video codecs (coder/decoders) known as H.261 or Px64 which is read as "P times 64" (referring to multiples of 64 kbit/s). Finally ratified in 1991, H.261 makes use of an algorithm called Px64 which standardizes the way that codecs decode a compressed video signal. A discrete cosine transform, motion-compensation, and a differential pulse code modulation algorithm allow high levels of compression to be achieved.

H.261 is aimed at Common Intermediate Format (CIF) technologies and accommodates both the North American NTSC video standard and the European PAL protocol. H.261 covers two video formats: the 352 by 288 CIF and the 176 by 144 Quarter CIF (QCIF). A transfer rate of 2.2 Mbit/s is needed to play a CIF file at 30 fps and QCIF requires 560 kbit/s. Thus compression ratios of 35 to 1 and 8.75 to 1 are required to transport CIF and QCIF images over 64 kbit/s lines. Px64 achieves these ratios using intraframe and predictive compression which works because very little motion takes place during a typical video conference.

CCITT working groups are developing standards to deal with 16 kbit/s compressed audio, multipoint conferencing, and encryption, which are not dealt with in H.261. It is likely that the standards will be ratified by the end of 1992.

Fractal Compression

Fractal image compression uses fractal geometry, a new mathematical discipline, to achieve extremely high compression rates, resolution independence at decompression, and superior image quality. Fractal compression can be looked at as a description or modeling language.

Fractal technology is capable of providing compression at ratios from 2500 to 1 and up for still video, and 100 to 1 and up for full-motion video, in contrast to ratios of 30 to 1 or less for either form of video using JPEG.

Using image processing techniques such as color separation, edge detection, spectrum analysis, and texture variation, images are broken up into fractals, or shapes that are repeated throughout the image. The result is a mathematical model of the image unrelated to fixed points (pixels) or segments as is used for algorithms based on the DCT.

It takes less data to describe an image with fractal compression than it does with DCT so fractal achieves greater compression ratios. The mathematical models created during compression describe points and shapes—not bit images. Because they are regenerated from fractal formulas, rather than decoded from a representation of the pixel map, as in JPEG, fractal images are scalable and resolution-independent. The apparent quality of fractal images is independent of the resolution at which the images were scanned. Thus it is possible to rescale fractal images to fill the screen or just a small window. It is possible to zoom in on the fractal image almost indefinitely without obvious loss of detail.

Fractal compression is being proposed to the standards bodies as an extension to JPEG and MPEG by Iterated Systems, Inc.

MHEG

In addition to coding standards such as JPEG and MPEG, standards are needed for the higher layers of the multimedia application development process. The Multimedia and Hypermedia Information Coding Expert Group (MHEG) is developing bit-stream specifications for multimedia and hypermedia applications, that will result in good real-time performance on any platform, based on object-oriented methods. Version 2 of the

MHEG working documents, dated July 1990, defines a partial object hierarchy of both basic and composite objects and covers input, output, interaction, and linking. MHEG includes synchronization (between objects, or using marks or conditions), buffer memory, input objects like buttons or menus, and interactive objects such as prompts.

HyTime

The application of the Standardized Generalized Markup Language (SGML, ISO 8879) led to HyTime which was balloted in 1991 as ISO/IEC Committee Draft 10744. HyTime allows digital multimedia applications to be encoded in a linear stream, including all document structure, hypermedia linking, synchronization, and timing. Bit string representation is used for interchange. Multimedia objects can be referenced from the main part of a document.

A series of events and "batons" are used to control time, and virtual time can be mapped into real time. The Text Encoding Initiative draws on HyTime to describe multimedia and hypermedia documents and performance.

AUTHORING TOOLS

Authoring software is the glue that binds together the multiple media in multimedia applications or titles. Multimedia development tools differ from traditional software development tools in that they deal with a much wider variety of data formats and content types. The authoring version of an authoring software package is a development tool that is used to create, integrate, and orchestrate interactive multimedia titles. A run-time version of the same software is usually required for playback.

Authoring software comes in many different flavors. Most packages are designed to be used by nonprogrammers and all allow the user to write complex instructions without using a programming language such as C or Pascal.

Historically, there have been two primary development tool application categories: CBT and business presentations. In addition, authoring software has either been "scripting language" oriented (i.e., similar to traditional programming languages such as C or Pascal but specialized for creating applications) or "system" oriented (i.e., higher level user interface for nonprogrammers).

Authoring software first appeared in the 1970s in the CBT (military) industry. Today there are over 100 CBT-specific authoring tools on the market, with the majority supporting MS-DOS or Microsoft Windows platforms. CBT authoring software supports complicated nonlinear branching and is usually capable of tracking, recording, and scoring interactive student queries and responses. CBT authoring software began as "scripting languages" but has primarily evolved to "authoring systems."

There are more than 60 business presentation authoring tools on the market, with the majority focused on the Macintosh environment. Many provide authoring control over specific digital media such as animation, audio, or video. For example, Macromind Director is directed at animation. Even though most employ graphical front-ends, scripting languages are often included to create more complex programs. Presentation authoring tools are usually less powerful than CBT authoring tools in their primary user interface mode.

In addition to CBT and presentation authoring tools, there are several recent products that specifically support the development of graphical, object-based windowing applications (e.g., Claris HyperCard for the Macintosh and Asymetrix Toolbook for Windows 3.0). These products can also be used to create hypertext and hypermedia programs.

Multimedia authoring is complicated by the fact that not only are there multiple media, but multiple platforms, multiple environments, and multiple compression technologies. Multimedia applications can have distinctly different design requirements and thus require distinctly different authoring tools.

MULTIMEDIA TIMELINES

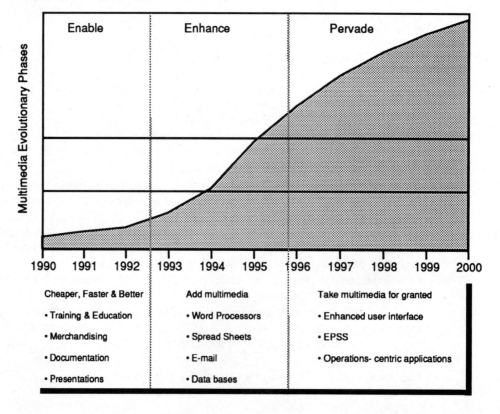

Figure 9-24. Multimedia will enter a phase of rapid growth by 1994–1995 because most of the impediments will have disappeared.

Market acceptance of multimedia for presentation-centric applications began in the mid-1980s with the availability of the personal computer and authoring systems that made it relatively easy to develop solutions. The personal computer was used as a controller for peripheral or ancillary analog devices such as videodisc players. As stated above, the emergence of multimedia as a capability to be exploited in day-to-day business operations hinges on an all-digital personal computer and networking environment.

Multimedia has entered the enhance phase of evolution as shown in Figure 9-24. Content- and presentation-centric applications are available in relative abundance and are experiencing a period of rapid growth. Many more businesses are looking to multimedia for more effective training, merchandising, and business presentations. CD-ROM based applications are enjoying rapid growth, especially in content-centric applications for documentation, manuals, references, policies and procedures, etc.

Although leading-edge companies have begun to implement EPSS and just-in-time training applications on a trial basis, we have not yet reached the pervade stage, where multimedia is taken for granted. Rapid growth is expected by the middle of the decade and it will depend on the convergence of several computing and networking technologies.

Five products and/or services must be available if multimedia is to succeed this decade

• Computing platforms with multimedia extensions and peripheral systems

• Audio, image, and video compression standards

• Storage systems capable of providing random access to massive data files with high transfer rates

• Transport systems capable of moving time-dependent media types at multi-megabit per second speeds, with no distance limitation at a reasonable cost

• Authoring tools that can be used by the subject matter expert with little or no support

The figures in the following sections are timelines for computing platforms, compression schemes, storage systems, transport systems, authoring tools and applications.

Computing Platforms

Computing platforms and peripherals are evolving rapidly to meet the needs of multimedia computing as shown in Figure 9-25. By 1995, all new personal computers will be multimedia capable and many of the existing systems will be upgraded. Each of the "bytes" depicts the point in time at which products are available at a reasonable price. The buyer will feel that the value received can easily be justified. For example, CD-ROM drives can be purchased through mail order firms for $400 or less. The price is expected to continue to fall with volume production. Although CD-ROM XA will be available at the beginning of 1993, it is not clear that it will be a major factor in the market. The price and performance of standard CD-ROM devices is being improved significantly and they will dominate the market. By 1995, high-speed CD-ROM devices will be available that impose no restrictions on our ability to play back full-screen, full-motion video.

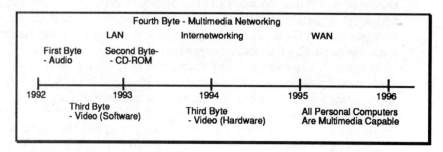

Figure 9-25. Evolution to multimedia provides the next major growth spurt for the personal computing industry.

Compression Schemes

The outcome of the various compression scheme efforts has not resulted in a clear winner. All of the current candidates are improvements but they will likely face stiff competition from fractal or wavelet technologies. Picture quality, image size, storage, and bandwidth continue to be issues with compression based on DCT. Fractals and wavelets will provide much higher levels of compression for the same image quality. Figure 9-26 notes that compression standards based on fractals and wavelets should be expected in 1996. Apple, IBM, and Microsoft will adapt their respective image and video extensions to take advantage of improvements in this area. Although it will not be included in the first release of Video for Windows, Microsoft has licensed fractal technology from Iterated Systems, Inc. in 1991.

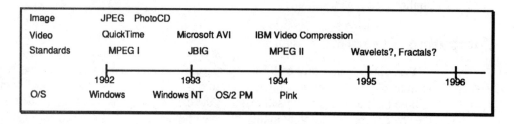

Figure 9-26. Compression schemes will continue to evolve before multimedia computing adopts a single standard.

Storage Systems

Digital Equipment demonstrated a multimedia-capable server at DECWORLD '92 and sources close to IBM point to similar systems from IBM. All suppliers of network servers will announce products in 1993 with storage and input/output capabilities needed to handle dynamic media and images. Further, the storage systems will be capable of interworking with all of the multimedia computing platforms.

Starlight Networks, Inc. announced StarWorks in the third quarter of 1992 with availability in the fourth quarter. The StarWorks software transforms an i486 EISA computer into a video application server that supports 20 simultaneous DVI users on DOS or Windows PCs and Macintosh computers. This is equivalent to a simultaneous networking capacity of 25 Mbit/s and 12 hours of video storage on 6-gigabyte Winchester disk drives.

Transport Systems

The intelligent hub and multiplexer vendors announced ATM-based products in 1992 with availability in 1993 or later. While there is little pent-up demand for such products in most organizations, it is important that the current planning process account for potential implementation of office- and operations-centric applications in 1994 and 1995. The superhubs or switched hubs introduced in 1992 and 1993 allow the buyer to preserve investments in network interface cards (NICs) and networking software. These new devices allow network managers to provide dedicated network bandwidth where and when it is needed. When combined with the capabilities of StarWorks from Starlight Networks, networked multimedia applications can be implemented for large numbers of users. The migration of existing LANs to broadband will drive the requirement for broadband services in the wide area network.

Figure 9-27 indicates that the LECs will begin to offer SMDS in 1993 but it will not be available on a nationwide basis until the IECs begin offering it in 1994. Both steps are significant as they are precursors to the implementation of BISDN in 1995.

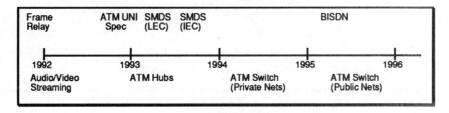

Figure 9-27. ATM deployment in LAN environments will create demand for BISDN services.

Although widespread deployment of BISDN will take 5 to 10 years, other services will be available in the interim. The pace will be dictated by the demand created by the implementation of multimedia and other applications that need high-bandwidth service. At present the demand for broadband services is being driven by growth in the number of users on LANs and by increases in the bandwidth requirements of individual users.

Authoring Tools

The current vendors of authoring tools are well aware of the potential bonanza that awaits those firms that provide tools to the masses. The market for such tools has been restricted to the professional developer or author until recently. Marked improvements in ease of use of authoring tools is being accompanied by multimedia extensions to operating systems that make it easier to implement multimedia applications. The capabilities and ease of use of QuickTime means that almost anyone can add motion video to an application. By 1994–1995, authoring tools and applications will enable the information knowledge worker to fully exploit multimedia in day-to-day office communications.

Applications

Audiographics, groupware, and desktop video applications are leading the way to networked multimedia as shown in Figure 9-28. The timeline depicts the feasibility of each application area from a cost, value, and technical point of view. Continued growth is expected for CBT and other presentation-centric applications. Office- and operations-centric applications such Lotus' Notes and EPSS, respectively, will gain momentum with a rapid growth phase beginning in 1994–1995.

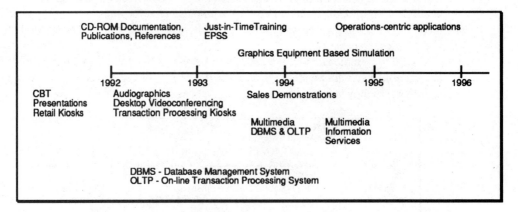

Figure 9-28. Multimedia applications will be implemented based on technical feasibility, cost and value.

The current recession is a manifestation of major shifts caused by a move to a global economy. The restructuring of organizations is irreversible and means that business must learn to operate with fewer people. More timely information, improved lifelong learning requirements and access to better tools means that various forms of EPSS applications will be implemented on a widespread basis. The should prompt an explosion in the number of operations-centric applications by the middle of the decade.

REFERENCES

Apple Computer. 1991. Blueprint for the Decade, An Overview of Apple technology and strategies. Cupertino, CA: Apple Computer, Inc.

Baggi, Denis L. 1991. Computer Generated Music. *Computer* 24(7):6-9 July 1991. © 1991 IEEE.

Boudette, Neal. 1992. IBM steps up multimedia push. PC Week 9(20):20.

Bunzel, Mark, and Morris, Sandra. 1992. *Multimedia Applications Development.*. New York: McGraw-Hill.

Fox, Edward A. 1991. Advances in Interactive Digital Multimedia Systems. *Computer* 24(10):9–21. October 1991. © 1991 IEEE.

Haber, Lynn. New image buzzwords: JPEG and JBIG. Network World 8(7):41,55. Copyright February 18, 1991 by Network World Inc., Framingham, MA - Reprinted from Network World.

Isbouts, Jean-Pierre. 1991. A Producer's Guide to Multimedia Authoring for CD-I. *MULTIMEDIA & VIDEODISC MONITOR* IX (3): 26–27.

Kessler, Gary C. 1991. Service for your MAN. LAN Magazine 6(10):47–49.

Le Gall, D. 1991. MPEG: A Video Compression Standard for Multimedia Applications. *Communications of the ACM* 34(4):46–58.

Leghart, Paul M. 1991 Day of reckoning looms for desktop OS winner. *Software Magazine* 11(14):68(8)

Rogers, Mark. 1991. O-ROM Premieres New Generation of Read-Only Optical Technology, *Computer Technology Review®*, Fall 1991 Edition: 61–7

Salamone, Salvatore. Users see clear value in image networking. Network World 8(9):1,39–43. Copyright February 18, 1991 by Network World Inc., Framingham, MA - Reprinted from Network World.

Stallings, William. 1991. Broadband ISDN: a standards update. Network World 8(11):49–52. Copyright March 18, 1991 by Network World Inc., Framingham, MA - Reprinted from Network World.

Walters, Stephen M. 1991. BISDN: Flexible Bandwidth for the Public Networks. Bellcore *Digest of Technical Information* 8(1):1–11.

Welty, William B. 1990. The Multibillion Dollar Video Game. Menlo Park, CA. Volpe, Welty & Company

10

Conclusions

PROMISES AND CHALLENGES

Multimedia is happening—the tide is unstoppable! Technology "push" is coming from both the consumer electronics and personal computer industries. Market "pull" is coming from leading-edge companies that recognize the need to increase the competence of their organizations in the face of mounting foreign competition.

The personal computer industry is undergoing an incremental evolution that will eventually revolutionize the business environment. The impact will be as significant as that generated by the currently omnipresent personal computer itself. As a result of the revolution, the personal computer may become an appliance in the home which is used for day-to-day applications. The personal computer is leading the way—creating a new role for computers, stimulating development of multimedia servers, and building demand for broadband networks.

The personal computer industry is confronted with a serious problem—the market for core products is saturating rapidly. There is a vast array of companies manufacturing personal computer products. They range from traditional, integrated companies such as IBM and Apple Computer, to the makers of IBM clones such as Compaq, AST Research, Dell Computer, and others, to the cottage industry based on the motherboards manufactured in the Far East.

Intense competition has seriously eroded the profit margins of all of the companies. At the same time, there has been little opportunity to add new functionality. Multimedia computing provides an opportunity to add new capabilities such as sound and motion video. New life is being breathed into the personal computer industry. Again there is opportunity to innovate and to distinguish among products based on function instead of price alone. Product enhancements by personal computer and workstation manufacturers are accelerating the growth of multimedia.

PROMISES

The Personal Communicator

The information-oriented, computer-based devices of the future have been termed "personal digital assistants or PDAs" by John Sculley of Apple Computer and "digital information devices" by Bill Gates of Microsoft Corporation. Whatever the name, these declarations point to a major shift in the role of the personal computer. With the integration of multimedia capabilities, the personal computer will primarily be used for information access and exchange, rather than computing.

Today information access or exchange is based on text, image, audio, or video in the form of books and reports, magazines, and radio and television programs. By combining the intrinsic interactivity of the personal computer with multimedia capabilities, the multimedia-capable computer becomes an excellent vehicle for communication.

The purview of information publishers—the print, radio, and television broadcast, plus the motion picture and audio and video tape industries—is now open to developers in the personal computer industry. A whole new area of applications for personal computers has been created. In business environments, information exchange applications are dominated by electronic mail and similar services. When combined with emerging networks capable of handling audio and video information streams, these new applications will touch most individuals in our society.

Reaching the Masses

In modern business life, employees face a conundrum. On one hand, they have great difficulty finding the information they need to do their tasks promptly. One the other hand, they are inundated with information, much of which is irrelevant. In this information age; almost everyone is reaching out for information or sending it to other interested parties. The term "information overload" no longer applies to the future, but certainly applies now. Information knowledge workers cannot cope with all the information that is presented to them. It is difficult to separate the relevant from the absurd. As the personal computer becomes the personal communicator, designed explicitly to assist the information exchange process, everyone is likely to have some use for it.

The personal communicator may appear as an appliance. Individuals may have several personal communicators, each of which is targeted at unique applications. For example, one might be an electronic travel guide containing local, state, or national maps, restaurants, train and plane schedules, and other travel-related information. Another personal communicator might contain a wide variety of recipes with motion video demonstrations of critical cooking steps. Individuals may own and use multiple personal communicators, each having unique information-handling capabilities. Ease of use will be the key to ubiquity.

Improved Human/Machine Interfaces

The use of dynamic media such as sound and motion video will lead to more natural human/machine interfaces. Many people are intimidated by the computer keyboard. At best, keyboards are a very inconvenient input mechanism for most users. Voice input and output is not available at this time. Apple Computer's Knowledge Navigator video showed a future notebook computer that has voice input and output capabilities. Voice input will extend the use of the personal communicator to many more users. High-quality sound and motion video will enhance the output capabilities of the computer. These more natural ways of interaction will lure more users to the new way of communicating.

Multimedia computing will be used in all areas of communication including entertainment, information access, presentations, and office applications. The personal computer has already been used with great success in the entertainment industry. Several hundred personal computer games are continually being improved with better-quality voice, music, animation and video. Similarly, musicians use their personal computers for recording, editing, and mixing to provide a new musical experience.

Users will have access to information in hypermedia books and magazines that contain full-motion video and audio clips. The information will be published on a compact disc (CD) so it can be played back on most personal computers. Products such as Compton's Multimedia Encyclopedia and Microsoft's Bookshelf are early examples of new forms of information sources.

In the business environments, all applications will take advantage of the multimedia capabilities of the emerging personal communicators.

The Emergence of a New Industry

The publishing industry will sustain the most significant transformation. Print-based publishing is not likely to disappear, but publishing on CD-ROM and networked information services will emerge as a powerful force. The electronic analogs of magazines, books, and papers will be distributed on CDs with messages that are more emphatic, more entertaining, and potentially more personal. Networked multimedia services will evolve from the base of America Online, CompuServe, and Prodigy to provide personalized multimedia news, market information, and competitive information to every workstation.

Integrated Networks

The implementation of Asynchronous Transfer Mode (ATM) technology and Synchronous Optical Network (SONET) transmission facilities makes it feasible to integrate image, audio, and full-motion video with data on a single, homogeneous network that can be accessed by personal computers through a single communications port.

This integration is key to realizing the personal communicator based on the personal computer. One can expect this technology to start appearing in intrabuilding and environments in 1993. By 1995 the authors expect to see ATM switches deployed in the public switched network.

Virtual Access

The Smithsonian Museum has approximately one-half of 1 percent of the total amount of artifacts and information it possesses on display at any time. The rest of the items are in crates or storage and are only available to research scholars. Further, the small amount of information on display is accessible to the small fraction of the population who are able to visit the Smithsonian

Broadband networks based on ATM technology and the personal communicator will make it feasible to "view" the entire Smithsonian collection by accessing a multimedia database from the home or business. It may not be quite as good as actually being there but it will be at least as good as seeing the collection on a television program. There are many opportunities to take advantage of virtual access so the authors expect to see a broad set of applications in this area.

Transformation of the Work Environment

Businesses today face some significant key challenges. The work force needs to be continually updated about new products and new business processes. Employees must keep up with product environments that undergo rapid change. More employees need to operate in global markets in a more timely manner. All employees can be empowered by effective and frequent communication of corporate goals, objectives, and performance.

Many organizations recognize there is a skill gap in North American business that can only be addressed by lifelong learning programs. U.S. businesses must upgrade their number one asset—the American worker—to regain a competitive edge in global markets.

The application of networked computers present an opportunity to change training from an event to a learning process. Electronic Performance Support Systems (EPSS) can provide task-specific information and learning modules to employees when, how, and where they are needed. The objective changes from training employees to increasing the competence of the work force. Access to relevant information, expert systems, and support systems can lead to significant improvements in productivity and effectiveness by bringing all employees closer to the customer. This is the promise of an effective communication machine.

CHALLENGES

The most prolific mechanism for information delivery and exchange is paper. The personal communicator needs to match key characteristics of this medium if it is to become ubiquitous. The personal communicator does not need to replace paper and probably never will. However, it is incumbent on the industry to match the key characteristics to help ensure success.

The promises of multimedia will not be realized unless the following challenges are met.

Usability

The personal communicator needs to be extremely easy to use. Ease of use is the most difficult challenge facing the industry. It should require very little effort and activity on the part of the user to get started and to achieve useful results. The user should be able to use one or two buttons or voice commands to obtain meaningful results. The computer should be able to organize the information to suit a particular user. After all, it is supposed be personal.

Utility should not demand interaction by the user. Interaction should be by choice and not by necessity. The user of a personal communicator must not be forced to interact to access information that is needed on a routine basis. Filtered information that matches the interest profile of the individual should be presented automatically. Interaction should allow users to get more value and explore new areas of interest. More value will be obtained because the information will be personalized.

Platform Independence

Personal computers have made significant advances over the past 10 years. They can be used for a wide variety of applications by all types and sizes of organizations. However, there are many kinds of computers, each of which has different performance and functional capabilities. Different computers are selected for different applications.

Information should be usable on any computer so that an individual can access and manipulate the information any place, any time. This calls for a high degree of standardization across computer platforms, operating systems, user interfaces, and application programs. A multimedia presentation created on a Macintosh using Aldus' Persuasion should be accessible on a PC clone under Windows NT or on an Ultimedia system or on a Unix workstation.

The personal computer industry has no experience with this degree of standardization but needs to face this issue to achieve the level of platform independence reached by the consumer electronics industry. A CD or an audio tape or a VHS video tape can be played on machines made by any manufacturer. Similarly, it must be possible to access multimedia information on CDs on any personal communicator. The authors believe the industry will cooperate to meet this challenge. As a result, the industry will serve the mass consumer market in addition to the "elite" personal computer user.

Cost

The cost of information to the end user must be affordable. One of the factors that reduces the cost of information in newspapers and magazines is the participation of advertisers. Broadcast television is free because advertisers bear all of the expense. The authors believe that advertisers need to continue to participate as information is provided in multimedia formats. Advertising dollars are needed to reduce the cost of capturing, storing, and providing access to multimedia information to the mass market.

Books, manuals, and documentation are much less expensive to publish on CD-ROM than on paper. However, the cost of the personal communicator needed for playback is still an impediment to mass market success. Since the cost of the computer platform is expected to decrease by 50 percent over the next 2 years, the affordability issue will cease to be an issue over time.

Authoring Tools

The final issue is related to the tools that are available to capture and manipulate information for multimedia applications. Paper only requires pencil or pen and mechanical aids that can be used by anyone, anywhere, any time. Authoring tools must accommodate any type of application on any platform, using any standard compression technology under any windowing environment.

The personal communicator demands two different types of authoring tools. One must allow any information knowledge worker to create presentations, training modules, multimedia reports, etc. in the context of normal day-to-day activities. The quality level will be consistent with the types of memos, reports, and presentations in business today. Video clips will not meet the production levels of a company presentation or a feature movie. The authoring tools need to be as easy to use as the application tools that are popular today.

Subject matter experts who prepare training modules for large audiences, product presentations, or multimedia publications need authoring systems that allow them to achieve higher quality. The tools will probably be more robust with more features and will possibly be more difficult to use. The tools must allow subject matter experts to deliver professional-quality material without creative support from multimedia professionals.

In neither case should the author or creator need the support of programmers or systems analysts to create the multimedia solution.

THE BOTTOM LINE

The multimedia phenomenon has been covered with increasing frequency over the past 5 years. During that period, a number of companies in the computer industry with the support of the silicon foundries have struggled to move their respective businesses into a new boom period through technology push on the multimedia wave. Hundreds of millions of dollars have been spent on compression devices, better authoring tools, and audio and video capabilities. A large chapter of this book is dedicated to the technology infrastructure that is being created. While this investment is necessary, it is not sufficient. Applications for these new capabilities have been slow to develop. As a result, the market pull necessary for rapid growth is still in the future.

The high technology companies that generated the technology push have tried to "kick-start" markets for their products. Issues such as the need for lifelong learning programs, information overload, and global competitiveness have emerged in the search for the market pull that must accompany technology push in order to achieve periods of rapid growth. As noted above, multimedia is still in the enhance phase of acceptance which is characterized by low volume and relatively high cost. This is the proving ground for the concept, and for answering fundamental questions about multimedia, why and how it should be used, and by whom. As applications move into the business milieu, there is much to be learned about the power of multimedia and the challenges that lie ahead. At this point technology push is delivering multimedia-capable computers and networks, and we are beginning to see true market pull.

The effort to implement the multimedia applications described in previous chapters is significant. There is a still a gap between the perspective of individuals in the multimedia community who understand the potential of available multimedia technology and what constitutes a "killer application" in business environments. This gap must be closed before multimedia applications become pervasive. Closure implies a close relationship between customers and suppliers at a minimum and suggests that there will be a be a new wave of high growth for companies that provide system integration services. The success of multimedia is intimately linked to the implementation, operation, and support of the infrastructure needed for business operations-centric applications.

The success of multimedia in business is dependent on the following factors.

- An understanding of the process that is to be optimized including performance and costs objectives, in the context of the user

- Effective measures that demonstrate the increased productivity, reduced costs, and/or increased revenue that results from implementing the solution

- The successful integration of a myriad of technology building blocks that satisfy the requirements of the application and implementation of systems that are easy for the target audience to use

Multimedia and Networking Glossary

Animation - A synchronized sequence of graphics that conveys action.

ANSI (American National Standards Institute) - A nonprofit organization that has two primary functions: First, it coordinates private sector activities in the development of national standards and decides on the eligibility of standards to be called American National Standards; and second, it acts as a national clearing-house and coordinator for voluntary standards in the United States.

Application program interface (API) System software that provides resources that programmers can use to create user interface features such as pull-down menus and to route programs or data to LANs.

Asymmetric System - A video system that requires more equipment to store,process, and compress a digital image than it needs to decompress and playback. Intel's DVI™ and Philips/Sony's CD-I™ systems are asymmetric in full fidelity mode.

ATM (Asynchronous Transfer Mode) - An international standard being developed by CCITT for the transport of voice, data, image, and video that is independent of rate, media and services. ATM provides a simple, fixed length packet or cell composed of destination address, priority, and service type to self route packets through the network. ATM will operate at T1, T3, FDDI and SONET rates.

Authoring System - The software development environment used to create a multimedia application or title. A run-time version of the same software is usually required for playback.

A/UX - Apple Copmputer's version of the UNIX operating system.

Bit map - The representation of a video image stored in the computer's memory. Each picture element (pixel) is represented by bits stored in memory.

BISDN (Broadband Integrated Services Digital Network) - An integrated services digital network operating at bandwidths of 1.5 Mbit/s and above. Three data rates will be available to Broadband ISDN subscribers: Full duplex services at 155 and 600 Mbit/s; and asynchronous service at 155 Mbit/s from the subscriber to the network and 600 Mbit/s from the network to the subscriber.
  Information will be transferred across the network using the Asynchronous Transfer Mode on SONET transmission facilities.

BRI - See ISDN BRI.

Bridges - An internetworking device that links local and remote local area networks. It operates at the media access or MAC layer of the network, which is within the Data Link Layer of the OSI model. Bridges are protocol independent.

C A high level programming language widely used by professional programmers. It is highly portable and produces efficient, fast-running programs.

C++ A high level programming language developed by AT&T's Bell Laboratories. Based on its predecessor, C, it is an object-oriented programming language that combines the benefits of C and the modularity of object-orieented programming.

CBT (computer-based training) - The use of computers for interactive instruction, education or training.

CCITT (The International Committee on Telephone and Telegraph) - A permanent organ of the International Telecommunications Union (ITU), which is a specialized agency of the United Nations. The CCITT was founded in 1954 for the purpose of promoting and ensuring the operation of international telecommunications systems.

CD-I™ (Compact Disc Interactive) - A consumer-oriented CD format standard for compact disc-based multimedia playback systems that supports graphics, animation, audio and images in addition to text, that was developed by NV Philips and Sony.

CD-ROM - A read-only optical storage technology that uses compact disks. CD-ROM disks can store up to 650 Megabytes of data.

CD-ROM XA (Compact Disc Read-Only Memory Extended Architecture) - A CD format that adds interleaved audio to data within the basic CD-ROM format.

CDTV (Commodore Dynamic Total Vision) - A consumer-oriented CD-based interactive multimedia player based on the Amiga 500 that supports text, graphics, animation, audio and images.

Client-server - A form of local area network-based computing in which the user station, or client, requests data and performs processing and the network server provides services, such as file transfer, communications , or printing.

Codec (Codec/Decoder) - A device that converts an analog signal such as voice to a digital stream and compresses it and sends it over a digital line. Another codec reverses the process at the receiving end.

Common Channel Signaling - The use of a separate channel dedicated to the purpose of signaling and used to manage multiple information channels simultaneously.

Composite Video - A video signal that combines all color and timing components of the picture.

CPE (Customer Premises Equipment) - Equipment resident at the customer's site that interfaces to a telephone network.

Digital Signal - An information signal which has a limited number of states. Voice and video, which usually originate in analog form, can be converted to digital signals. Voice is converted using pulse code modulation (PCM) to 64 kbit/s, which is DS-0. The public network is comprised of a hierarchy of digital signals.

DS-0 (Digital Signal - 0) - The lowest level of digital signal at 64 kbit/s, equivalent to one voice circuit. The digital signal hierarchy describes the protocols, framing format and frequency for various levels of transmission products.

DS-1 (Digital Signal - 1) - DS-1 refers to T1 (1.544 Mbit/s) transmission and can be multiplexed into 24 DS-0's.

DS-3 (Digital Signal - 3) - DS-3 refers to T3 (44.736 Mbit/s) transmission and can be multiplexed into 28 DS-1's.

DVI® (Digital Video Interactive) - Intel's proprietary technology based on programmable chips for high level compression of full motion video.

ECMA (European Computer Manufacturers Association) - ECMA was formed in 1961 to coordinate the work of making various computer standards compatible. Members are European companies which develop, manufacture and market data processing machines used to process digital information for business, scientific, control or other purposes. ECMA is a very active liaison member of both CCITT and ISO.

ESP (Enhanced Service Provider) - Companies that provide services over common carrier transmission facilities used in interstate communications, which employ computer processing applications that act on format, content, code, protocol or similar aspects of the subscriber's transmitted information; provide the subscriber additional, different or restructured information; or involve subscriber interaction with stored information.

FDDI (Fiber Distributed Data Interface) - FDDI is a token-ring LAN with an optical transmission rate of 125 Megabaud and a data rate of 100 Mbit/s. An FDDI LAN can have a total perimeter of 100 kilometers and accommodate up to 500 stations. A CBEMA committee, accredited by ANSI, is responsible for U.S. development of FDDI standards. The specification is being updated to include single-mode fiber and to cover compatibility and interconnection with SONET.

Flash Memory - Flash memory is a nonvolatile memory medium (it "remembers" even when the power is turned off) that can easily be updated. This credit card-sized package will be used to replace floppy and hard disk drives in portable personal computers in the future. Flash memory cards substantially reduce the computer's power consumption (when compared with traditional mechanical disk-drive memories).

Frame Relay - A fast packet signaling and data transfer mechanism between intelligent end points (such as LANs) and an intelligent network. Incoming data is examined to determine its destination and routed on a packet-by-packet or frame-by-frame basis. Frame relay is being specified to operate at speeds from 56 kbit/s to 1.544 Mbit/s. Efforts are underway to increase the operating speed to 44.736 Mbit/s.

Full-Motion Video - Video sequences or systems that provide the number of images per second to afford the illusion of smooth motion. This is often defined as the rate of standard video signals in the U.S. (30 frames per second) and in Europe (25 frames per second).

Graphics - One frame or a sequence of frames, of artificially produced material for a computer display (normally "drawn" with bit-mapped images).

Group 3 - Digital facsimile equipment per CCITT Recommendation T.4. (Sends an A4 or 8.5 x 11 inch page in a half minute over a voice grade line.)

Group 4 - Digital facsimile equipment per CCITT Recommendations T.5 and T.6. (Uses public data networks and their procedures for essentially error-free reception. May also be used on the public switched network with an appropriate modulation process.)

GUI (Graphical User Interface) - A user interface that uses a mouse and a bit-mapped graphics display to make basic computer operations substantially easier for the user. Standard features include alert boxes, a clipboard, the desktop metaphor, dialog boxes, scroll boxes, on-screen display of fonts, "what-you-see-is-what-you-get" (WYSIWYG) on-screen page presentation and multiple on-screen windows.

Hypermedia - A method for delivering information that provides multiple connected pathways through a body of information, allowing the user to jump easily from one topic to related or supplementary material, which may be text, graphics, audio, images or video.

IEC (Inter-Exchange Carrier) - A common carrier that provides long distance services and inter-LATA services, for example, AT&T, MCI and US Sprint..

IMA (Interactive Multimedia Association) - A nonprofit organization that specializes in multimedia technology with more than 170 members from diverse fields including IBM, Sony Corp., N.V. Philips, and Intel Corp.

Image - One frame of an exact likeness of a real entity. This may be a photograph, a single television frame or some other reproduction of a real event.

ISDN (Integrated Services Digital Network) - A digital network that is evolving from the existing telephony network, which provides end-to-end connectivity to support a wide range of both voice and non-voice services. User access is via a limited set of standard multi-purpose interfaces.

ISDN B-Channel - A 64 kbit/s channel accompanied by timing, intended to carry a wide variety of Information streams, such as voice encoded at 64 kbit/s, data information at rates less than or equal to 64 kbit/s, and voice encoded at rates less than 64 kbit/s alone or combined with other digital information streams.

ISDN BRI (Basic Rate Interface) - An ISDN user-network interface with two B-Channels and one D-Channel, 2B+D. The bit rate of the D-Channel is 16 kbit/s.

ISDN D-Channel - A 16 or 64 kbit/s channel carrying control and signaling information and as an option, packetized information.

ISDN PRI (Primary Rate Interface) - An ISDN user-network interface with multiple B-Channels and one D-Channel. The bit rate of the D-Channel is 64 kbit/s. When a 1.544 Mbit/s primary rate interface is provided, the structure is 23B+D.

JBIG (Joint Bi-level Imaging Group) - A working group established to develop a standard for compressing bi-level images such as black-and-white photographs or pages of text. Since distortion is no acceptable for these types of images, JBIG is a lossless compression technique.

JPEG (Joint Photograph Experts Group) - A working group established to develop a standard for compressing and storing images in digital form. JPEG is a lossy image compression technique that proceeds on a pixel by pixel basis.

LATA (Local Access and Transport Area) - With the AT&T consent decree, 164 court-approved LATAs were established. Local calls within the serving area of a Bell Operating Company (BOC) are also referred to as intraexchange, intraLATA calls.

Latency - In networks, latency is the delay associated with data packets passing through multiple networks hops. A delay occurs each time a data packet is retransmitted through a network switch, router, or bridge.

Leased Lines - Leased lines provide point-to-point or multipoint-to-point (known as multidrop) services, and offer no network switching. Leased lines have no call setup time and transmission speeds up to 45 Mbit/s are available now. In future, with SONET, speeds of 155 and 600 Mbit/s and higher will be available.

LEC (Local Exchange Carrier) - Within their service area, LECs provide many services in addition to basic exchange service. All may provide long distance service between exchanges within their LATAs. LECs provide transport services, which allows the movement of information within the LATA. In addition, they provide access to long distance carriers.

MPEG (Motion Picture Experts Group) - A working group established to develop a standard for compressing and storing addressable video in digital form.

OC-N - SONET operates at speeds that are multiples of 51.84 Mbit/s which is Optical Carrier-1 or OC-1. OC-3 is a channel at 155.52 Mbit/s and OC-12 is 622 Mbit/s

Pixel (Picture Elements) - Pixels are the individual elements that comprise the video image. The number of pixels per line and the number of vertical lines varies depending on the video mode.

PCM (Pulse Code Modulation) - A technique for converting an analog signal into a digital bit stream for transmission. Voice is converted to a 64 kbit/s on a global basis for transmission by public network carriers.

PRI - See ISDN PRI.

RBOC (Regional Bell Operating Company) - Under the AT&T consent decree, ownership and control of about 80% of the Bell System's assets was assumed by seven regional Bell holding companies. Bell companies are prohibited from providing "information services", manufacturing telecommunications equipment and engaging in long distance communications between and among 164 court-delineated, "local access and transport areas" (LATAs). The seven RBOCs are Ameritech, Bell Atlantic, Bell South, Nynex, Pacific Telesis, Southwestern Bell, and US West.

Routers - An internetworking device for connecting local area networks that divides a network into logical subnetworks so that data travels the most efficient routes possible. The router relies on protocols, such as OSI and TCP/IP to determine the optimal route for data packets.

Signaling - The exchange of control information between elements of a telecommunications network for the purpose of managing the information channels provided by the network.

SMDS (Switched Multi-Megabit Data Service) - A public, packet switched data service that provides LAN-like performance and features over a metropolitan or wide area. The service concept was developed by Bell Communications Research based on the IEEE 802.6 standard being developed by the Institute of Electrical and Electronic Engineers for Metropolitan Area Networks. SMDS will operate initially at 1.544 and 44.736 Mbit/s and will be integrated with broadband ISDN some time after 1992.

SONET (Synchronous Optical Network a.k.a. Synchronous Digital Hierarchy) - A fiber optic transmission system based on multiples of a 51.84 Mbit/s building block that will be used to transport SMDS and BISDN services. Speeds will range from 51.84 Mbit/s to more than 13 Gbit/s. The SONET standards developed by the CCITT provide for basic compatibility between different optical-line systems and define the parameters for setting up a local fiber network and enabling it to interconnect with similar networks via optical links.

SS#7 (Common Channel Signaling System Number 7) - An out-of-band signaling protocol designed to pass routing information between switches and routing centers in high-speed backbone networks. To implement SS#7, carriers must build a separate signaling network parallel to the information carrying network, using special signaling switches.

Although not specifically developed by CCITT for ISDN, SS#7 is a natural fit for ISDN switch-to-switch signaling requirements. ISDN deployment is predicated on ubiquitous deployment of SS#7 facilities. In a digital environment, SS#7 allows the telephone companies to provide other new intelligent services.

Symmetric System - A video system that is capable of compressing/storing and decompressing/playing back digital video.

STS-N (Synchronous Transport Signal) - In reference to SONET, an electrical signal that is converted to or from SONET's optical signals, where N is a multiple of 51.84 Mbit/s. The 51.84 Mbit/s building block was designed to allow 'mapping in' of a DS-3 channel, and includes transport overhead which tells how each byte should be processed.

T-Carrier - A digital transmission system standardized by AT&T for short and medium distance transmission. T-Carrier is a PCM system using 64 kbit/s for a voice channel.

T1 (T-Carrier) - A digital transmission system that operates at 1.544 Mbit/s, allowing 24 voice channels to be multiplexed onto a single line. T1 is a standard method of interconnecting digital communications in the North American telephone industry.

T3 - A digital transmission system that operates at 44.736 Mbit/s, allowing twenty-eight T1 links to be multiplexed on a single line.

Videodisc - An optical disc used for storage and retrieval of images or video and sound. A video disc player is required to play back the video disc on a personal computer or a standard television monitor. Storage capacity is up to an hour of high quality, full motion video plus two audio tracks that can be played separately or together. There are two distinct formats, CLV and CAV:

• CLV (Constant Linear Velocity) videodiscs which provide up to one hour of extended play per side and are good for linear viewing.

• CAV (Constant Angular Velocity) videodiscs which provide thirty minutes of extended play per side but allow random frame access, fast and/or slow motion playback, scanning (displaying occasional frames as it traverse the disc), and search by specific frame. These features are critical for true interactive videodisc applications.

Index